Studies in British Transport
History 1870-1970

Studies in British Transport History 1870-1970

Derek H. Aldcroft

David & Charles
Newton Abbot London Vancouver North Pomfret (Vt)

ISBN 0 7153 6505 3

Set in 11/13 IBM Journal
and printed in Great Britain
by Compton Printing Limited
Pembroke Road Stocklake Aylesbury Buckinghamshire
for David & Charles (Holdings) Limited
South Devon House Newton Abbot Devon

Published in the United States of America
by David & Charles Inc
North Pomfret Vermont 05053 USA

Published in Canada
by Douglas David & Charles Limited
3645 McKechnie Drive West Vancouver BC

Contents

     in Diesel and Electric Traction   243

12   The Changing Pattern of Demand for
     Passenger Transport in Post-war
     Britain — D.H. Aldcroft and P.J. Bemand   263

13   Reflections on the Rochdale Inquiry
     into Shipping   275

     Appendices   297

     Index   303

Introduction

There is no shortage of writers on transport history. Each branch of transport sports a large following of enthusiasts whose pens toil ceaselessly, judging by the large number of items that appear in print each year. Much of the writing reflects a certain amount of nostalgia and personal reminiscence which, to use Kellett's words, has given rise to books 'intended to be wallowed in rather than read, and certainly not to be studied, to be used for convenient reference, or to serve as the basis for further work'.[1] However, though many such writings lack the substance and documentation that appeal to the academic mind, many of them do contain useful material which can serve to illustrate or support a particular thesis. For example, the second volume of Dow's work on the Great Central provides some marvellous insights into the attitudes and motives which dominated the mind of Sir Edward Watkin, and as such tell us a great deal about the nature and calibre of railway management in the Victorian era.[2] Similarly, many of the House histories sponsored by the shipping companies, despite their obvious shortcomings, often furnish illumination about the personal characteristics of the men who ran them and thereby help to explain why the companies acted in the way they did. In short, such works should not be rejected out of hand by the academic scholar even though in many cases they may be of limited use to him.

Transport history as an academic discipline has developed in a rather *ad hoc* manner, more as an off-shoot of other disciplines — notably economic history and engineering —

than as a subject in its own right. Yet in the past couple of decades it has done much to establish its own identity. The subject now boasts three journals in this country: two of these cover transport history in general, namely the *Journal of Transport History* which has a strong international flavour, and *Transport History* whose interests are concentrated on the British scene; the third journal, *Maritime History*, is exclusively devoted to shipping.

Of course not all the writing on transport history finds its way into these specialised journals. Indeed, much new work has appeared either in book form or in publications not concerned specifically with transport matters. The range and quality of some of the recent writings suggest that academics are giving much more serious attention to the subject than was previously the case. The reasons for this growing interest vary. One possibility is the greater availability of primary records, particularly for railway history. Another has perhaps been the enormous growth in transport economic studies in the last decade or so which has served to kindle interest on the historical side. Here the use of sophisticated techniques of analysis has no doubt encouraged their application to the historical context, notably in the form of econometric history. Or could it be simply that past neglect of transport history by academics has provided young scholars with an ideal opportunity to sharpen their talents in a field not already well trodden by the great minds?

A preliminary exploration of some of the more recent literature gives ground for satisfaction that good progress is being made in several departments of transport history. As might be expected, the railways seem to have come in for more than their fair share of treatment. Here interest has been focused primarily on investment and financial aspects, the railways' contribution to economic growth and one or two other matters. Several authors have investigated the sources of railway capital and the impact which the raising of large amounts of money had on the English capital market. Broadbridge's study of the Lancashire & Yorkshire

Railway[3] provides detailed insight into the diverse sources
from which finance was raised, while a host of articles have
covered similar territory including the oft-neglected Irish and
Scottish sectors.[4] One particular aspect which has received
much attention of late is the way in which the capital market
responded to the growing demands made by the railways
(including the development of provincial stock exchanges),[5]
while several time series of aggregate railway investment have
been produced.[6]

No less important are the contributions on the decision-
making and managerial aspects of railway history. R.J. Irving,
for example, has recently examined some of the determinants
of investment and innovation of the North Eastern and
London & North Western Railway Companies,[7] while G.
Channon has investigated the motives behind the Midland's
decision to push through to London.[8] However, perhaps the
most welcome piece of work is that by Gourvish who tackles
the rather neglected aspect of internal managerial problems
involved in the day-to-day running of the railways from the
standpoint of Mark Huish at the London & North Western.[9]
This is undoubtedly a pioneer study which will serve as a
model for future writers in this field. Other interesting contributions include articles on railway trade unionism, the
railways' interests in steamship services and the role of the
Government with respect to railway amalgamation.[10]

But it is the growth men who have really stolen the show.
What has attracted most interest over the last decade has been
the way in which railways contributed to economic growth
in the nineteenth century. Were they crucial to Victorian
prosperity as many would have us believe, or could we have
done without them? Several partial attempts were made to
settle the issue by examining the impact of railways on
different sectors of the economy but the issue as a whole
was still left somewhat diffuse.[11] A much more precise
quantitative assessment finally appeared in 1970 when
Hawke, following the pioneering work of American scholars
Fogel and Fishlow, attempted a penetrating and sophisticated

analysis of the railways' contribution to national income.[12]
At last we were given an aggregate figure: if the railways had
been dispensed with it would have been necessary to compensate for the loss of about 10 per cent of the national income
in 1865. Though the final figure was tentative and the means
by which it was derived left room for improvement it did
seem that the railways' contribution to the growth of the
economy was far from negligible.[13]

Finally, the influence of railways on urban development
has also been the subject of serious study. On this topic the
centrepiece study is undoubtedly Kellett's magnificent
volume[14] which shows in intricate detail (almost as if the
author had lived the period) how the railways dissected and
intersected some of our great cities (London, Manchester,
Birmingham, Glasgow and Liverpool) and the problems and
social costs created for those unfortunate enough to get in
their way. This is a classic and pioneer work, the counterpart
in a sense of Hawke's work though in a different context.
Apart from Kellett's volume there have been numerous
shorter studies; many of these concentrate on one particular
town as, for example, Simpson's careful study of Glasgow.[15]
Jack Simmons's wide-ranging tour of railway cities provides
an admirable background to the subject.[16]

This of course does not exhaust the recent work on
railway history but the above references do provide an idea
of the greater interest shown in the subject over the last few
years. There are, moreover, still plenty of worthwhile
opportunities for further research in this sector. It is, for
instance, surprising that no decent business history of a
railway company has yet been written despite the great
collections of company records now available to historians.[17]
Or again, the operating policies of the railways, especially
after 1870, have been rather neglected; it would be interesting to know just how the railway companies justified the
building of so many uneconomic branch lines in the latter
half of the nineteenth century. Very little has been written
about the railways' ancillary activities — canals, steamship

services, hotels and the like. And there is much work still to
be done on the railways' pricing policies and their investment
decision-making procedures. These and many other issues
provide a good quarry for scholars in the future.

Canal, river and road transport have received much less
attention than the railways. For the early period there has
been one very sound study of the turnpike road system,[18]
one or two detailed articles on river navigation, notably those
by Unwin and Wilson on the Aire and Calder,[19] and relatively
little on canals. Road haulage and road passenger transport
have not received much attention either,[20] though one cannot
forget the masterly study of London's transport system in
the nineteenth century published a decade ago.[21] For the late
nineteenth century and through to the development of motor
transport recent work is very thin on the ground. Writings by
enthusiasts of the new form of locomotion have not been
lacking but there has been little in the way of serious study.
The early development of road haulage in the motor era has
been almost completely neglected — indeed for this sector
one is still heavily dependent on Gilbert Walker's *Road and
Rail* first published some 30 years ago (1942). The road
passenger side has fared little better; true, the number of
writings grows each year but, as Hibbs has shown in his
recent bibliographical survey of the literature,[22] many of the
publications are of only passing or marginal interest to the
serious student. The same author's popular history of bus
services provides plenty of detail about the individual companies and the men who ran them but the study lacks
depth and substance in economic matters.[23] One very interesting, though overlong, volume by Plowden[24] is worth
mentioning since it illustrates the implications of the motor
car and the way it has influenced the legislative process.

Shipping has produced some very commendable efforts in
the last decade or so though there is still no standard text for
the nineteenth century. This gap is flanked on either side by
two excellent volumes by Davis and Sturmey.[25] On productivity,
costs and technical change in ocean shipping a series of distin-

guished analytical articles spans the period from the late seventeenth century through to the end of the nineteenth.[26] Virtually
singlehanded Professor Hyde has pioneered the study of shipping business histories in a series of excellent volumes,[27] while a
number of his former students have contributed to our knowledge of the structure and financing of shipping operations.[28]
Moreover, some useful work on shipping has appeared in
writings not devoted specifically to the subject, as in the
case of Jackson's book on Hull.[29] There is still much work to
be done in this field, notably on the shipping conference
system[30] and the impact of company mergers before 1914,
while coastal shipping still awaits its historian. One difficulty
in this respect compared with the railways is that access to
company records is not easily obtainable; a recent guide to
some of the material that is readily available, both company
and other sources, should provide helpful assistance to intend-
ing authors.[31]

For the remaining sectors of transport there is little of
note to report. Aviation remains a sadly neglected area,
especially for the period up to 1939.[32] Nor has the study of
infrastructures — roads, docks and airports — found many
takers. There are one or two exceptions: a useful two-volume
study of Bristol port has recently appeared,[33] while
Professor Hyde, with his volume on Liverpool,[34] has provided
a splendid launching to a new series on Britain's ports. But
there is still an urgent need for good general historical
surveys of these facilities.

Despite the current activity in transport history the scope
for further worthwhile research is still considerable. There
are many fields of study that should prove particularly
rewarding, including shipping conferences, the impact of
technical change on transport costs, the determinants of
transport demand, the contribution of canals and roads to
economic development and the role of the independent airlines, to name only a few. It is clear from the recent literature
on the subject that the type of transport history required is
changing. Detailed factual studies for their own sake are no

longer adequate or acceptable. More explicit reference needs to be made to the way in which transport systems operate, for example how pricing and investment decisions are made and what determines innovation, and the contribution they make to economic growth.

Some would argue that the broader issues cannot be settled until much more work has been done at the micro level. Here then is the case for more good business histories, among other things. But the economist or macro-economic historian cannot wait that long; he would probably argue that it is possible to produce the outline canvas and leave the details to be filled in later. With his economic tools and explicit reference models the process can be short-circuited so that the building blocks do not have to be laboriously constructed one at a time. While there are virtues in both approaches it seems more than likely that both sides may learn one from the other. The business historian, for example, may sharpen his exposition and its utility by using the concepts and tools of the economist, while the latter may in turn benefit from the more detailed and historically accurate labours of the historian. To take a case in point: Hawke's analysis of the railways' impact would undoubtedly have been strengthened had he been able to draw upon a more coherent body of evidence with respect to canal rates. Despite all the effort that has gone into canal history in the past no worthwhile investigation has been made into the structure of canal freight rates. In other words, the answers to some of the major issues in transport history, as with many other historical issues, are more likely to be solved by mutual co-operation between economic historians with different approaches to the subject than by the strained relationships which have existed in the last decade or so.

NOTES

1   J.R. Kellett, 'Writing on Victorian Railways: An Essay in

Nostalgia', *Victorian Studies* (1962)

2   G. Dow, *Great Central: The Dominion of Watkin* (1962)

3   S. Broadbridge, *Studies in Railway Expansion and the Capital Market in England, 1825-1873* (1970)

4   See especially, E.S. Richards, 'The Finances of the Liverpool and Manchester Railway Again', *Economic History Review*, 25 (1972); J. Lee, 'The Provision of Capital for Early Irish Railways, 1830-53', *Irish Historical Studies*, 16 (1968); W. Vamplew, 'Sources of Scottish Railway Share Capital before 1860', *Scottish Journal of Political Economy*, 17 (1970), and 'Banks and Railway Finance: A Note on the Scottish Experience', *Transport History*, 4 (1971); T.R. Gourvish and M.C. Reed, 'The Financing of Scottish Railways before 1860: A Comment', *Scottish Journal of Political Economy*, 18 (1971) and the 'Reply' by Vamplew in the same issue

5   M.C. Reed, 'Railways and the Growth of the Capital Market', in M.C. Reed (ed), *Railways in the Victorian Economy* (1969), and 'George Stephenson and W.T. Salvin: The Early Railway Capital Market at Work', *Transport History*, 1 (1968). See also J.R. Killick and W.A. Thomas, 'The Provincial Stock Exchanges, 1830-1870', *Economic History Review*, 23 (1970)

6   G.R. Hawke and M.C. Reed, 'Railway Capital in the United Kingdom in the Nineteenth Century', *Economic History Review*, 22 (1969); A.G. Kenwood, 'Railway Investment in Britain, 1825-1875', *Economica*, 32 (1965); B.R. Mitchell, 'The Coming of the Railway and United Kingdom Economic Growth', *Journal of Economic History*, 24 (1964)

7   R.J. Irving, 'British Railway Investment and Innovation, 1900-1914; An Analysis with Special Reference to the North Eastern and London & North Western Railway Companies', *Business History*, 13 (1971)

8   G. Channon, 'A Nineteenth Century Investment Decision: The Midland Railway's London Extension', *Economic History Review*, 25 (1972)

9   T.R. Gourvish, *Mark Huish and the London & North Western*

Railway: A Study of Management (1972); see also his earlier article, 'Captain Mark Huish: A Pioneer in the Development of Railway Management', *Business History*, 12 (1970)

10 G. Alderman, 'The Railway Companies and the Growth of Trade Unionism in the Late Nineteenth and Early Twentieth Centuries', *The Historical Journal*, 14 (1971); P.S. Gupta, 'Railway Trade Unionism in Britain, C.1880-1900', *Economic History Review*, 19 (1966); B.F. Duckham, 'Railway Steamship Enterprise: the Lancashire and Yorkshire Railway's East Coast Fleet, 1904-14', *Business History*, 10 (1968); T.R. Gourvish, 'The Railways and Steamboat Competition in Early Victorian Britain', *Transport History*, 4 (1971); G. Channon, 'The Aberdeenshire Beef Trade with London: A Study in Steamship and Railway Competition, 1850-69', *Transport History*, 2 (1969); P.J. Cain, 'Railway Combination and Government, 1900-1914', *Economic History Review*, 25 (1972)

11 B.R. Mitchell, 'The Coming of the Railway and United Kingdom Economic Growth', *Journal of Economic History*, 24 (1964); W. Vamplew, 'The Railways and the Iron Industry: A Study of the Relationship in Scotland', in M.C. Reed (ed), *Railways in the Victorian Economy* (1969); and 'Railways and the Transformation of the Scottish Economy', *Economic History Review*, 24 (1971)

12 G.R. Hawke, *Railways and Economic Growth in England and Wales, 1840-1870* (1970)

13 Hawke's work is discussed in Chapter 1

14 J.R. Kellett, *The Impact of Railways Upon Victorian Cities* (1969)

15 M. Simpson, 'Urban Transport and the Development of Glasgow's West End, 1830-1914', *Journal of Transport History*, NS 1 (1972)

16 J. Simmons, 'The Power of the Railway', Chapter 12 in H.J. Dyos and M. Wolff (ed), *The Victorian City: Images and Realities* (1973)

17 For a very handy survey of the available material see G. Ottley, *Railway History — A Guide to Sixty-one Collections in Libraries and Archives in Great Britain* (1973)

18 W. Albert, *The Turnpike Road System in England, 1663-1840*

(1972)

19   R.W. Unwin and R.G. Wilson, 'The Aire and Calder Navigation', a
      series of four articles in *The Bradford Antiquary*, 42 (1964), 43
      (1967), 44 (1969) and 45 (1971)

20   One little study of the response of Pickfords to the railways
      deserves a mention: G.L. Turnbull, 'The Railway Revolution and
      Carriers' Response: Messrs Pickford & Company, 1830-50',
      Transport History, 2 (1969)

21   T.C. Barker and M. Robbins, *A History of London Transport*,
      Vol 1: *The Nineteenth Century* (1963). The second volume on
      the twentieth century is eagerly awaited

22   J. Hibbs, 'The History of the Motor Bus Industry: A Bibliograph-
      ical Survey', *Journal of Transport History*, NS 2 (1973)

23   J. Hibbs, *The History of British Bus Services* (1968)

24   W. Plowden, *The Motor Car and Politics, 1896-1970* (1971)

25   R. Davis, *The Rise of the English Shipping Industry in the
      Seventeenth and Eighteenth Centuries* (1962) and S.G. Sturmey,
      British Shipping and World Competition (1962)

26   D.C. North, 'Sources of Productivity Change in Ocean Shipping',
      The Journal of Political Economy, 76 (1968); G.M. Walton,
      'Sources of Productivity Change in American Colonial Shipping,
      1665-1775', *Economic History Review*, 20 (1967), 'A Measure
      of Productivity Change in American Colonial Shipping',
      Economic History Review, 21 (1969), 'Productivity Change in
      Ocean Shipping after 1870: A Comment', *Journal of Economic
      History*, 30 (1970), 'Obstacles to Technical Diffusion in Ocean
      Shipping, 1675-1775', *Explorations in Economic History*, 8
      (1970-1); R. Knauerhase, 'The Compound Steam Engine and
      Productivity Changes in the German Merchant Marine Fleet,
      1871-1887', *Journal of Economic History*, 28 (1968); C.K.
      Harley, 'The Shift from Sailing Ships to Steamships, 1850-1890;
      A Study in Technological Change and its Diffusion', in D.N.
      McCloskey (ed), *Essays on a Mature Economy: Britain after 1840*
      (1971)

27   F.E. Hyde, *Blue Funnel* (1956); *Shipping Enterprise and Management 1830-1939: Harrisons of Liverpool* (1967); Sheila Marriner and F.E. Hyde, *The Senior John Samuel Swire, 1825-98* (1967). A volume on Cunard is eagerly awaited

28   P.N. Davies, 'The African Steam Ship Company', F. Neal, 'Liverpool Shipping in the Early Nineteenth Century', and D. Williams, 'Liverpool Merchants and the Cotton Trade, 1820-1850', all in J.R. Harris (ed), *Liverpool and Merseyside: Essays in Economic and Social History of the Port and its Hinterland* (1969); P.N. Davies and A.M. Bourn, 'Lord Kylsant and the Royal Mail', *Business History*, 14 (1972)

29   G. Jackson, *Hull in the Eighteenth Century: A Study in Economic and Social History* (1972), especially Chapters 3, 4, 6

30   One of the very few studies on this aspect is that by Chiang Hai Ding, 'The Early Shipping Conference System of Singapore, 1877-1911', *Journal of South East Asian History*, 10 (1969)

31   P. Mathias and A.W.H. Pearsall (eds), *Shipping: A Survey of Historical Records* (1971)

32   A very useful book on technical development and its implications is that by R. Miller and D. Sawers, *The Technical Development of Modern Aviation* (1968)

33   W.G. Neale, *At the Port of Bristol*, Vol 1: *Members and Problems, 1848-1899* (1968); Vol 2: *The Turn of the Tide, 1900-1914* (1970)

34   F.E. Hyde, *Liverpool and the Mersey: An Economic History of a Port, 1700-1970* (1971)

1 Railways and Economic Growth[1]

First published in The Journal of Transport History, *NS 1 (1972)*

The last decade or so has witnessed one of the liveliest debates among economic historians to date, namely the controversy concerning the new economic history or the debate about methodology in history. Indeed almost as much has been written about the virtues or otherwise of the 'new' methodology as on the subject itself. The debate is now becoming somewhat sterile and it is not the purpose here to add to the growing volume of literature in this respect. But for the sake of clarity it is important to get the record straight by way of a few observations about the 'new' art, or should we say science?*

Briefly and simply stated the new economic history lays primary emphasis on measurement and pays specific recognition to the relationships between measurement and theory. It involves the application of economic, statistical and accounting tools to specific problems of economic development. The economic tools provide the means by which to construct a model or theory which can then be tested for its validity by the application of statistical analysis. There is nothing very novel in this procedure as far as contemporary problems or those of the recent past are concerned. To take a simple example: economic theory postulates that there is some positive relationship between production and productivity movements. The validity of this proposition can be, and has been, tested by applying statistical analysis to the observed data.

---

* I appreciate the valuable comments made by Professor H.J. Dyos

Clearly the methodological techniques are anything but new.[2] Perhaps the chief departure lies in the fact that in recent years young and energetic scholars, mainly American, have been applying known techniques on an extensive scale to problems of specification in major areas of historical debate. Thus to try and determine the endless and inconclusive descriptive debates about such major issues as the economics of slavery, the role of the railroads in American development, and the impact of declining exports on the growth of the British economy in the later nineteenth century, the new economic historians have sought to formulate explicit propositions and have then proceeded to test their validity. Correct specification is a crucial factor in such studies and for this reason theory is used to identify the explanatory variables for which quantitative information is required and sometimes to derive evidence about those variables for which information is not readily available.[3] Frequently the device of a simulation model is employed to determine what might have happened had certain events not taken place. By constructing a counterfactual situation or hypothetical past, for which invented data are supplied, it is possible to measure the difference between observed data (that is reality) and the predictions of the model.[4] A well-known example has been the attempt to project the likely developments in transportation and economic activity in America in the absence of railroads.[5]

That these studies have yielded more than trivial findings is testified by the results so far produced.[6] Other branches of history have not remained unaffected by such developments — they have certainly been caught up in the trend towards quantification — but for the most part the use of advanced techniques has been confined to economic history.[7] In so far as historians have used quantitative techniques at all they have used only descriptive statistics and fairly elementary methods and have tended to eschew problems involving model building and the use of sophisticated statistical techniques.[8] It is evident however that a more scientific approach to the analysis of historical problems is emerging, a trend no doubt encouraged by similar advancements in related disciplines.[9]

Such developments have not gone unchallenged, though given the rather innocuous and yet potentially rewarding nature of the 'new' methodology it is sometimes difficult to comprehend what all the fuss is about. Unfortunately the general debate has centred not on the important issues such as the nature of the methods and tools to be used in such analyses; rather it has either taken the form of a somewhat sterile discussion on peripheral issues, eg whether this particular type of history is new or not, or else it has consisted of a frontal attack on the whole concept of the new economic history. The latter has been couched in terms of a basic incompatibility between theory and history but so far it has failed to register any really convincing arguments to justify rejection of the basic methodology. Fritz Redlich, one of the severest critics, argues that econometric history is simply quasi-history on the grounds that it involves the use of hypothetical models or counterfactual propositions which are alien to history, that in turn these cannot be verified precisely, and finally that the methods used are anti-empirical.[10] None of these points of criticism can stand the test of close scrutiny. The substance of the argument rests on the line against counterfactuals but these are germane to all historical enquiry whatever the mode of investigation. Few historians could claim that at one time or another they have not posed the question 'What if such and such had not happened then . . .?' Or to put it in a more concrete form: 'What would have happened to the British economy if there had been no return to the gold standard in 1925 (or alternatively, a return at a lower parity)?' On numerous occasions historians have asked this particular question, but the answers have consisted largely of a series of intuitive guesses as to what might have taken place. No specific solution can be derived until the proposition is put to the econometric test.

In other words, to reject the use of the counterfactual would be to destroy much of the base of historical enquiry.

The opponents of the new approach are clearly on weak ground therefore in taking stance against the counterfactual concept, especially since, as Murphy has pointed out, 'the whole purpose of testing counterfactuals . . . has been to please historians'.[11] And after all, the new economic historians have not been engaged in constructing weird and wonderful counterfactuals that are so abstruse as to be divorced completely from reality, but have primarily concerned themselves with making explicit and testing those which have been thrown up by traditional historical enquiry. Thus as Professor Fogel, the leading practitioner of econometric history, makes clear: 'the difference between the old and new economic history is not the frequency with which one encounters counterfactual propositions, but the extent to which such propositions are made explicit. The old economic history abounds in disguised counterfactual assertions'.[12]

Critics have also argued that quantitative and econometric methods are of limited value because of the inadequacy of the historical data. Such methods are obviously not appropriate to every historical situation and where historical data are inadequate or imprecise their application would yield limited results. Yet while few would contend that a scientific approach can get over this problem satisfactorily ' . . . it hardly follows that, when the sources are suspect or the facts incomplete, an impressionistic, subjective approach can surmount these difficulties'.[13] In any case it is perhaps insufficiently appreciated that the use of scientific tools provides scope for a certain amount of data reconstruction and enables the maximum use to be made of what information is available. Thus, if the historical data are satisfactory, then to contend that impressionistic and subjective judgements are better than the findings derived from a scientific analysis of the facts is surely going too far. Those historians who cannot accept this proposition are simply confirming that they do not wish to make the best use of their resources. While at the other extreme, where the data are completely unsuitable for scientific analysis it is questionable whether they can be used very fruitfully by any type of historian.

If the critics of the new approach have failed to come up with any powerful arguments against it this does not mean that the findings and methods of the new economic history have to be accepted without question.[14] In due course some of the results achieved may be subject to modification in the light of new data or the application of more powerful tools of analysis, while the methods themselves are constantly open to refinement. But whatever its present limitations it is clear that the new approach offers the prospect of obtaining far more definitive answers to some of the hitherto unresolved historical problems regardless of whether or not all historians are anxious to know the solutions.[15]

Transport history has gained a place of some prominence in the rise of the new economic history. It is true that the first major formulations were made in the late 1950s when Conrad and Meyer investigated the economics of slavery,[16] but the subject really sprang to life in the mid-1960s with the publication of two profound works on US railroads by Fogel and Fishlow.[17] These set out to determine exactly what contribution the railroads made to economic growth by measuring their social saving, ie the difference between the actual cost of shipping goods in a particular year (1890 and 1859 respectively) and the alternative cost of freighting the same commodities in the absence of railroads. The results came as something of a shock to many historians who had previously believed in the overwhelming importance of railways as an agent of economic growth. At the most the social saving derived from railroads amounted to between 4 and 6 per cent of national income, representing approximately one year's delay or more in the growth of the economy.[18]

The railways have been made the subject of the first new economic history written in this country. Following in the footsteps of Fogel and Fishlow, Dr Hawke has produced a work which will no doubt remain a model of its kind. It is certainly a more wide-ranging and intensive study than that of Fogel, though the approach and method of analysis are

very similar. As with Fogel and Fishlow, Hawke's main objective is to determine the importance of railways in the economy
of England and Wales. The study is centred on the year 1865
and the questions posed are straightforward: 'To what extent
did the economy depend on railways in 1865?, to what extent
could the national income of 1865 have been attained without
the innovation of railways?, and what were the social returns
to investment in railways?' These questions he approaches
through a calculation of the social saving derived from the
railways, measured as the difference between the actual cost
of transport services in any one year provided by the railways
and the alternative cost of the same services in the absence of
railways (p 31). The main social savings calculations for passenger and freight traffic are produced in Chapters II-VII. The remaining chapters investigate the linkages from railways to
other sectors of the economy to see if these resulted in any
contribution to economic growth which has not been picked
up or recorded in the direct social savings calculations. The
last chapter summarises and assesses the findings.

For convenience the main results may be summarised
briefly. In aggregate the railways probably contributed about
10 per cent of the national income in 1865: in other words,
had they been dispensed with it would have been necessary
to compensate for the loss of about one tenth of the national
income. The social savings on freight traffic derived from the
railways amounted to 4.1 per cent of the national product
(most of which came from coal and minerals), while in the
case of passengers the railways increased production possibilities by between 2.6 and 7.1 per cent depending on the
assumptions made about the degree of personal comfort. Dr
Hawke recognises that the social savings calculations may
understate the impact of the railways if they induced in other
sectors of the economy changes that favoured economic
growth. Thus additional calculations are required to measure
any technological external economies that the railways made
available to people and firms acting as other than transport
users. For instance, the provision of railway services might

induce in a particular industry a greater degree of concentration of production resources, or encourage the adoption of new techniques, and these could result in a fall in real production costs which would not be recorded in the social savings calculations. After a fairly intensive survey of the possible indirect repercussions of the railways on other industries, on the labour force and the influence of railway pricing policy and productivity movements etc, he finds that little addition needs to be made for externalities, so that in the absence of the railways the loss to national income would not have been much greater than 10 per cent. Finally, the railways provided a socially rewarding, if financially unattractive, investment; the social internal rate of return averaged 15-20 per cent between 1830 and 1870, a return not likely to be exceeded by an alternative use of resources.

These then are the basic findings. At this point many obvious questions spring to mind: What is their significance? How reliable are the results? Is the method of calculation sound? It would however require more than a short article to do full justice to the volume, for after reading each chapter several queries and criticisms are immediately raised. I shall therefore focus attention on one or two broad issues. First it is essential to assess the significance of the findings and their comparability with American experience. Second, the reliability of the data used and the calculations themselves require some comment. And third, some observations will be made on the basic methodology and assumptions underlying the study.

If we accept the finding that dispensing with the railways would have involved the loss of 10 per cent of the national income in 1865, we must then assess the significance of this figure. Hawke only addresses himself very briefly to this issue and admits, perhaps somewhat grudgingly, that the railways did have a considerable impact on the economy. Unfortunately we have no other yardstick, at least within the context of the British economy, with which to make an assessment, but from our knowledge of the structure of the Victorian economy it seems unlikely that any other innovation or sector could have had such a large impact on the economy. One of the largest sectors in the later nineteenth century was building and construction, but this rarely accounted for more than about 4 per cent of national income and the social return from this sector was hardly likely to have been larger than that of the railways. However, as Hawke notes, this does not necessarily imply that the railways were crucial to the development of a wide range of other industries.

Many writers, when reviewing the work, have naturally enough made direct reference to the US results, and even Hawke himself makes the comparison. Against Fogel's 5 per cent saving for 1890 the 10 per cent for this country appears large. There are of course obvious reasons why there should be a difference: for example, water transport was much cheaper relative to rail in America than in England. Even so it is doubtful whether any really meaningful comparison can be made since the bases on which the two sets of calculations are made are somewhat different. Originally Fogel computed the social saving on agricultural commodities and it was only in a later article that he crudely estimated the savings on non-agricultural commodities and adopted Fishlow's figures for savings in passenger traffic.[19] Thus his aggregate saving of some 5 per cent of the national income cannot be regarded as a very firm result. Moreover, unlike Hawke who does not specify what changes might have taken place in non-rail transportation had the railways not been built, Fogel postulates feasible extensions to the canal network in America. The effects of these are apparently embodied in the final social savings calculations and this would inevitably lead to a lower value compared with that for England and Wales. For these reasons it would be unwise to press the comparison of the results unduly.

In any case, despite Hawke's impressive and wide-ranging inquiry one cannot help but feel somewhat sceptical about the end product. It may be that he has arrived at about the right order of magnitude in his social savings calculations but this could be more through fortuitous accident than conscious design. This is not intended as a criticism of the author's scholarship or the care and lucidity with which he presents his findings. It represents, rather, doubts as to the procedure and assumptions adopted in the study. These can be conveniently dealt with under the following headings: (1) coverage, (2) use of data and (3) methodology.

Although much more comprehensive than Fogel's original study, Dr Hawke's analysis still contains some gaps, the effect of which is probably to underestimate the value of the social savings. For example, no evaluation is made of the productive time savings as a result of faster travel by rail, while the economic effects of carrying mail are not even considered. More important, the study is incomplete in two respects: first, the author does not examine all the leads and lags between railways and other sectors of the economy; and second, no attempt is made to show what the economy would have been like had the railways not been created. Possibly this is asking too much of any one author to undertake but until we have answers on these points a final assessment of the impact of the railways cannot be made.

As far as the first point is concerned Dr Hawke does investigate some of the linkages in the second part of his study: these include the effects of the railways on the coal, iron and a few other industries, and on the capital market, the location of industry and the labour supply. For the most part he finds that the railways were not crucial to the development of other sectors and that most of the gains are already included in the direct social savings calculations. It is doubtful however whether all the technological externalities have been taken into account properly. The brick, stone and timber industries are dismissed in a couple of pages, while engineering and construction are barely considered. Even for those sectors which are discussed in some detail one gets the impression that Dr Hawke is too readily inclined to dismiss their significance. The influence of the railways on managerial techniques and on the development of the capital market and the investing habit, for instance, are probably underestimated.[20] Moreover, although he considers the additional gains over and above the social savings calculation to have been small, no precise estimates are given and the final result simply contains a rather vague 'guesstimate' as to what they might be. Finally, some aspects are not considered at all, such as the wider implications of the railways on the social and urban development of the country. It is possible that the larger town and urban groupings resulting from railway development led to economies in the administration of local governments which are not reflected in the social savings calculations. As Fogel recognises, 'No evaluation of the impact of railroads on [American] development can be complete without a consideration of the cultural, political, military and social consequences of such an innovation.'[21]

The above considerations suggest that the social savings may have been underestimated. The implications of the second point noted above are more difficult to determine. Hawke does not hypothesise what would have happened in a non-rail economy, though such an enquiry is crucial to the interpretation of the real social savings derived from the railways. It is probable that in the absence of the latter resources would have been devoted to expanding the non-rail transport network (canals, coastal shipping and roads), and depending on whether this resulted in increasing, falling or constant costs compared with those under a rail/non-rail transport system the social savings would be increased, decreased or remain the same respectively. It is difficult to determine precisely what would have happened since so much depends on the assumptions made. American experience suggests that the social savings would have been reduced given a further extension of the canal network, though this is probably not a very useful guide in view of the wide discrepancy in cost structures between water and rail transport between the two countries.[22] However, it seems plausible to assume that extensions and innovations in the non-rail transport sector (eg the development of more efficient road vehicles)[23] would have resulted in falling costs in this sector and thereby offset some of the potential gains from the introduction of railways.

All this is admittedly hypothetical, but not until we know the alternative resource costs under dynamic conditions can we determine the real social savings derived from building the railways. As Hawke rightly points out in his introductory chapter, the concept of social saving is the *ex post* analogue to the *ex ante* concept used in cost-benefit studies and if the latter had been applied at that time to railway investment the alternative use of resources would have had to be taken into account.[24]

Doubts must also be expressed about the selection of data and the basis of some of the calculations. The yearly estimates of social savings which are made for both passenger and freight traffic for the years 1840-70 (to 1890 in the case of freight) are derived from extrapolations on the base year of 1865. Constant real costs are assumed for alternative modes (mainly canals for freight and coach for passengers) so that the multiplicand remains the same for each year. The estimates of the costs of alternative transport modes are derived in a very crude manner indeed. In the case of freight traffic the cost figures of only two canals are considered, the Leeds & Liverpool, and the Kennet & Avon, and these range from 0.12d to 0.6d per ton-mile. A vague compromise of 0.4d is then selected which is supposed to represent 'as reasonable an estimate as the evidence presently available permits'(p 84). To this is added the derived cost of shipping by canal (1.5d), which again is based in fragmentary scraps of data, and an allowance for slightly longer shipments by canal. The final result produces the hypothetical non-rail cost of 2.3d per ton-mile which when multiplied by the total ton-mileage gives the non-rail cost of goods transport. The social saving is then derived by subtracting the rail cost from the result.

There are several grounds for concern here. The data on non-rail costs are compiled on the basis of very slender

evidence and it is extremely doubtful whether they are
reliable enough for the purposes to which they are put.
Second, it is assumed that the costs of canal transport remain
constant through time and for all commodities so that for
each year the cost multiplier is the same for all types of traffic.
This may not affect the aggregate social savings calculation
materially but it could make a considerable difference to the
sectoral breakdown. It is difficult to believe, for instance,
that it cost about four times as much to carry coal by canal
than by rail. Third, only canal transport is considered as an
alternative to rail but some freight also went by road and sea
where costs varied considerably compared with the canals. In
parts of Lincolnshire, for instance, road cartage of agricultural
freight was charged at the rate of 6d per ton-mile as against
1d per ton-mile by rail in the early 1840s,[25] while in Scotland
the median charges per ton-mile for minerals (1860s) were as
follows: carts 5.21d, canals 3.86d, east coast sea routes 1.47d,
and west coast sea routes 0.66d.[26] These rates do not of
course reflect real costs but if similar orders of magnitude
prevailed in costs to those reflected in the rates charged by
different modes it suggests that some allowance must be made
for non-canal transportation when computing the social
savings.

Similar criticisms are applicable with respect to the calculations for passenger traffic. Here the alternative mode is
coach travel; water transport is dismissed as an unsuitable
alternative though in this case the neglect is probably not one
of great moment. But again the cost data for coach travel are
based on very limited evidence. Two sources only are used,
those of Lardner and the Royal Commission on Railways of
1867. The former equated first-class traffic with inside coach
travel and second- and third-class with outside coach travel,
but the relevant rates are not specified in detail. The Royal
Commission equated first-class rail traffic with 'posting' at a
cost of 2s per mile, second-class traffic with inside coach
travel and the rest with outside coach travel at 4d and 2½d
per mile respectively. These values are assumed to reflect real

costs — a somewhat dubious assumption — and the resultant
calculations produce lower and upper limits of the social
savings in personal travel, a large element of which is derived
from increased comfort. Apart from the crudeness of the
data used it is questionable whether the corresponding classes
between rail and coach are correctly specified. Given the fact
that all forms of rail travel were superior in speed and comfort
to any by road and, in addition, that no allowance is made
for productive time savings, then even the upper estimates
probably underestimate the social savings as presently
calculated. Finally, both in the case of freight and passenger
traffic Hawke uses a constant cost money multiplier for conveyance by alternative modes but the railway receipts (costs)
are kept in current prices.

Other criticisms could be made on this score, eg regarding
the derivation of the ton-mileage and passenger-mileage
statistics. Much of the data is derived from fragmentary scraps
of evidence or extrapolations from single 'authoritative'
estimates, and it is doubtful whether they are always adequate for the purposes at hand. The author acknowledges the
paucity of information (though in some cases he has not cast
his net very wide) and the inexactitude of some of his estimates. Nevertheless, he expresses a surprising degree of
confidence in some of the results: 'It would be surprising',
he says with reference to his estimates for rail output, 'if
later research shows any of these figures to be greatly
misleading' (p 77).

We have already touched upon some of the more detailed
points of analysis and it now remains to discuss the methodological problem in broader terms. In some respects this is
the issue which gives grounds for most concern. One reason
for this is that Dr Hawke never really explicitly states his
methodological approach in detail at the start. Admittedly he
follows close on the heels of Fogel and Fishlow and there is
a very useful appraisal of their techniques in the introductory
chapter. But given the criticisms which he and other writers
have made about their methods of analysis and assumptions it

is a pity that he does not clarify the issue for his own subsequent analysis. Instead the reader is left to pick up the assumptions one by one as he works through the chapters and even then they are not always made very explicitly. As a result some methodological ambiguities arise which have quite serious implications.

In order to establish the benefits of an innovation such as the railways it is necessary to know the marginal costs of both rail and all alternative transport modes. It is then possible to derive a value for the real resource saving of the innovation, as opposed to the direct financial savings to transport users, as follows: $(MC_a - MC_r)Q$ where

MC_a = the marginal cost of carrying traffic on alternative modes
MC_r = the marginal cost of carrying traffic by rail
Q = the quantity of traffic to be carried

However, though relatively simple in theory[27] there are certain practical difficulties involved in the application. Normally, and especially for the nineteenth century, it is difficult to determine the structure of marginal costs in transport very accurately and so it is often necessary to use some price variable as a proxy for marginal costs. This would be all right so long as prices charged by all carriers were equal to their respective marginal costs but this is unlikely to be the case. Second, if an accurate estimate of social savings is to be made some assumption must be made about the likely movement of marginal costs as traffic is diverted from one transport mode to another. For small incremental shifts at the margin this presumably would not pose much of a problem, but for large diversions in any one year it would not be possible to extrapolate from the existing cost data.

It would appear that Hawke makes several assumptions with regard to costs: that the relevant costs used reflect marginal costs of carrying traffic; that rail receipts are equivalent to rail resource costs; and that costs per ton-mile

on alternative modes remain constant. Now these assumptions
are either questionable or inconsistently applied throughout
the study. There is no explicit statement on the marginal cost
concept and the treatment of this problem varies from one
transport mode to another. In the case of canal transport some
attempt is made to distinguish between non-rail charges and
non-rail costs though whether the latter can be regarded as
the true marginal cost for canals, given the crude manner in
which it is estimated, is another matter. However, for road
and rail transport marginal costs are assumed to be equivalent
to rates charged. Now although for road transport this may
have been true in some cases, at least where rail competition
forced road charges down towards marginal costs, for the
railways this was clearly not so unless they were making zero
profits. In any case, since the railways did not know the
marginal costs of their individual services 'it is still less
plausible to relate the average of the individual rates to marginal costs' (p 291); in which case it is surely unrealistic to use
rail receipts as a measure of resource costs. The final assumption,
that of constant costs of non-rail transport, is particularly
dubious. Given the increasing diversion of traffic to alternative modes it is clearly somewhat implausible to assume that
their costs remained constant, but this brings us back again
to a consideration of the changes which would have occurred
in the non-rail sector in the absence of railways.

There can be no denying that Dr Hawke has produced a
most scholarly and intellectually stimulating volume which
will provide a focus of debate for some years to come.
Furthermore, it is also a very informative piece of work con-
taining much of interest to those readers who are not specially
interested in quantitative and econometric techniques of
analysis. There is a surprising amount of information and
factual material (some of it not always very relevant to the
main theme of the volume) on all manner of topics, including
not only the railways themselves, but also employment,
agriculture, various industries — especially iron — and the
capital market. In fact the book would provide a very useful

starting point for a study of the mid-Victorian economy, though its value in this respect is certainly not enhanced by the derisory index of less than three pages.

Nevertheless, in the light of the above considerations it can be argued that a precise estimate of the social savings from the railways still remains to be made. The study leaves several points open to question which give rise to some doubt about the credibility of the findings. Without performing the necessary calculations it is impossible to say whether Dr Hawke has overestimated or understated the gains from the railways, but it is clear that considerable refinement and modification of the analysis are required before we can be confident that we have the final result. It may be, as one critic of Fogel has hinted, that it is asking too much to ask 'What if there had been no railroads . . .?'[28] Whether this is correct or not one thing is certain: the railways will never be the same again since the advent of Fogel, Fishlow and Hawke.

NOTES

1   G.R. Hawke, *Railways and Economic Growth in England and Wales, 1840-1870* (Oxford, 1970)

2   Even with respect to historical problems. Before the war Beveridge, for instance, was using regression analysis in his investigations of the trade cycle

3   For a lucid exposition of the techniques see H.J. Habakkuk, 'Economic History and Economic Theory', *Daedalus*, C (1971)

4   The 'newness' of this is not the use of the counterfactual, which is implicitly incorporated in much traditional historical enquiry, but the fact that the counterfactual is made explicit and quantified. M. Desai, 'Some Issues in Econometric History', *Economic History Review*, XXI (1968)

5   R.W. Fogel, *Railroads and American Economic Growth: Essays in Econometric History* (Baltimore, Md, 1964). So far most of

the counterfactual exercises relate to America though Smelser
attempted a reconstruction of the social structure of Lancashire
in the absence of an industrial revolution. N.J. Smelser, *Social
Change in the Industrial Revolution: An Application of Theory
to the Lancashire Cotton Industry, 1770-1840* (1959)

6   The literature is too extensive to quote in full but a useful collec-
tive survey of recent work can be found in R.W. Fogel and S.L.
Engerman, *The Reinterpretation of American Economic History*
(New York, 1971). See also the papers and bibliographical
material in R.L. Andreano (ed), *The New Economic History*
(New York, 1970). For a short and useful summary of current
achievements and the scope for further enquiry see A. Fishlow
and R.W. Fogel, 'Quantitative Economic History: An Interim
Evaluation: Past Trends and Present Tendencies', *Journal of
Economic History*, XXXI (March 1971)

7   J.M. Price, 'Recent Quantitative Work in History: A Survey of
the Main Trends', *History and Theory*, Beiheft 9 (1969).
Quantitative work is nothing new in economic history and some
economists have turned their hand to this kind of work, though
many economic historians prefer to regard this as a branch of
applied economics

8   W.O. Aydelotte, *Quantification in History* (Reading, Mass, 1971),
28. Though Professor Aydelotte's conception of what is involved
is perhaps somewhat oversimplified (see p 44).

9   In urban history, for instance, more explicit questions are being
asked and new techniques adopted including the application of
sociological theory and the use of quantitative materials and
statistical methods. See S. Thernstrom and R. Sennett, *Nineteenth-
Century Cities: Essays in the New Urban History* (Yale, 1969), vii,
and S. Thernstrom, 'Reflections on the New Urban History',
Daedalus, C (1971), 370. In other disciplines, notably geography,
the use of more scientific techniques of analysis has made considerable progress. See H.C. Prince, 'Real, Imagined and Abstract
Worlds of the Past', *Progress in Geography*, III (1971), for an
extensive review of recent research

10   F. Redlich, ' "New" and Traditional Approaches to Economic
History and Their Interdependence', *Journal of Economic
History*, XXV (1965)

11 G.G.S. Murphy, 'On Counterfactual Propositions', *History and Theory*, Beiheft 9 (1969), 16

12 R.W. Fogel, 'The New Economic History: Its Findings and Methods', *Economic History Review*, XIX (1966), 655

13 Aydelotte, op cit, 52

14 Nor should the above argument be construed as an attempt to re-- ject the utility of traditional economic history. Quantitative analy- sis clearly has limits as well as limitations and it is certainly unlikely to produce much technological obsolescence among traditional economic historians. In any case the polarisation of the two groups has surely been pressed too far, and both have much to offer each other. An impassioned plea for more co-operative effort and the termination of the divide between the two opposing methodological camps has recently been made by H.W. Richardson, in 'British Emigration and Overseas Investment, 1870-1914', *Economic History Review*, XXV (1972), 100, 108

15 It would seem that some are not. Professor A. Schlesinger, Jnr, for instance, has written that 'almost all important questions are important precisely because they are not susceptible to quantita- tive answers' — 'The Humanist Looks at Empirical Social Research', *American Sociological Review*, XXVII (1962), 770

16 A.H. Conrad and J.R. Meyer, 'The Economics of Slavery in the Ante-Bellum South', *Journal of Political Economy*, 66 (1958) and 'Economic Theory, Statistical Inference and Economic History', *Journal of Economic History*, 17 (1957)

17 Fogel, op cit; A. Fishlow, *American Railroads and the Trans- formation of the Ante-Bellum Economy* (Cambridge, Mass, 1965)

18 This represents a very emasculated summary of the main findings, some of the points of which will be elaborated below

19 R.W. Fogel, 'Railroads as an Analogy to the Space Effort: Some Economic Aspects', *Economic Journal*, LXXVI (1966), 39-40

20 See T.R. Gourvish, 'Captain Mark Huish: A Pioneer in the Development of Railway Management', *Business History*, XII (1970), and J.R. Killick and W.A. Thomas, 'The Provincial

Stock Exchanges, 1830-1870', *Economic History Review*, XXIII (1970)

21   Fogel, *Economic Journal*, loc cit, 40 n 2

22   In the United States railway services were cheaper than those of England and Wales, but since relative water costs favoured America even more, the impact of the railway was less

23   This is not so impractical as it sounds. By the early 1830s steam carriages had been developed to the extent that they offered one of the cheapest and quickest forms of travel over short distances. Had the railways not appeared it is conceivable that much greater improvement in the mode of land carriage would have taken place. See Walter Hancock, *Narrative of Twelve Years' Experiments (1824-1836) Demonstrative of the Practicability and Advantages of Employing Steam Carriages on Common Roads* (1838), 3-5, 97

24   On this point see Paul A. David, 'Transport Innovation and Economic Growth: Professor Fogel on and off the Rails', *Economic History Review*, XXII (1969), 513

25   Samuel Sidney, *Railways and Agriculture in North Lincolnshire. Rough Notes of a Ride over the Track of the Manchester, Sheffield, Lincolnshire and Other Railways* (1848), 13

26   Wray Vamplew, 'Railways and the Transformation of the Scottish Economy', *Economic History Review*, XXIV (1971), 51

27   To obtain a precise formulation for social savings certain other variables need to be taken into account but for present purposes these need not concern us here. See P.D. McClelland, 'Railroads, American Growth, and the New Economic History: A Critique', *Journal of Economic History*, XXVIII (1968)

28   McClelland, loc cit, 121

2 The Efficiency and Enterprise of British Railways, 1870-1914

First published in Explorations in Entrepreneurial History, 5 *(1968)*

Despite an immense amount of literature about British railways, little has been attempted in the way of analysing the efficiency and enterprise of railway undertakings in the period after the construction of the main network between the 1870s and 1914. In fact only one book of any note has been published and that was written nearly half a century ago by the economist George Paish.[1] Since then little interest has been shown in the subject apart from a few comments made recently by Kindleberger in an article dealing with the question of obsolescence and technical change in British industry.[2] Yet the subject deserves a full-scale study. The scope of the present essay is much more modest, however, since it only attempts to scratch the surface of a very broad topic. In fact the following comments arise partly out of research the author has been doing into the question of innovation and enterprise in British industry in the later nineteenth century.[3] The chief object of the exercise is to outline the main issues in the hope that it will provoke other scholars to make more detailed analysis.

Even today it is difficult to find a satisfactory measure of efficiency for the service industries since there are so many intangible elements which defy precise quantification. For the nineteenth century the problem is more complex because of the limited nature of the statistical data. However, two series are available, one relating to profitability and the other to labour productivity, details of which are produced in Tables 1 and 2. Both these seem to indicate that from the 1870s or early 1880s the railways' operating performance was deteriorating steadily. The percentage of working expenditure to gross receipts rose steadily from around 50 per cent in the period 1860-80 to 63 per cent in the years immediately prior to World War I; the rate of return on paid-up capital fell from a peak of 4.41 per cent in 1870 to an annual average of 3.42 per cent between 1905 and 1909. The productivity index shows a similar trend. Compound rates of growth for selected periods have been worked out from the Phelps Brown productivity index (total railway traffic divided by the numbers employed) which is based on the Hoffmann production data. Although this is only a fairly crude index, the fall in the rate of growth of productivity is sufficiently large as to rule out any possibility of statistical error being solely responsible for the downward trend. Whereas in the period from 1860-1 to 1879-80 labour productivity on the railways rose by 1.59 per cent per annum, in the following three decades between 1880-1 and 1909-10 it averaged no more than 0.17 per cent. In other words, productivity on the railways remained practically stationary in the three or four decades before 1914.

The question is why did diminishing returns set in during the later nineteenth century? Was it inevitable that they should do so in a maturing service industry, and if so in what ways could the railways counteract the trend? Briefly the argument which follows will suggest that though diminishing returns were to some extent inevitable given the nature of the traffic and other conditions, there is a good case for maintaining that the railways did not pay sufficient attention to improving their techniques of operation. Some of the factors which retarded innovations will be presented briefly in the final section.

The deterioration in the operating ratio was not necessarily a true reflection of a decline in efficiency on the part of the railways. It was partly the result of a rapid rise in working expenses in relation to gross earnings; between 1880 and 1906 the former rose by 116.6 per cent as against 79 per cent for gross earnings. This was the product of unfavourable

TABLE 1
RECEIPTS AND EXPENSES OF BRITISH RAILWAYS, 1870-1912

	Gross Receipts	Working Expenses	Net Receipts	Percentage of Net Receipts to Total Paid up Capital	Percentage of Working Expenditure to Gross Receipts
	£mn	£mn	£mn		
1860	27.7	13.1	14.5	4.19	47
1870	45.0	21.7	23.3	4.41	48
1880	65.4	33.6	31.8	4.38	51
1885	69.5	36.7	32.7	4.02	53
1890	79.9	43.1	36.7	4.10	54
1895	85.9	47.8	38.0	3.80	56
1900	104.8	64.7	40.0	3.41	62
1905	113.5	70.0	43.4	3.42	62
1910	123.9	76.5	47.3	3.59	62
1912	128.5	81.2	47.3	3.55	63

Source: Railway Returns of the Board of Trade

TABLE 2
AVERAGE ANNUAL GROWTH RATES OF LABOUR PRODUCTIVITY ON BRITISH RAILWAYS

Quinquennial Averages		Long-Term Rates	
1860/61-1864/65	4.3	1860/61-1879/80	1.59
1865/66-1869/70	2.23	1865/66-1879/80	0.92
1870/71-1874/75	1.53	1870/71-1879/80	0.27
1875/76-1879/80	−1.0		
1880/81-1884/85	−1.1	1880/81-1909/10	0.17
1885/86-1889/90	0.41	1880/81-1889/90	−0.35
1890/91-1894/95	−1.52	1885/86-1909/10	0.02
1895/96-1899/1900	1.02	1890/91-1909/10	−0.08
1900/01-1904/05	−0.58		
1905/06-1909/10	0.78		

Based on the productivity series given by E.H. Phelps Brown and S.J. Handfield-Jones, 'The Climacteric of the 1890s: A Study in the Expanding Economy', *Oxford Economic Papers* (October 1952), 294 trends in costs of both a short- and long-term nature. Running costs rose rapidly in the late nineteenth century and it was at this time that the decline in the operating ratio was greatest. In the 1890s, for example, the cost of labour in the running part of the locomotive department rose by 43 per cent while rates and taxes doubled; and in the five years 1896-1901 the cost of coal doubled.[4] These short-term changes in running costs were superimposed on a long-term unfavourable trend in working costs which, we suggest, can largely be attributed to the nature of the traffic and the type of services provided in the later nineteenth century. After the 1870s the extension of the railway network consisted largely of the building of branch and suburban lines together with the provision of relatively expensive services and conveniences for passengers and traders. All of these entailed an outlay in costs and an increase in the labour supply disproportionate to the increase in receipts and traffic which accrued from them. In other words, average unit costs of operation increased and labour productivity declined because the unit cost of operation on the new services was greater than that of the main line network. For example, the unit costs of operation on many branch lines, particularly those serving remote areas, were high in comparison with costs on the rest of the railway system because of the lower density of traffic. Much suburban line traffic was also less profitable than originally anticipated since a good deal of it consisted of workmen travelling at reduced fares. The returns were fairly small while the peak-hour nature of this traffic necessitated a heavy outlay in rolling stock and labour, part of which remained underutilised during slack periods. And as the Great Northern found when dealing with the large daily traffic flow to London, suburban services could become an embarrassment if they began to interfere with the more profitable main line traffic.[5] Similarly the nature of the goods traffic was changing towards a greater number of small consignments and shorter hauls which tended to raise the cost of handling. A chief goods manager of a leading railway company reported that:

'In order to work with as little capital as possible and to minimise the risks from changes in market conditions, the retailers and local agents keep but little stock on hand and depend upon quick transit for the execution of the orders they receive. As a consequence, instead of large consignments as formerly, the railway companies are called upon to convey small separate lots at more frequent intervals and with extreme expedition and regularity of service.'[6] Moreover, an increasing proportion of the railways' total traffic consisted of the cheaper grades of traffic, including passengers and freight carried at special fares or reduced rates, and coal which was carried at a very low margin of profit. In 1914 something like 80 per cent of the rates quoted by the railways were exceptional (below the standard rate), while coal accounted for about one third of the total freight traffic. Finally, in this period the railways were providing a far wider range of facilities and services than ever before, often with little additional cost to the consumer. To improve the safety and comfort of passenger travel, for example, they were obliged to introduce more expensive rolling stock which involved relatively greater maintenance and running costs. Whereas in 1863 a railway carriage cost the Great Western £250 at the most, by the 1890s the company had to pay over £1,000 for an eight-wheeled upholstered, gas-lit coach.[7]

It is important to bear in mind that all these factors tended to affect the railways' balance sheets adversely (mainly the expenditure side) at the very time when railway charging powers were being made increasingly inflexible by parliamentary control. This meant that the possibility of passing on the increased costs to the consumer was limited, especially as regards goods traffic. The Railway and Canal Traffic Act of 1894 prevented the companies from raising freight rates above those in force at the end of 1892 unless they could justify the increase to the satisfaction of the Railway and Canal Commission. This seriously restricted the freedom of the companies to vary their charges, especially in an upward direction for 'although permitting in principle the discretion

of the companies to vary their charges within the statutory
maxima, the Act tended to make the actual rates in force
become both the maximum and minimum rates'.[8] In fact the
companies were placed in a very difficult position. They were
reluctant to demand increases in freight rates since, if
challenged, they had to prove that there had been an increase
in the cost of conveying the freight exclusive of the cost of
carrying and dealing with passenger traffic. In practice, however, it was virtually impossible to segregate joint costs; the
statistical data collected by the railways were inadequate to
provide a solution to this problem,[9] while the method of
charging adopted by the legislation of 1894 provided little
incentive to determine rates on the basis of operating costs
alone. Consequently few demands were made to raise rates.
Those that were made were rarely accepted, and no relief was
afforded until 1913 when they were allowed a flat rate increase of 4 per cent to cover the cost of a recent wage award.

It has been argued that parliamentary control also prevented a general lowering of rates on the grounds that if any
reductions made proved unprofitable it would be difficult to
get them raised again. It is very doubtful, however, if rates
were as 'sticky' in the downward direction as often imagined.
Certainly the standard rates remained more or less the same
but since traders took every opportunity to secure reductions
by way of exceptional rates the general trend was downward.
If the number of exceptional rates is anything to go by, it
would seem that freight charges were still being reduced after
1894. Within the short space of twelve months, one company
alone arranged sixty-three thousand special rates and, as we
have seen, by 1914 the bulk of the rates quoted by the railways were exceptional or below standard. Thus the railways
got the worst of both worlds; as unit costs of operation rose,
the overall average level of rates charged was declining.
According to one authority, the average receipts per ton fell
from 32.19d to 27.76d between 1892 and 1907.[10] Whether
intended or not, the overall effect of the rate-making
machinery of 1894 was to limit the freedom of the railways

to vary their charges at a time when costs of operation were
escalating upwards.

The inhibiting restrictions of the legislation might not have
been so bad had a more scientific method of fixing rates been
introduced. But apart from the concession of tapering mileage
rates it provided little opportunity or incentive for the companies to base their rates on actual costs of operation.
Generally speaking, rates continued to be determined in much
the same way as they had been in the past

> by the nature and extent of the traffic, the pressure of com-
> petition, either by water, by a rival route, or by other land
> carriage; but, above all, the companies have regard to the
> commercial value of the commodity, and the rate it will bear,
> so as to admit of its being produced and sold in a competing
> market with a fair margin of profit.[11]

Thus the time-honoured principle of low rates for cheaper
commodities and higher rates for more valuable commodities
was maintained. It might be of course that certain low-valued
commodities were cheap to carry while certain high-valued
goods were expensive; but as one transport economist has
pointed out 'such an indirect correspondence between
charges and costs was largely fortuitous'.[12] Admittedly,
scientific costing was a difficult concept to apply to the
railways due to the joint determination of many costs. But
at a time when average costs were rising, in part because of
the extension of the railway network into more unproductive
fields,[13] the need for a proper cost plus discriminating pricing
policy was all the more urgent. Net revenue on the more
marginal traffic was lower than the average since the rates
charged did not reflect the fact that costs of operation were
higher than elsewhere on the system. Thus an increasing proportion of the traffic and services (both passenger and freight)
was being subsidised by the more profitable sections of the
network. 'The failure of revenue to cover costs in some
directions was made good in others by the exercise of
monopoly power to make revenue there much more than

cover costs.'[14] It follows therefore that the restrictive provisions of the legislation of the early 1890s, together with the
absence of any explicit stipulations regarding scientific pricing
policies, forced or even encouraged the railway companies to
retain the benefits (?) of cross-subsidisation far longer than
was desirable. It was not until the growth of road transport
threatened seriously the fortunes of the railways that the
futility of their pricing policy was fully brought home.

If, as it seems, it was difficult for the railways to recoup
increased costs by varying their charges, the only other
alternative was to reduce working expenses and increase
productivity by improving operating performance. Certainly
there seems to have been plenty of scope for technical improvements. Railway traffic was increasing in both volume
and density; measured on the basis of receipts per route
mile,[15] the density of traffic (goods and passengers) on the
British railway system rose by over 30 per cent between
1880 and the early twentieth century.[16] Now it is axiomatic
that railway traffic ought to be handled more economically
as it grows in volume and density. Briefly economical management consists in keeping down the train mileage, keeping
up train loads and reducing operating costs to a minimum.
Apparently, however, British railways made little effort to
improve the handling of their traffic in this period.

The deterioration in the railways' operating performance
attracted much attention in the later nineteenth century,
especially from railway shareholders and a number of
eminent authorities. The American E.B. Dorsey, the English
economist George Paish, and the MP and shareholders'
watchdog Burdett-Coutts made detailed comparative studies
of American and British railway systems.[17] Despite the inadequacy of the statistical data, they all came to the conclusion
that the efficiency of Britain's railway system left much room
for improvement. They were appalled at the high unit cost of
moving freight and passengers on English railways compared
to American railways, and they concluded that considerable
savings could have been achieved had more economical

methods of handling traffic been adopted. Both Paish and Burdett-Coutts were of the opinion that by 1900 there had been virtually no improvement in operating efficiency. The majority of British passenger and goods trains were loaded no more heavily than in 1880 while unit costs of operation were greater. During the same period, American railroads had achieved considerable reductions.

The differences between British and American operating practices were brought out clearly by Paish in a detailed comparative study between the London & North Western and the Pennsylvania railroads. As Table 3 (see p 40) shows, the cost of moving a ton of goods one mile on the former system rose by 24 per cent between 1880 and 1900 whereas the Pennsylvania secured a reduction of 33 per cent. Over the same period the cost of conveying one passenger one mile increased by 11.5 per cent and fell by 13 per cent respectively. Paish argued that these differences were due largely to the fact that the London & North Western had made little progress in improving its methods of handling traffic in this period. In 1900 the average quantity of goods and passengers carried per train was almost exactly the same as it had been twenty years earlier. The average passenger train load was still no more than sufficient to fill one carriage while freight trucks were often moved with loads of less than one ton. The average freight train load of the London & North Western was a mere 68.6 tons as against 486.6 tons for the Pennsylvania railroad. This company's train loads were in fact heavier than those of any other British company barring the Lancashire & Yorkshire. Compared with the latter, the British company ran 45 per cent more trains over one mile of its track to carry 79 per cent less traffic per mile. Had the North Western in 1900 carried train loads of freight and passengers as heavy as those of the American company, its expense would only have been £3.5 million instead of £8.1 million, and its net earnings would have been greater by £4.6 million.

It is only fair to point out, of course, that American

TABLE 3

EARNINGS AND EXPENSES PER TON-MILE

	1880	1900	Percentage Charge 1880-1900
Pennsylvania Railroad			
Receipts per ton-mile	0.459	0.27	−41.2
Expenses per ton-mile	0.270	0.181	−32.9
Net earnings per ton-mile	0.189	0.089	−52.9
London & North Western			
Receipts per ton-mile	1.190	1.189	0.0
Expenses per ton-mile	0.554	0.686	+23.8
Net earnings per ton-mile	0.636	0.503	−20.9

methods of handling traffic were not wholly applicable in Britain since the nature of the traffic was somewhat different. The pattern of traffic on British railways — short hauls and small consignments — provided less scope for the introduction of costly capital equipment which might not be fully utilised. In fact, it has been suggested that some of the alleged short-comings of British railways were due as much to the nature of the traffic as to bad management.[18] This argument can be stretched too far, however, for as Paish pointed out, even when allowance is made for the density of traffic, the smaller consignments and the shorter hauls of the English railroad compared with the American,

> there can be no doubt that our lines are woefully behind. All the considerations that can be thought of, and which should be made for our English lines, cannot justify a train load of only sixty-eight tons against the Pennsylvania's four hundred and eighty-four tons. Everyone who gives careful consideration to the subject will admit that with the expenditure of a relatively small amount of capital upon reducing gradients and upon increasing the size of our toy trucks, and by the exercise of reasonable care in the loading of trucks and trains, an enormous improvement can be effected.[19]

The delay in the adoption of new techniques in handling

traffic was most noticeable on the freight side. Modern marshalling yards and large trucks, for example, were conspicuous
by their absence. Apart from the new marshalling yards at
Crewe, Wath, and Edge Hill (Liverpool), few attempts were
made to redesign and improve freight handling facilities at
railway terminals where congestion prevailed.[20] Similarly,
large-capacity trucks were almost completely neglected. The
eight- and ten-ton 'toy' truck remained the standard down to
1914, and even by the 1930s twenty-ton wagons represented
only 3 per cent of the total stock of mineral wagons. The
average load of the ten-ton goods wagon was a mere 2.83
tons; yet it had been recognised for many years that the small
wagon was inefficient and that considerable economies could
be made by using the twenty-ton instead of the ten-ton truck.
It has been estimated that for a capital cost increase of 50 per
cent the earning capacity is doubled, current maintenance
costs are reduced by 25 per cent per ton-mile, shunting costs
fall and locomotives can handle payloads up to 25 per cent
greater.[21]

Though the nature of the traffic no doubt determined to
some extent the type of service provided, it is clear that the
failure of the railways to modernise their techniques meant
they sacrificed many economies. Freight continued to be conveyed in very small lots at low speed to a multiplicity of
stations or depots, and much of the traffic originated and
terminated in single-wagon consignments. The consequences
have been described in the Beeching Report which is worth
quoting at length:

> . . . the wagon became the unit of movement and through
> working of trains was largely suppressed. Instead, nearly all
> freight moved by the staging of wagons from marshalling yard
> to marshalling yard, with variable and cumulative delays in
> them, so that the overall journey was bound to be slow and
> unpredictable.
>
>   Thus in order to provide for a large measure of rail partici-
> pation in country-wide collection and delivery of small con-
> signments, which the railways were never particularly well

suited to do, and which they only did because the horse-drawn
cart was worse, the railways threw away their main advantages.
They saddled themselves with the costly movement of wagons
in small numbers over a multiplicity of branch lines, where
there were too few wagons moving to make good trains. At the
same time, they sacrificed the speed, reliability, and low cost
of through-train operation even on the main arteries.[22]

A number of other improvements or innovations might be
mentioned which did not gain widespread adoption. Few
freight wagons were fitted with automatic brakes or oil axle
boxes which permitted faster running and more economical
operation of freight movement. Standardisation of rolling
stock was neglected. An official report in 1918 mentioned
the existence of no less than two hundred different types of
axle boxes and over forty variations of the ordinary wagon
hand-brake; nearly every railway company had adopted
different types of springs and axles. 'In no other country has
individuality been allowed so much free scope, with the result
that British Railways are severely handicapped, and the working of them not as economical as it might be.'[23] Only limited
attention, moreover, was given to the question of improving
the efficiency of the locomotive. In 1938 a speaker at the
Institution of Electrical Engineers recalled how when he
joined the railways at the beginning of the century 'the price
of locomotive coal was still so low that the majority of
railways did not consider it worthwhile to undertake research
on the locomotive considered as a heat engine, with a view to
more economical design'.[24] Some even expressed the view
that there was little new to learn about the locomotive since
'it [had] got to about the end of its tether as regards
improvement . . .'[25]

Wartime control demonstrated conclusively that there was
much slack to be taken up in the railway system. With less
rolling stock and a depleted labour force, the railways moved
more traffic annually between 1914 and 1918 than they had
done before the war. Although the statistical returns relating
to this period have never been published, it is clear that

unified working brought about revolutionary changes in the techniques of handling traffic, particularly goods traffic. Steps were taken to eliminate the light loading of wagons and to concentrate loads by allocating traffic between certain points to specific routes. Congestion at sidings and terminals was lessened by regulating as far as possible the flow of traffic to coincide with the rate at which it could be dealt with at the receiving points. A considerable amount of through running was arranged for locomotives handling troops and supplies, though the extent to which this could be accomplished depended very much upon the railway workers' ability to identify and handle the track and rolling stock of companies other than their own. To obtain more effective use of the available wagon capacity, a pooling of railway-owned goods wagons was brought into operation. By this system, wagons previously returned empty were reloaded at or close to the point of discharge. Thus the number of wagons running empty was greatly reduced and the train mileage correspondingly cut down. Particular attention was paid to the movement of coal which before the war constituted about one third of the total freight traffic of British railways. In conjunction with the Coal Controller, a careful inquiry was made into the pattern of coal movements in the UK, and as a result a Coal Transport Reorganisation Scheme, designed to eliminate all unnecessary handling of coal, was drawn up and put into operation in 1917. This arrangement was very successful for it is said to have saved about seven hundred million ton-miles per annum, reducing considerably the pressure on railway rolling stock.

Though the gains achieved in wartime were substantial, it might well be argued that what could be done in time of emergency under unified control was unlikely to be achieved in peacetime when the railway companies were free to do as they chose. To some extent this is true though it in no way exonerates the companies for their failure to improve the efficiency of their undertakings before 1914. In any case, there were many technical improvements which the com-

panies could carry out individually and without collective
action. In fact, a few of the more enterprising railway companies, such as the Caledonian, the Great Eastern and the North
Eastern, did try to reform their methods in the late nineteenth
and early twentieth century. The most progressive company
was the North Eastern which, in the early 1900s, introduced
larger wagons and improved its handling techniques. Between
1900 and 1909 the company brought into use nearly fourteen thousand wagons of over fourteen tons each, nearly half
of which had a capacity of more than twenty tons. Moreover,
the North Eastern was one of the first to collect comprehensive statistical data (eg ton-mile and passenger-mile statistics)
which enabled the company to find out how traffic could be
most economically and efficiently conveyed.[26]

Progressive companies were, however, few and far between
and in general best practice techniques were not widely
adopted by the railway companies before 1914. If, as we
have suggested, diminishing returns could have been checked
in part by improvements in operational efficiency, why then
were the railways so slow to innovate? They could not
excuse themselves on the grounds of ignorance since best
practice techniques were fairly well known and employed
extensively by American railroads.

It has often been argued that the pattern of British railway
traffic was not conducive to the adoption of modern methods
of operation as employed by American railroads. Pratt, for
example, maintained that the small consignments and short
hauls on the British system prevented the railways from taking
advantage of larger wagons.[27] It is quite true that the pattern
of traffic was different and that it was less adaptable to
American methods. But it would be completely erroneous to
explain the lack of innovation on these grounds alone. In the
first place, some companies did take steps to introduce new
methods and this in itself suggests that reform was by no
means impossible. Secondly, it can be argued that it was up
to the railways themselves to take the initiative in reorganising
their traffic movements so that more economical methods of

operation could be employed. Thirdly, insofar as the pattern of traffic was fragmented and therefore unsuitable to new techniques, the railways were in part to blame. In the past the railways had paid too much attention to satisfying the individual wants and requirements of their customers irrespective of the costs involved. Railway users in Great Britain enjoyed a far wider range of services and facilities than their counterparts in other countries. Only British railways tolerated such conveniences as separate dining cars, or low demurrage charges which encouraged traders to use wagons as warehouses. Such facilities were no doubt one aspect of qualitative improvement; but many of them were expensive to provide and the additional cost fell on the railways rather than on their customers. Thus whatever their defects, in terms of service British railways were probably unsurpassed anywhere in the world by 1914; but to achieve this distinction they sacrificed much in the way of economies.

Innovation of course posed problems of investment and the capital cost might be sufficiently high as to deter the railways from making changes. Because the fixed capital equipment of the railways was highly interrelated both internally and externally, the capital cost of a particular innovation, eg larger wagons, was in the long run much greater than the cost of the initial equipment. Innovation in one sector would not only have required the adaptation of other parts of the railway system but would also have involved the alteration of some of the installations outside the railway system. In other words, the height of bridges, the short radius of curves, and the layout of stations, docks and coal staithes set the limits within which an increase in the size and weight of locomotives, wagons, and coaches could be made. In this respect, Britain suffered from being a pioneer in industrial development. In America where the shipping ports, iron and steel works and other installations had developed simultaneously with the railways, the appliances at the ports and works had been made to fit in with the modern appliances of the railway companies. But in Britain the railway companies had to adapt their equipment to the old and crude conditions already existing or started while the railways were still in their infancy. Stated simply, the difference was that American installations could take twenty-ton or larger wagons whereas the British could not. The chairman of the Caledonian Railway was not exaggerating when he observed that

> there is not, at the present time, a single shipping port, iron and steel work, or gaswork, or any work in Scotland, capable of dealing with a 'waggon' of a carrying capacity of thirty or even twenty tons of coal, and there are not half a dozen collieries in Scotland whose appliances for separating coal are capable of admitting a waggon of the height of a thirty ton waggon.[28]

What in effect this amounted to was that technical progress on the railways was determined very much by the rate of progress elsewhere.

Financial interrelatedness was not the only problem however; the railways were faced with the question of what has been termed institutional relatedness,[29] a situation which was reflected in the division of ownership of some of the rolling stock. Many railway wagons were privately owned, a legacy no doubt from the early days when traders were expected to provide their own rolling stock. Altogether over one half the wagons used on British railways were privately owned, 90 per cent of which belonged to colliery companies.[30] The opposition of the colliery owners to the introduction of larger wagons is well known, but private ownership in itself was not necessarily responsible for the fact that their wagons were ten-tonners, since few collieries were equipped for dealing with large trucks. Hence even had the railways owned all the coal cars, there is no reason to assume that it would have made much difference to the rate of technical progress since the railways would still presumably have been faced with the problem of persuading colliery owners to alter their screens, sidings, and so forth to accommodate the new equipment. Co-operation in this matter was difficult because

of the problem of apportioning joint costs and gains between
the respective parties.

Problems of allocating investment costs did not arise in
every case however. In fact much improvement could have
been made without the problem of joint costs arising had
traders in general been more willing to accept reform. As
Sherrington observed: 'Traders who cry out that the level of
British railway rates is too high should remember their own
continuous opposition to the adoption of a system which has
always been the practice on railways abroad.'[31] Reform to
them meant the loss of some of the facilities which they had
enjoyed. The British traders' preference for delivery in small
lots and their unwillingness to pool orders made it difficult to
streamline the methods of handling freight. As the Chairman
of the Great Northern Railway Company pointed out in 1903:
'The question [of reform] does not entirely rest with the
railway companies. We have been doing our best for some
time past to induce our traders to help us to introduce the
economies which can be effected from the use of larger
wagons.'[32]

On the other hand, the attitudes and policies of the railroad leaders were not exactly conducive to reform. They
devoted far too much time and energy to building up vast
railway empires, and as a consequence they neglected the
question of efficient operation. Dow, for example, in his
history of the Great Central suggests that had Watkin been
less obsessed with the aggressive expansion of his railway
empire he might have given more attention to the consolidation and improvement of the property he already controlled.[33]
Similarly the Great Northern allowed its suburban business
to grow up haphazardly, and it spent on competitive extensions — far from its main line — the money so badly needed
at the London end where there was a rich field for urban
traffic.[34] Such policies were a product of the fierce
competition which existed among many railway companies.
Inevitably it necessitated securing as much traffic as possible
whatever the cost. Hence the companies were forced to

duplicate facilities and promote uneconomic lines and services.
But in so doing they lowered their average net returns since
the proportionate cost of providing the more marginal
facilities was greater than that for the main-line system as a
whole. Indeed in some cases the marginal cost of the additional facilities was greater than the marginal revenue which meant
in effect the railways were making a loss on parts of their
system.[35]

The attitude of the railways to reform was reflected in the
lip service they paid to collecting proper statistical data. For
many years railway economists, particularly Acworth and
Paish, had urged the companies to compile returns relating to
factors such as ton-mileage, passenger-mileage, train loads,
and wagon-mileage since the information currently collected
was 'almost useless except for the purpose of showing the
profits earned and the dividends distributed.'[36] It appears
that railway accounts were drafted by persons still under the
influence of the promotion and construction period in railway history with little conception of the economic science of
transportation. If the railways were to be run scientifically
and economically it was essential that such data should be
collected. In turn, it could be argued that reform was delayed
simply because railway managers and directors had not got
the statistical information which would show them where
the system needed pruning or modernising to make it more
efficient. Indeed it is only recently that British railways have
ascertained exactly which parts of the system are uneconomic.
Yet until the collection of adequate data was made compul-
sory by parliamentary legislation just before World War I,
few companies attempted to do anything about the matter.
Many companies were reluctant to spend time collecting data
which they regarded as of limited value. The Committee on
Railway Accounts was informed by the Chairman of the
London & North Western that in his opinion such statistics
were 'worthless and absolutely useless'.[37] If this view was
typical of the other railway companies, it is not surprising
that improvements in railway-operating practice only made

slow progress in the years before 1914.

The comments made in this paper are only intended as a preliminary introduction to the study of railway-operating practice in the period 1870-1914. Although diminishing returns were in part inevitable owing to the extension of the railway network into less productive areas, it is suggested that the railway companies could have offset this tendency had they developed more scientific methods of handling their traffic. There are a number of reasons to account for the relatively slow pace of technical progress, but possibly one of the most important was the fact that railway managers and directors were still influenced by the construction phase of railway history, and hence they were more interested in extending their empires than in operating their undertakings on a scientific basis. It is to be hoped that a more thorough study of the records of individual companies will support or reject some of the general conclusions presented here.

NOTES

1   This book was originally published in article form in *The Statist*, G. Paish, *The British Railway Position* (1902)

2   C.P. Kindleberger, 'Obsolescence and Technical Change', *Bulletin of the Oxford University Institute of Statistics* (August 1961)

3   See the author's 'The Entrepreneur and the British Economy, 1870-1914', *Economic History Review* (August 1964) and 'Technical Progress and British Enterprise, 1875-1914', *Business History* (July 1966)

4   L.C.A. Knowles, *The Industrial and Commercial Revolutions in Great Britain During the Nineteenth Century* (1944), 282

5   T.C. Barker and M. Robbins, *A History of London Transport*, Vol 1: *The Nineteenth Century* (1963), 214-21, for a good discussion of the point made here

6   E.A. Pratt, *Railways and the Nation* (1908), 380

7   D.E.C. Eversley, 'The Great Western Railway and the Swindon Railway Works in the Great Depression', *University of Birmingham Historic Journal*, 2 (1956), 182

8   A.M. Milne and A. Laing, *The Obligation to Carry* (1956), 31

9   This point is discussed more fully later

10   W. Bolland, *The Railways and the Nation* (1909), 44

11   G. Findlay, *The Working and Management of an English Railway* (1891)

12   J.R. Sargent, *British Transport Policy* (1958), 42

13   That is by extending the railway network into areas where traffic was relatively sparse or by providing extra facilities or services. This applies equally to passenger traffic

14   Milne and Laing, op cit, 31

15   This of course is a rather crude way of measuring density but in the absence of passenger-mileage and ton-mileage statistics etc, it is the only alternative

16   See *Departmental Committee on Railway Accounts and Statistical Returns*, Minutes of Evidence, Memo by W. Burdett-Coutts, Cd 5052 (1910), 322

17   G. Paish, *The British Railway Position* (1902), E.B. Dorsey, *English and American Railroads Compared* (1887), and Burdett-Coutts' Memorandum to the *Departmental Committee* (1910)

18   W. Ashworth, *An Economic History of England, 1870-1939* (1960), 125

19   Paish, op cit, 51

20   See O.S. Nock, *The London and North Western Railway* (1960), 72, 91-3; and H. Ellis, *British Railway History*, Vol II: *1887-1947* (1959), 236

21   K.G. Fenelon, *Railway Economics* (1932), 172

22   *The Reshaping of British Railways*, Pt I: *Report* (HMSO, 1963), 24-5

23   *Report on the Standardisation of Railway Equipment*, Cd 9193 (1918), 3

24   Quoted in K.H. Johnston, *British Railways and Economic Recovery* (1949), 142

25   *Report of the Tariff Commission*, Vol 4: *The Engineering Industries* (1909), para 579

26   *Departmental Committee on Railway Accounts and Statistical Returns*, Cd 5052 (1910). Evidence of Philip Burtt, 7 April 1908, QQ 5079-5108

27   E.A. Pratt, *Railways and their Rates* (1906), 97

28   Paish, op cit, 117; see also S.E. Parkhouse, 'Railway Freight Rolling Stock', *Journal of the Institute of Transport* (September 1951), 215

29   See Kindleberger, loc cit

30   *Report on Private Traders' Railway Wagons in Great Britain* (HMSO, 1919)

31   C.E.R. Sherrington, *A Hundred Years of Inland Transport, 1830-1933* (1934), 235

32   C.H.Grinling, *The History of the Great Northern Railway, 1845-1902* (1903 ed), xii

33   G. Dow, *Great Control*, Vol II: *Dominion of Watkin, 1864-1899* (1962), 164

34   Grinling, op cit, xv

35   It is possible, though I have not been able to verify it, that some railway companies actually confused gross and net revenue which could lead them into assuming that all they had to do was to

acquire as much traffic as possible irrespective of cost and this would raise their returns. It would of course increase *gross* revenue but not necessarily *net* revenue

36   W.M. Acworth and G. Paish, 'British Railways: Their Accounts and Statistics', *Journal of Royal Statistical Society*, LXXV (June 1912); see also J. Danvers, 'Defects of English Railway Statistics', ibid, LI (1888), and W.M. Acworth, 'English Railway Statistics', ibid, LXV (1902)

37   Cd 5052 (1910), op cit, 326-7

3 British Shipping and Foreign Competition: The Anglo-German Rivalry, 1880-1914

First published in D.H. Aldcroft (ed),
The Development of British Industry and
Foreign Competition 1875-1914 *(1968)*

I

Whatever criticisms might be levelled against British industry in general in the latter half of the nineteenth century, few if any apply to the shipping industry. After the Civil War, when the American challenge was finally thrown off, Britain's mercantile marine emerged as the largest and most powerful fleet in the world. It accounted for just over one-third of the total world ocean-going tonnage (and a considerably higher proportion of the world's steam fleet) and, although its nearest competitor was still America, the latter's share of the world tonnage had been reduced from 19 to 9 per cent in the decade 1860-70. The rapid adoption of the new techniques in shipbuilding and ship propulsion, namely iron, steel and steam, ensured the maintenance of this supremacy almost uninterrupted down to the early twentieth century. At the outbreak of war the British mercantile marine was the largest, the most up-to-date and the most efficient of all the fleets in the world. It still accounted for one-third of the world fleet, and nearly one-half the world's steam fleet, and it was almost four times as large as its nearest and most powerful rival Germany *(see Table 1, page 54).* The vessels on the UK Register consisted, moreover, of the largest and most efficient type of ships. Britain sold her old vessels to foreigners and equipped herself with the latest models. Every year around 5½ per cent of the total fleet was disposed of, two-thirds of which were sold to foreign flags. As a result of this policy 85 per cent of the tonnage on the Register in 1914 had been built since 1895 and just over two-thirds since 1900.

TABLE 1: *Tonnage of Merchant Shipping Owned by Various Countries*
(million net tons; percentages of total world fleet in brackets)

Country	1860	1870	1880	1890	1900	1905	1911
United Kingdom	4.66 (35.06)	5.69 (33.9)	6.57 (32.9)	7.98 (35.8)	9.30 (35.5)	10.73 (34.8)	11.70 (33.8)
British possessions*	1.05 (7.9)	1.46 (8.7)	1.87 (9.4)	1.71 (7.7)	1.45 (5.5)	1.59 (5.2)	1.83 (5.3)
Germany	—	0.98 (5.8)	1.18 (5.9)	1.43 (6.4)	1.94 (7.4)	2.47 (8.0)	3.02 (8.7)
Norway	0.56 (4.2)	1.02 (6.1)	1.52 (7.6)	1.71 (7.7)	1.51 (5.8)	1.48 (4.8)	1.65 (4.8)
France	0.97 (7.2)	1.07 (6.3)	0.92 (4.6)	0.94 (4.2)	1.04 (4.0)	1.39 (4.5)	1.46 (4.2)
US (excl. Great Lakes tonnage)	2.55 (19.2)	1.52 (9.1)	1.35 (6.8)	0.95 (4.3)	0.83 (3.2)	0.95 (3.1)	0.87 (2.5)
Russia	—	—	0.47 (2.3)	—	0.63 (2.4)	0.66 (2.1)	0.74 (2.1)
Sweden	—	0.35 (2.0)	0.54 (2.7)	0.51 (2.2)	0.61 (2.3)	0.72 (2.3)	0.77 (2.2)

TABLE 1: *Continued*

Country	1860	1870	1880	1890	1900	1905	1911
Denmark	–	0.18	0.25	0.30	0.41	0.48	0.54
		(1.1)	(1.2)	(1.3)	(1.6)	(1.6)	(1.6)
Netherlands	0.43	0.39	0.33	0.26	0.35	0.41	0.57
	(3.2)	(2.3)	(1.7)	(1.2)	(1.3)	(1.3)	(1.6)
Spain	–	–	0.56	0.62	0.77	0.74	0.79
			(2.8)	(2.8)	(2.9)	(2.4)	(2.3)
Italy	–	1.01	0.99	0.82	0.95	1.03	1.11
		(6.0)	(4.9)	(3.7)	(3.6)	(3.3)	(3.2)
Japan	–	–	0.09	0.15	0.86†	1.3†	1.8†
			(0.05)	(0.61)	(3.3)	(4.2)	(5.1)
World Total	13.29	16.8	19.99	22.27	26.21	30.85	34.63

*   Includes Canada, Newfoundland, Australia, New Zealand, British India and all colonial territories
†   These figures refer to gross tonnage. The percentages for these years are therefore somewhat higher than they should be

Source: Board of Trade, *Progress of Merchant Shipping Returns*

In terms of world trade carried and ships built, Britain's superiority was equally pronounced. By the early twentieth century British ships were carrying around one-half the sea-borne trade of the world whilst in the twenty-five years before the war we built two-thirds of the new ships that were launched.

This brief summary shows clearly the dimensions of Britain's seapower in the few decades before 1914. In some respects, however, the data give a somewhat misleading impression of the extent of Britain's supremacy. From the early 1880s, and in some cases even earlier, Britain's mono-poly of the carrying trade was being increasingly challenged by the growth of foreign fleets. The impact of foreign competition is brought out clearly from the figures for entrances and clearances of shipping in the ports of various countries. It can be seen from Table 2 *(opposite)* that the British share fell, sometimes substantially, between 1880 and 1911 in most of the short-haul European and Scandinavian trades, whilst competition also increased sharply in the home trade. On the other hand, on most of the long-distance routes Britain maintained her position fairly well and, in some cases, eg New Zealand, her share of total clearances actually increased during these years. The British position remained strongest and almost unchallenged on the Empire routes, for even by 1913, 94 per cent of the trade between the UK and the Empire was carried by British ships. On some of the long-haul, non-Empire trades, however, British shipping was beginning to feel the effects of foreign competition. This is particularly true of the Chilean trade where the British share dropped sharply until the turn of the century. The same could also be said of the North Atlantic run though the data on entrances and clearances for America do not appear at first sight to support this statement. The figures do not, however, adequately reflect the importance of the passenger trade in which competition from the Germans was particu-larly severe in the late nineteenth and early twentieth centuries. Moreover, if the figures for steam shipping alone

TABLE 2: *British Share of Entrances and Clearances at Ports in Selected Countries, 1880-1911*

	1880 %	1900 %	1911 %
UK	70.4	63.7	58.9
Germany	38.1	26.9	23.0
Holland	49.8	41.7	30.5
Sweden	13.5	9.9	5.4
Belgium	59.4	44.6	44.1
France	40.6	40.6	36.1
Italy	34.3	n.a.	28.7
Norway	11.8	10.9	9.8
Portugal	63.0	56.8	47.6
Denmark	11.4	7.8	5.1
US	51.7	52.8	50.1
Japan	n.a.	38.9	30.5
Argentine	37.8	29.3	33.5
Chile	79.9	50.1	50.7
Canada	65.4	61.0	69.9
New Zealand	88.0	91.8	96.8
South Africa	85.6	89.8	80.0
India	79.1	79.0	76.6
British possessions	87.1	90.5	91.9 (1905-08)

Source: Board of Trade, *Merchant Shipping Returns*

are considered, it will be found that the British share of entrances and clearances in the United States trade fell from 68 to 51 per cent between 1880 and 1911. Since steam-propelled shipping was by far more predominant than sail on this run from the late 1880s, it seems not unreasonable to accept the steam data as an indication of Britain's relative decline.

A more detailed breakdown of the entrance and clearance statistics into national, British and foreign flags is presented in Appendix 1 *(page 298)*. This provides some guide as to the source of competition as between national and foreign fleets in particular countries. In at least four countries for which data are available, namely Sweden, Germany, Japan and Argentina, the fall in the British share was largely due to the successful competition from the national fleets of the

respective countries. But in most other countries where competition was at all severe, the British were being displaced by
foreign rather than national flags, though occasionally, as in
the case of Chile, it was a combination of the two. Furthermore, in practically every country where foreign lines were
the major threat to British shipowners, the relative importance of the national fleets declined *pari passu* with the
British. This would seem to indicate that the chief source of
competition was from the four countries which managed to
dislodge the established position of British shipping from
their own ports. Two of these, Argentina and Sweden, can be
ruled out immediately since their fleets were far too small
even by 1914 to offer really serious competition in other than
local ports. Although the Japanese fleet increased more
rapidly than most others in this period, it was still very small
by 1900 and, even though it became the third largest by
1914, it was employed mainly in ousting the British from
local waters rather than competing for trade in neutral or
third markets.[1]

By a process of elimination, therefore, the German fleet
emerges as the only possible contender of any importance in
the mercantile field. Germany was the only country which
managed to raise its share of world shipping significantly in
these years (*see Table 1*), and by 1914, with a fleet of just
over three million tons net, it was the second largest in the
world. By comparison with the British fleet it was, of course,
still quite small, but despite its size it was capable, partly
because of the efficient way in which it was organised, of
offering an effective challenge to Britain's maritime supremacy in many parts of the world. By the early twentieth century
the German fleet was operating on nearly all the major trade
routes, and in many foreign ports the German flag
assumed a prominent position. It was, perhaps, more effectively deployed in some trades than others, especially on the
North Atlantic and parts of Africa, but there is no doubt
that from the British shipowners' point of view German
shipping was becoming a serious menace and one that could

not be ignored. Contemporary comments by shipowners and the mercantile press confirm the view that it was German shipping that offered the most serious source of danger to British shipping. As early as 1891, the *Shipping World* reported in its leader column that 'Today there is no question that the chief competitor we have on the seas is Germany.'[2] There were, in fact, few references to foreign competition in later years which failed to mention Germany as the main enemy.[3]

Germany then was Britain's chief competitor and the discussion which follows will mainly be devoted to an examination of Anglo-German mercantile rivalry. The obvious way of dealing with this topic would be to examine the nature of competition in specific areas, but this method is rejected on the following grounds. In the first place, a comprehensive treatment would prove too lengthy and it is doubtful whether any worthwhile conclusions would emerge simply from the presentation of a large number of case studies. Secondly, the lack of suitable data precludes a thorough discussion of competition on every major trade route. Much work still remains to be carried out on British shipping in this period, and until the shipping companies are willing to open up their archives, the necessary raw material remains secret. Instead, therefore, it was deemed more useful and appropriate to follow a thematic or analytical treatment of the factors which assisted or promoted the growth and competitiveness of German shipping. These can be divided into two broad groups: the first includes the benefits or advantages derived from Government assistance in the form of subsidies, rebates, etc, and lower wage costs. The second category comprises policy or promotional factors used by German shipping lines to enhance their position, eg use of the conference system, rate cutting and organisation and operation of their enterprises. Each of these factors will be considered in turn and, where appropriate, particular reference will be made to areas in which conflict between British and German shipping lines occurred. Where possible, the reaction of British shipowners will be taken into account.

II

Most countries in the latter half of the nineteenth century
paid subsidies to their shipping lines. The types of subsidy
varied a great deal. Concealed subsidies in the form of payments for the carriage of mail were very common in Britain and
on the Continent. In fact, British policy was largely confined
to subsidising ships for postal and Admiralty purposes, and
apart from the special aid given to the Cunard Company early
in the twentieth century for the construction of two crack
liners, no purely navigational bounties were made in this
country. Experience abroad was somewhat different, the system of subsidisation usually being far more elaborate and
complex. France and Japan, for example, granted both
navigational and constructional bounties, the terms of which
were revised frequently. Apart from payments made for the
carriage of mail which by all accounts were quite small,
Germany had three types of bounties; these comprised
payments made to shipowners for specific purposes and two
classes of indirect subsidies, namely special railway rates for
exported goods which allowed shipping lines to quote low
through rates of freight, and special customs facilities for
imports destined for use in shipbuilding yards.[4]
   Many contemporary commentators, including shipowners
of course, were convinced that subsidies were the main cause
of the growth of foreign shipping fleets. *The Economist* in
1911 stated categorically that the expansion of Germany's
shipping in recent years was due to no small extent to the
policy of general subsidisation.[5] Even Sir Robert Giffen, the
Board of Trade statistician, had expressed a similar view
somewhat earlier.[6] It is extremely doubtful, however,
whether this judgement is wholly correct. No systematic evidence has been brought forward to support the case either
for or against, so that most of the observations made have
been at best impressionistic. Admittedly the data available are
scanty and the problems of comparison formidable, but it is

possible to reach tentative conclusions by a careful examination of the material.

The most obvious starting point is to deal with the direct subsidy payments to shipping lines since these are fairly easy to identify quantitatively. Comparisons between countries are obviously difficult, especially with mail subsidies since it is not clear what proportion was paid for actual services rendered. But most mail payments, especially the British, were fairly lavish and usually contained a concealed subsidy. The figures in Table 3 *(below)* include all subsidies whether navigational, constructional or for the carriage of mail.

TABLE 3: *Subsidy Payments to Mercantile Marines of Various Countries*

	1901		1907	
	Total Subsidy Payment	Subsidy Per Net Ton	Total Subsidy Payment	Subsidy Per Net Ton
	£	s d	£	s d
United Kingdom	1,003,401	2 2	791,755	1 4
Germany	440,470	4 6	392,160	2 9
France	1,787,271	34 6	2,528,028	36 0
Russia	374,590	11 9	414,273	11 9
Japan	—	—	886,104	—
Italy	—	—	695,596	14 0
Austro-Hungary	—	—	566,500	24 9

Sources: *Select Committee on Steamship Subsidies*, H of C, 385, 1902, App 36; *Return on Steamship Subsidies*, H of C, 359, 1907; and *Report on Shipping Subsidies in Foreign Countries*, Cd 6899, 1913

It can be seen that in terms of subsidies per ton of shipping owned, the payments were very small indeed in both Britain and Germany. German subsidies, it is true, were higher than the British, but the difference is not great enough to be more than marginally significant. Moreover, account must be taken of the fact that the bulk of the German subsidies were paid to two companies for specific services. The North German Lloyd received annually £165,000 and £115,000 for its East Asian and Australian services respectively, whilst the

German East African Company was paid £76,500 for its
African operations.[7]

It is important to note that, apart from very small payments
for the carriage of mail, the North German Lloyd received no
financial aid at all for its North Atlantic services, yet it was in
this field that it proved to be Britain's most serious competitor. It could be argued, of course, that the Atlantic service
stood to gain indirectly from the subsidies which were granted
to other branches of the Company. But in view of the fact
that the subsidised services were extremely uneconomic, this
line of reasoning is incorrect. Basically the East Asian and
Australian services were established for prestige purposes, and
the subsidy of 1885 had been designed to encourage regular
communication with these areas where British shipowners
maintained a virtual monopoly. Certainly the subsidy assisted
the growth of German shipping and trade with these regions,[8]
but at considerable cost to the German Exchequer and
the NDL. Between 1886 and 1896 the Company made a loss
of 5.25 million marks on the services despite a subsidy of
44.3 million from the German Government. Had it not been
for the subsidy, the directly subsidised fleet would have made
a ruinous loss of 49.5 million marks.[9] Thus, the establishment
of regular services to the Far East and Australia was a costly
business, and at best it only secured a marginal share of the
British trade. Even if competition increased in these areas,
British shipowners had little cause to complain, since the P &
O line was almost as heavily subsidised as the NDL. The
British company received no less than £330,000 per year for
its services to India, China and Australia which worked out
roughly at 5s 6d per mile. On a comparable basis, the NDL
received 5s a mile for its East Asian operations and 6s 8d for
the Australian service.[10]

German entry into the East African shipping trade can be
attributed to the subsidy policy. In the late 1880s the
German East African colonies depended almost entirely on
foreign shipping though there were no direct shipping services
with Europe. A law of 1890 earmarked £45,000 for the

establishment of a regular line to East Africa,[11] and as a
result the German East Africa Company was established with
a capital of six million marks, four-fifths of which was held
by the German banks. The creation of this company at that
particular time was possibly determined by the fact that the
year before the first direct British service had been started by
the British India Line which received £15,000 per annum from
the British Government. Rivalry between the two companies
was short lived, however, since the latter service was discontinued in 1892 after having incurred losses of £30,000 per
annum.

This left the German company with a virtual monopoly of
direct shipping services between Europe and East Africa. The
venture was far from being a profitable one, however. By the
end of 1893 losses totalled more than one million marks and
dividends were out of the question.[12] Two factors were
responsible for this unpromising beginning. Although the
subsidy terms were fairly generous, the State laid rather
onerous conditions upon the Company the effect of which
was to take back part of what it gave. All State traffic was to
be carried at a discount of 20 per cent on normal rates, and
since initially the greater part of the traffic was under State
auspices, this was obviously not a lucrative proposition. But
rather more important was the fact that the trade of East
Africa was still very small and could not support a separate
steamship line. According to Brackmann, only in three years
during the first fifteen years of the Company's existence did
the value of goods transported between Germany and East
Africa by the line amount to more than one-half the value of
all goods transported by the Company.[13] In other words, in
most years more than 50 per cent of the Company's traffic
was derived from countries other than East Africa. It was the
limited nature of the East African trade which eventually
forced the Company to enter South African waters and
compete against the British.[14]

Whilst it cannot be denied that Germany's shipping services
to East Asia, Australia and East Africa were materially

assisted by Government subsidies — in fact, without them they would most surely have been discontinued — it is very unlikely that British shipowners lost much as a result. The North German Lloyd never became a formidable competitor in Australia or in China and Japan, and in any case, as we have already noted, the major British company was on roughly an equal footing as far as financial aid was concerned. East Africa never held much appeal for shipowners in this country, and after the failure of the British India service, interest waned completely. The absence of a direct British service probably caused Britain to lose about £5 or £6 million worth of trade with East Africa a year, an amount hardly worthy of the expense of a subsidised line.[15]

It is impossible, therefore, to attribute the growth and competition of German shipping to the Government's subsidy policy. Subsidies were not large in comparison with other countries and payments were confined to one or two particular services. According to Meeker, less than 4 per cent of the net tonnage of Germany's merchant fleet received direct subventions in 1894.[16] Furthermore, the subsidised services were certainly far less prosperous and competitive than the non-subsidised ones. The contrast is particularly marked if one considers the strength of the German companies on the unsubsidised North Atlantic route. There were, of course, many other countries which subsidised their shipping, some much more lavishly than Germany. But the results achieved were disappointing, to say the least. France's subsidy policy was one of the most generous, yet its results were disastrous, since it greatly favoured the construction of sailing vessels whilst scarcely any large ocean-going steamers were built.[17] In fact, probably the only country which achieved any degree of success with subsidies in the pre-1914 period was Japan.

Direct payments were not the only form of subsidy which German shipowners received. It was frequently alleged that they were assisted materially by preferential railway rates which were granted by all German State railways to goods exported from inland places of Germany on through bills of

lading. This allowed the German lines to quote very low
combined sea and rail rates which had no equivalent in Britain.
The actual rates for sea carriage were usually the same as the
British, but the difference in favour of German combined
land and sea rates of freight as a result of subsidised rail
charges could be quite considerable. For example, the cost of
sending a ton of rails from Oldenberg to Hamburg was 3s 4d
on the East African tariff and 3s 2d on the Levant as against
8s 4d for the carriage of the same commodity from Birmingham to Liverpool, a slightly shorter distance. In some
instances German railway tariffs for exported goods were
only one-third the comparable British rates.[18]

It is doubtful, however, whether such preferential treatment
was either as extensive or as effective as many contemporaries
would have us believe. A number of witnesses before the
Select Committee on Steamship Subsidies and the Royal
Commission on Shipping Rings complained about the harmful effects of this practice and stated that German policy was
to have a through rate everywhere.[19] These judgements were
probably based on limited experience. Certainly they were
common in the East African and Levant trades, and in the
case of the East African Company, they were an important
factor in enabling it to gain an entrée into the South African
trade. As we have already seen, this Company had not been
very successful in its East African operations and late in 1893
it launched a concentrated attack on the English lines in
South Africa by establishing a direct link with Pretoria,
Johannesburg and Durban. This onslaught was assisted by the
negotiation of special through rail and sea rates from Germany
which allowed the quotation of very low freight rates. But
low freights were not the only weapon which the Germans
used to compete with the British. The Company's second line
of attack was to increase the size of its fleet so that it could
start extra services to the Cape via the Atlantic route and
match the speed of the English lines. This competition proved
too much for the latter and they were soon anxious to come
to terms with the German line in order to avoid a costly rate

war, though initially the two main English lines, the Union
and Castle companies, had prepared plans to take the war
into the enemy's camp.[20] The resulting agreement proved a
victory for the German East African Company since the
English lines conceded most of the Company's wishes. By
the terms of the agreement the English conference system
was altered in such a way that shippers would not forfeit
rebates if they shipped by the German line. The Union line,
which during the rate war had lowered its rates from Hamburg
to South Africa, raised them again and agreed not to run a
regular service to Zanzibar. Furthermore, the English lines
agreed not to compete with the German line in East African
waters. In return, the German company limited its sailings to
South Africa via the Atlantic.[21]

   Entry into the South African trade and the victory over
the British lines did not make the German company a really
prosperous undertaking. But conditions certainly improved:
traffic increased from 1894 onwards and the Company was
able to make better use of its enlarged capacity. Financially
the Company also fared better: in the later 1890s a small
surplus on trading operations began to accrue and dividends
were paid for the first time in 1895. Compared with most
other German lines, the East African was still in a very weak
state, but its position had certainly improved as a result of
gaining a foothold in the South African trade. But the
Company's strength was not sufficient to counter effectively
a combined attack of the English lines after the Boer War.
The Union-Castle lines, having amalgamated their interests in
1900, fought to regain their position in South Africa, and
according to Brackmann, 'Nichts liessen die englischen
Linien unversucht, um der deutschen Reederei die
Südafrikafracht fortzunehman.'[22] They sent ships to
Hamburg, Belgian and Dutch ports to collect anything available at reduced rates of freight. Despite a rapid increase in
the size of the German company's fleet, it could only
manage to send out twenty-six steamers a year on the round
trip to Africa as against sixty-five English ships which sailed

from Hamburg. The competition became so fierce that by
1907 the German line was in no position to continue, and at
a shareholders' meeting a proposal was made that the Company be liquidated. This motion was not, in fact, carried but
the Company was forced to concede victory to the British
shipowners on terms favourable to the latter.

The details of the German East African line's relationships
with the British have been traced in some detail simply to
show that, despite a fairly generous direct subsidy and preferential treatment by the German railways, it was not sufficient
to overcome the combined opposition of the British lines in
South Africa, though it should be noted that the resources of
the German line were considerably less than those of their
competitors. Presumably, then, companies which secured
preferential through rates, but which did not have the additional benefit of a direct subsidy, such as the Levant line,
must have been in an even weaker position than the East
African Company to counter opposition from foreign shipowners.

More generally, it is doubtful whether preferential rates
were all that important in enhancing Germany's competitive
power. Apart from the two lines already mentioned, the only
other through rate concessions granted by the Government
were to the Bremen Atlas line in 1906 (for destinations in the
Mediterranean and the Black Sea)[23] and to shipowners trading
to South Brazil.[24] Moreover, even where such concessions
existed, it is by no means clear that all the freight carried by
the favoured lines was on through bills of lading. One witness
before the Royal Commission on Shipping Rings thought
that the quantity of cargo moving on through bills of lading
from the interior of Germany to South Africa formed only
a very small proportion of total shipments. In any case, such
preferential rates only assisted German shipping marginally.
They could not enhance its competitive power in British
ports or in neutral waters (ie in non-German or non-British
ports), and even in the home trade it might be argued that
much of the traffic would have been carried by German lines

whether through rates had been available or not. No doubt, orders for goods were placed with German in preference to British manufacturers in consequence of the cheaper through rates granted abroad, but the amount of trade lost in this way must have been very small indeed. Probably a much more effective weapon in attracting traffic were the cheap or fighting rates offered by German shipowners. This method of attack was frequently adopted, but usually as a temporary expedient, and generally it was in no way connected with the special concessions granted by German railways. This aspect is discussed in more detail later.

The only other element of subsidy was the preferential treatment accorded to materials for shipbuilding construction. The German customs tariff of May 1885 exempted from import duties nearly all materials destined for use in shipbuilding yards, whilst from 1895 onwards German railways gave preferential rates for the carriage of certain raw materials and partly manufactured articles used for the construction of German shipping. Such facilities were a very minor factor and could have had little effect in determining the strength of German competition. For one thing, shipbuilding materials were free of duty in Britain, so in this respect the two countries were on an equal footing. Secondly, they were probably much more of a boon to the German shipbuilding industry, which grew fairly rapidly after 1894,[25] than they were to the shipowners. German shipbuilding was still a fairly high cost industry in comparison with the British before 1914, and many German shipowners continued to take advantage of the better facilities offered in this country.[26] In this respect the subsidised lines were at a disadvantage since one of the conditions of the subsidy laws was that the ships had to be built in German yards.

Although British shipowners complained a great deal about the harmful effects of foreign subsidies, our analysis suggests that they were only of marginal importance in stimulating the growth and competitiveness of foreign mercantile marines. It is not without significance that the strongest and

most serious competitor was Germany, whose shipowners
received less in the way of direct and indirect bounties than
shipowners in other countries apart from Britain. In Germany
subsidies were on far too limited a scale to be an important
factor in the growth of that country's shipping. Occasionally,
as in the case of the East African Company, they assisted the
creation and development of a new undertaking, but even a
double-edged subsidy (direct payments and preferential rates)
was not sufficient to make this line really prosperous or to
enable it to withstand the attack of English opposition after
the Boer War. If anything, then, it could be argued that as far
as British shipping was concerned, foreign subsidies were
'blessings in disguise', for as one prominent shipowner, W.J.
Pirrie, told the Select Committee of 1902, 'They have stimulated British companies in the particular trades affected, to
move more quickly and keep more abreast of the times than
they might otherwise have done.'[27]

There were other factors besides subsidies which were said
to favour foreign (German) shipping as opposed to British.
British shipowners complained frequently that British vessels
were hindered by official Board of Trade regulations whilst
their wage and victualling costs were higher than abroad.[28]
It is true that various rules and regulations were imposed by
Parliament on British shipping from which foreign shipping
was partly exempt. These included such things as the load
line, life-saving appliances, inspection of provisions, crew
space, manning and cattle regulations. It is difficult to say
precisely how important these were in determining the costs
of operation of British ships. The general impression is that
they were a very minor element. On the other hand, according
to *Fairplay*, the combined effect of these regulations was to
impose a handicap of about 10 per cent on our shipping as
against foreigners.[29] A more thorough study prepared by Dr
Ginsberg for the British Association in 1901 suggested that
the difference in terms of cargo-carrying space amounted to
8.7 per cent in favour of foreign shipping.[30] He concluded,
however, by saying that though foreign regulations were

generally not as extensive or so strictly enforced as in this country, the total effect on the competing power of foreign ships of applying all our restrictions would be 'comparatively insignificant'.[31] This conclusion is particularly applicable to the latter part of the period since by then many countries were bringing their safety and manning regulations in line with those in this country.[32]

It is generally acknowledged that before 1914 wage and victualling costs were higher on British ships than on those operating under foreign flags. Precise international comparison of such costs are out of the question for this period since the data are extremely fragmentary and unreliable. But what evidence there is suggests that the cost of wages and provisions on British ships was up to 20 per cent above that on German vessels of a similar type and tonnage. This is, of course, only a very approximate estimate, but it does suggest that German shipowners might have had some advantage in this respect. The difference in costs can be largely accounted for by the higher wages paid to British seamen, the better scales of food and the higher manning scales in force on British vessels.[33]

The general conclusion which emerges from the discussion so far is that German shipping had no marked economic advantages over British shipowners. There were exceptions, of course. The operating costs of German vessels was probably on average lower largely because of lower wage and food costs. Unfortunately, it is impossible to give precise estimates of the difference in costs, but the margin in favour of German vessels might well have been quite small when all costs are taken into account.[34] In one or two trades, subsidies of one form or another no doubt assisted German shipping, but they cannot in any way be considered as a vital factor in the development of the German fleet. In other words, all these factors taken together probably only had a marginal effect in raising the competitive strength of German shipowners before 1914.

III

If our assumptions are correct it follows by implication that
the success of German competition was a product of skilful
policy and organisation on the part of German shipowners.
This does not necessarily imply that German shipowners
were any more efficient than their British counterparts,
though in some cases they may have been, but rather to
suggest that they adopted tactics which ultimately paid off.
One of these was the policy of rate-cutting and the use of the
conference system to serve their own ends.

Broadly speaking, the rise of German maritime competition
had by the early twentieth century resulted in a compromise,
expressed in a number of conference agreements, which left
the trade of the UK to British lines, whilst the latter abstained
to a certain extent from participating in the trade from the
Continent, especially from German ports, the implicit understanding being that outward freights from the UK and from
the Continent were to be approximately the same. In essence
the conference system was a defensive weapon and at times
it undoubtedly proved a handy device for avoiding costly
rate wars. But whether it was all that successful in bringing
recalcitrant German shipowners to heel, as some British contemporaries suggested, is somewhat doubtful.[35] It is true
that the Germans were eventually strong participants in the
conferences, but they were not always coerced into joining
by pressure from the British. German shipowners were often
anxious to join the conferences, and in some cases sponsored
them, in order to gain a stronger foothold in particular trades
whilst the British lines frequently compromised with the
Germans simply to prevent costly rate wars. Moreover, once
in, the Germans could hardly be said to have adhered strictly
to the rules of the conference system. The German lines
observed the agreements only insofar as it paid them to do
so, and they evaded the rules whenever important objectives
were at stake. As one official committee remarked, 'Every
weapon was used by the German lines not only to obtain
admission to the conference, but, when admitted, to extort

further concessions, not always justified by the magnitude of their trade.'[36]

Because of the secrecy which still shrouds the working practices of the conference system, and for that matter the operations of the shipping companies in general, it is impossible to provide a definitive account of the German shipowners' behaviour in the conference system. But the documentary evidence available suggests that the Germans not infrequently broke the rules of the game and in some cases, especially on the North Atlantic, they were the dominant players who called the tune.

Although German shipowners joined most of the conferences on the main trade routes, there usually existed an uneasy truce between them and the other members of the conference. From time to time they would withdraw from the agreement on some pretext or other and a rate war usually followed. In 1905, for example, a dispute arose between the P & O and the Hansa Company regarding the former Company's right to load at Antwerp for Calcutta and Bombay. Hansa wanted to debar the P & O from calling at Antwerp altogether, and the refusal of the British Company to cede to their demands resulted in the German line withdrawing from the Calcutta ring which it had joined in 1898. A rate war followed between the German line and the remaining members of the conference,[37] and some cargo rates were reduced by nearly 50 per cent. The Hansa line attacked the members of the conference on home territory by quoting very low rates from Middlesbrough and London to Calcutta, and at the same time secured the co-operation of an independent British company, the Well Line. The rate war lasted for over eighteen months, but eventually late in 1907 a settlement was made. The Hansa Company secured its original objective but little else since the agreement ensured that all members of the conference, whether British or foreign, were on an equal footing. In fact, the manager of the P & O flatly refused to allow the Germans to re-enter except on such conditions.[38]

In the South African trade there had been constant friction between the two parties and the agreement of 1907 was little more than a stop-gap measure. The East African line had accepted the conditions imposed by the British with ill grace, and in the following years demanded an improvement of the terms. A failure to gain satisfaction forced the Company to look round for an excuse to break the agreement and press their claims from outside the conference. It was known at the time that the South African Government was considering legislation to outlaw the rebate system and on these grounds the German East African Company withdrew from the conference at the beginning of 1912. Shortly afterwards the Union-Castle Company was informed that the rebate system was to be made illegal. The effect of these two events led to a complete collapse of the South African conference and an outright rate war ensued between all members. It was the East African Company, still the weakest member of the group, which first made overtures for a settlement, and in the following year all the East and South African shipowners concluded a new agreement. This made all freight rates similar for all lines and provided for spheres of interest in the African Continent. The Germans agreed not to load from England for South Africa whilst in return British shipowners allowed the Germans sole rights in the Continental-East African trade. This lessened friction to a minimum and, until the war, it proved a workable agreement.[39]

German competition in the South American trade took a slightly different form. Here the German shipowners tried to avoid an outright breakaway from the conference and as far as possible they carried on competition from within. Initially the early agreements in the River Plate and Brazilian trades had worked fairly smoothly. These had been concluded towards the end of the nineteenth century after severe competition had developed with the emergence of foreign lines, particularly the Hamburg-South American Company, in these regions. The principal basis of these agreements was absolute equality of rates from the UK and Continental ports. These rates were fairly strictly observed by all members, though occasionally cut rates were quoted from the Continent.

The main source of trouble occurred in the Brazilian trade when in 1900 the Hamburg-American line entered the area, by friendly arrangement with the Booth line, with one sailing per month from Hamburg to North Brazil. This service became a joint one between the Hamburg-American and Hamburg-South American lines in 1901 and, on the liquidation of the gentlemen's agreement with the Booth line in the following year, the Hamburg lines demanded a much larger share of the Brazilian trade. The British lines refused to co-operate and immediately a severe rate war broke out. The Hamburg lines invaded English ports with their steamers and within a matter of months the whole trade was disorganised and rates were reduced by about 40 per cent. By September 1902, however, the German lines, having been weakened elsewhere by competition, withdrew their ships from English ports and agreed to suggestions put forward by Booths for pooling the European traffic. Freight and passenger earnings from Liverpool, Antwerp and Hamburg were divided in the proportion of 70 per cent to the Booth line and 30 per cent to the Hamburg lines, which, for the latter, was a slight improvement on their previous share. In addition, freight and passenger charges were fixed by the agreement.[40]

Although these arrangements worked fairly smoothly, they did not entirely eliminate all competition from the German shipowners. Rates were fixed at such a high level that the incentive to undercut them was quite strong and this the Germans did on occasions. Alternatively they fetched cargo from Liverpool to Hamburg or Antwerp for shipment to Brazil at the current rate of freight. These practices were carried on within the conference system with little opposition from the English owners. The explanation was quite simple. Paradoxically it reduced competition. By allowing the Germans to take one or two advantages, the British lines were able to earn the full rate on their cargo. Had the British objected or counter-attacked, the result would have been a general lowering of all rates. As it was, limited competition in the conference satisfied both parties.[41]

Periodic rate wars both within and without the conferences were quite common on most of the major trade routes, and often the German shipowners were the chief offenders. At times the terms offered were so favourable that goods were sent from Britain to the Continent to take advantage of the low freights. The practice of cutting rates was usually only temporary, though occasionally conference rates were fixed at such a level as to induce undercutting. From the German shipowners' point of view it was a fairly effective method of gaining recognition and entry into the established stronghold and obtaining a greater share of the available traffic. Statistical proof of the latter is unfortunately very scanty, but there is no question that German shipping acquired an increasing proportion of the traffic in most of the trades in which they took an active interest.

The British shipowners' reaction to such competition varied a great deal. When severe rate wars ensued they had no option but to reply to the attack and hope that an agreement would soon be reached. Occasionally they tried to forestall any possible attack by quoting lower rates from the Continent than those from English ports. This method was adopted for cargo to the Persian Gulf in 1906, though without much success,[42] and in the New Zealand trade. In the latter case the two main English lines, Tyser & Shaw, Savill & Albion, shipped goods from Hamburg and Antwerp to New Zealand via London at rates considerably below those for British cargo direct, in the hope that the German companies would be discouraged from starting a direct service to New Zealand. But more often than not, the British lines were prepared to put up with a certain amount of competition and evasion of the conference rules rather than engage in a ruinous rate war which would have resulted if they had retaliated with the same weapons. Asked what his reaction would be if the Germans offered lower rates of freight to

Australia, the manager of the White Star line confessed that he would shut his eyes to it 'unless it became so big that I could not help looking at it. At the present time our object is not to bring about unnecessary friction with the Continental lines.'[43]

Although German participation in the conference system reduced competition, it certainly did not eliminate it. British shipowners probably fared better than they would have done had free competition prevailed, but conferences were by no means such a secure source of protection as many imagined. This reliance on a system which only partially contained the German opposition was partly responsible for the shipowners' reluctance to relinquish the rebate system, since it would deprive them of security against the Germans. Even merchants, whose opposition to the rebate system was fairly unanimous, were of the opinion that the rebates could only be abolished by international agreement, for as the chairman of the Australian Merchants' Committee pointed out:

> While the Germans continue to use the rebate system, it appears to me very doubtful whether it would be advisable to have any interference with it in our trade except by inter-national agreement. If by international agreement rebates were abolished abroad, in Germany especially, then I should be quite agreeable to see them abolished in this country, but I should be very sorry as a merchant to see rebates abolished in this country whilst they continued in Germany, because the inevitable result would be that the British cargo trade being unprotected by the rebate system would be open to the attacks of the Germans, while the German trade being protected by the rebate system would not be open to the reprisals of the British shipowners.[44]

IV

So far we have only discussed German competition on those routes where German shipping was still a minor participant, albeit an increasingly powerful one. But in one field, the North Atlantic passenger trade, where competition was more severe than anywhere else, Germany was a dominant partner

almost from the beginning of this period. It is true that after
the collapse of the American mercantile marine in the Civil
War, Britain for a short time held a semi-monopoly of the
traffic on this route. The bulk of the passenger traffic between
Europe and the United States and Canada passed through
this courtry, and in 1871 there were only one or two foreign
lines of any importance operating on the North Atlantic.
Within the next decade or so foreign competition grew very
rapidly indeed, and by the middle of the 1880s there were more
than twenty distinct lines maintaining regular sailings between
Europe and North America. Of the Continental lines, the
German Hamburg-American and the North German-Lloyd
were by far the most important. Even by the early 1880s
these two lines accounted for about 30 per cent of the total
westward passenger traffic, and they were rapidly encroaching
on the British position. In fact, these two lines formed the
backbone of the German shipping industry and within a short
space of time they became the largest shipping companies in
the world.[45]

The vast westward migration to the United States and
Canada in the latter half of the nineteenth century provided
ideal conditions for the rapid growth of liner companies.
Between 1860 and 1890 ten million people migrated to the
States mainly from Britain, Germany, Scandinavia, Holland
and Switzerland. In the remaining years before the war (1890-
1914) the total migration rose to fifteen million, the bulk of
this originating from central and south-eastern Europe.[46]
This change in the geographical pattern of migration tended
to favour the Continental shipping lines and, more particularly,
the German companies since the latter established special
migration or control stations along the eastern borders of
Germany to trap the emigrants as they crossed into German
territory.[47] Most of the emigrants travelled third class or
steerage, and the growing competition for this traffic
especially from the 1880s onwards led to a series of attempts
to regulate and pool the business.

The first attempt to form an agreement or conference in

this trade took place in 1886. By this time German influence had grown considerably in the North Atlantic passenger business, and the new director of the Hamburg-American Company's Passenger Department, Albert Ballin, was anxi ous to reduce the influence of the British lines competing or traffic at Hamburg. In order to wring concessions from the 'atter, Ballin attempted to break the English monopoly of the Scandinavian traffic by establishing a line between Stettin and New York in conjunction with a Danish firm. If this plan failed he threatened to attack the British in their own country by carrying steerage passengers either from Liverpool via Le Havre or from Plymouth via Hamburg. The British lines soon capitulated under these threats, and an agreement was made with the German lines in September 1886. Ballin agreed to withdraw the Scandinavian service and the German lines gained access to steerage traffic from English ports. A clearing house was set up in Hamburg to allocate passenger traffic between the British and German lines and minimum rates were fixed for passengers.[48]

Initially this arrangement worked quite successfully since there is little evidence of sharp disagreement between the respective parties in the first few years. In time, however, it became increasingly unsatisfactory. The British lines complained that they were not getting the share of the business to which they were entitled and they accused the Germans of not withdrawing completely from the Scandinavian traffic. A more serious objection to it from the German point of view was that the agreement excluded many foreign shipping lines which were competing for the passenger traffic of Europe. There was a general feeling among German shipowners, particularly Ballin, that a much wider and more comprehensive arrangement was necessary if competition on the North Atlantic was to be reduced to a minimum.

Accordingly in 1892 the first North Atlantic passenger line conference was formed by four companies, the North German-Lloyd, Holland-American, Hamburg-American and Red Star lines. Each line was allotted a certain percentage of the westbound steerage traffic from North European ports, and provision was made for the participation of the British lines. Members agreed to arrange their services in such a way so that the number of steeragers actually carried corresponded as nearly as possible with the numbers allotted by the contract. If the tonnage employed by a given line was increased, then the company was entitled to a stipulated increase per 1,000 tons in the number of steerage passengers carried, whilst if its tonnage declined, its allotted share was reduced. On the other hand, in the event of a company exceeding its allotted quota, it was obliged to take measures to bring about a readjustment, and if at the end of any year the annual steerage traffic of a given line exceeded the stipulated quota, it was required to pay to those lines that did not reach their quotas an agreed amount of compensation per excess steerage passenger. Consistent maladjustment between the actual traffic carried and the prescribed quotas was rectified either by manipulating fares or by revising the quotas. Passage rates for steeragers were laid down in the contract and could only be altered by a collective decision of the conference.

Essentially this was the basis on which pooling agreements were made for the North Atlantic passenger traffic for the next twenty years or so until the war terminated the agreements. Of course, the scope of the original agreement was much enlarged in later years as other lines joined and many separate agreements were made covering various classes of traffic, both west- and eastbound. Eventually there were some twelve separate agreements covering thirty different lines engaged in the Atlantic passenger traffic, including the Mediterranean Steerage Conference established in 1908. It would be quite impossible to discuss the detailed and exceedingly complex clauses of all these contracts. Basically, however, they followed the pattern of the original agreement outlined above.[49] In any case, from our point of view the most important points to consider are the effects of the pooling agreements on competition and the relationships of the British lines with the conference members. Most of the

comments will be confined to the westbound steerage conference since this was by far the most important of all the
agreements made.

It is difficult to make a precise assessment of the impact of
the pooling agreements since it is impossible for one thing to
acquire a complete set of statistics of the passengers carried
by each line.[50] Secondly, the working documents of the
conferences which still exist are not open to the general
public for inspection.[51] Consequently we are forced to rely
almost entirely on published, mostly contemporary, sources
for information about the operations of the pooling agreements. Much of this consists of very fragmentary evidence
and, except in a few cases, it was virtually impossible to
construct a reasonably reliable series of data which could be
used for comparative purposes. Nevertheless, despite the
inadequacy of the data, it is possible to make one or two
observations, though the reader should be warned against
placing too much reliance on them.

It seems fairly certain that the pooling arrangements
achieved a greater stability in passenger fares, though they
were probably maintained at a higher level than under free
competition. In the 1890s steerage rates were maintained
fairly well, and by the turn of the century they were on
average above those fixed in 1892. By 1913 they had fallen
somewhat, though they still remained above the 1892 level.
In view of the fact that the profit margin on steerage traffic
was quite small, this greater stability in rates, no doubt,
ensured the companies a more secure return and permitted
an improvement in the quality of service. The *Shipping World*
remarked that 'as a working agreement between the several
companies concerned . . . it has built up Transatlantic
traffic in a way that would otherwise have been impossible'.
Even the chairman of Cunard, a company which caused the
conference members a considerable amount of trouble, was
extolling the virtues of co-operation by 1913.[52] On the other
hand, it would be unwise to attach too much importance to
the apparent stability of passenger fares in this period. For

one thing they were generally much less volatile than freight
rates anyway, and at a time when improvements in service
were taking place, it is perhaps only to be expected that fares
for the Atlantic crossing would either remain firm or increase
slightly. Furthermore, the general impression of continuous
stability is probably misleading in itself. There is no index of
passenger fares and the comments above are based on data for
a few random years. It might well be, therefore, that the year
to year fluctuations in passenger rates were greater than the
figures suggest. This conclusion is in part confirmed by the
fact that the conference arrangements did not automatically
lead to permanent stability of rates. From time to time disputes
arose among the members, especially between the German and
British lines, regarding the division of traffic or the fares
charged. Invariably these disagreements led to rate wars, some
of which had disastrous results as far as the companies' profits
were concerned.

In fact, trouble broke out soon after the Pool Agreement
had been inaugurated. At first the British lines refused to
join the conference because they were dissatisfied with the
proportion (14 per cent) of the Continental traffic allotted to
them.[53] It followed, therefore, that they could no longer
adhere to the original understanding of 1886 with the
Germans, which meant in effect that the latter now had a
free hand as regards the Scandinavian traffic. This was not,
however, the immediate cause of the rate war. The strained
relationships were, in fact, aggravated by the outbreak of
cholera in 1893 which caused a sharp fall in the emigrant
traffic. Total passengers carried by all lines fell from
439,730 to 285,631 between 1893 and 1894, and some of
the Continental companies were hit very badly indeed. Competition for the diminished volume of trade brought rates
down sharply. Passenger fares were reduced by nearly 50 per
cent and, in an attempt to counter British competition, the
Germans re-entered the Scandinavian trade. By the end of
1894 most of the shipping companies engaged in the dispute
were ready to negotiate a truce, and in September of the

following year an agreement was finally signed by the four
Continental lines, the American line and seven British companies.[54] In effect this brought the British lines into the
pooling arrangements for the first time, though they accepted
a much reduced quota of the Continental traffic (6 per cent)
than they had been offered originally. In return, the Continental lines (mainly the German in this case) agreed to
withdraw from the Scandinavian traffic and to reduce their
callings at British ports.[55]

The British lines clearly got the worst of the bargain, but
they were prepared to acquiesce simply because the only
alternative appeared to be a prolongation of the costly rate
war. Moreover, since most of the important Continental lines
were already in, or about to join, the Pool, it would have been
difficult for the British shipowners to remain outside indefinitely. By this time the foreign lines, taken together, formed a
dominant influence in the passenger trade of the North
Atlantic and hence were in a strong position to dictate their
own terms.

Although the British lines, and particularly Cunard, were
dissatisfied with the new pooling arrangements, most of them
managed to maintain reasonably amicable relationships with
their Continental partners until the turn of the century.[56] In
May 1903, however, Cunard withdrew from the Atlantic
agreements. The causes of the rift were complex. Basically,
Cunard objected to the way in which the Continental lines
were trying to monopolise the European traffic, and in
particular the Company was annoyed about the methods
employed, namely the establishment of the frontier control
stations in Germany. But the more immediate cause of the
withdrawal was the agreement made between the Continental
companies and the Morgan Trust[57] early in 1903 to the
effect that each would safeguard the other's interests against
outside competitors. Not only was Cunard ignored in connection with this agreement but it appeared from the wording
that it was directly aimed against the British company.[58]

Cunard's departure from the conference did not

immediately precipitate the rate war. Rather it was sparked
off by the Company's subsequent negotiations with the
Austrian and Hungarian Governments to carry emigrants and
mail from Trieste and Fiume. In effect, these arrangements
gave Cunard virtually a monopoly of the traffic, and the
German lines, retaliating from what they thought was their
prerogative, carried the war into the rival camp by cutting the
Scandinavian rates. Inevitably this led to an all-round reduction
in western steerage rates and by 1904 they had been reduced
by two-thirds.[59] Eventually peace was restored in October
1904, though not before the companies concerned had sacrificed most of their profits for that year. Cunard's earnings,
for example, dropped from £248,563 to £61,588 in 1904.
Altogether it has been estimated that the crisis cost the
participant companies nearly £1 million.[60]

The subsequent agreement was only a temporary or make-
shift measure, however. All the lines agreed to restore their
rates to the level prevailing before the rate war and Cunard
rejoined the Pool. But a lasting arrangement was out of the
question and within a few months Cunard had withdrawn
from the conference again, largely on account of a failure to
reach an agreement over the Hungarian traffic. According to
Murken, the Cunard Company strengthened her position in
the period immediately after the rate war and could afford,
therefore, to pursue a more independent line of action. The
Hungarian and Austrian contracts made an appreciable difference to her overall position; the number of Continental
passengers carried by the Company rose from 1,267 to
35,705 between 1902 and 1906, and by the latter date they
accounted for nearly 39 per cent of the total passenger trade
of Cunard. Moreover, the technical and competitive
superiority of the Company was revealed in 1907 when the
Lusitania and *Mauretania* were launched.

Thus, when negotiations took place early in 1906 for a new
and more permanent pooling agreement, Cunard was in a
stronger position to press for better terms than she had
previously enjoyed.[61] The British lines as a whole (that is

including those transferred to the Morgan Trust) were allotted nearly 37 per cent of the total westbound traffic and the Cunard Company alone obtained nearly 14 per cent. This was excluding her Fiume service for which a special allowance was made. Nearly all the major lines operating on the North Atlantic joined the new Pool which was a more elaborate arrangement than the previous ones, for it included clauses relating to cabin traffic.

The strength of the conference was tested almost immediately since the economic crisis in the United States (1907-08) brought a very sharp reduction in emigrant traffic. In 1908 the number of steerage passengers travelling westwards was a mere 424,000 compared with nearly 1,400,000 the year before. The Continental companies were hit very badly indeed — the profits of the Hamburg-American Company were halved — and the British group had to pay them compensation.[62] Yet, though it proved the most serious fall-off in passenger traffic for many years, a rate war failed to materialise. Having survived the worst crisis since its inception in 1892, the pooling agreement functioned fairly smoothly in the following years although there were one or two minor crises caused by interference from shipping lines outside the Pool. It was not until 1913 that another serious rate war broke out.[63] This time the dispute arose out of a disagreement between the two German lines over their respective shares of the westbound steerage traffic. The Hamburg-American Company demanded an increase in its quota, but the other members of the conference, including the North German Lloyd, refused to sanction this. Despite innumerable meetings it was found impossible to reach an understanding with the recalcitrant company and early in 1914 the Pool was formally dissolved. Subsequently, westbound rates were reduced and the outbreak of military warfare a few months later ended the possibility of negotiating any new agreement.[64]

It is clear from this brief discussion that the history of the North Atlantic passenger agreements between 1892 and 1914

was far from being trouble free. No doubt the pooling arrangements acted as a restraining influence on the competitive zeal
of the constituent members, but they could not prevent the
occurence of bouts of severe competition when the lines
failed to agree on some particular issue. Moreover, the conference system did not prevent competition in service; in fact,
it might be argued that it shifted the emphasis towards
competition in this field. It is well known that the shipping
companies operating on the North Atlantic tried to outbid
each other by building bigger and better transatlantic liners
and offering additional service comforts to their passengers,
even to the steeragers. At times, however, one gets the
impression that the companies carried service competition to
excessive lengths.

Throughout the period the British lines maintained an
uneasy relationship with the continental members of the
Pool. Cunard, as we have seen, was never very happy with the
arrangements and was particularly suspicious of German
motives. These suspicions may at times have been well founded,
but in turn it could be argued that Cunard's actions were no
less reprehensible. Whether on balance the British lines
benefited from joining the conference, or in Cunard's case
from remaining outside it for part of the time, is difficult to
say precisely, owing to the fragmentary statistical data
available. But in Tables 4 *(see page 86)* and 5 *(see page 87)*
an attempt has been made to assemble roughly comparable
figures for a number of years. Taking the British and Canadian
lines together,[65] it can be seen that they maintained their
relative share of the westbound cabin and steerage traffic
(including the Mediterranean traffic) between 1903 and 1913
after having suffered a sharp loss in the previous twenty years,
a loss which can be attributed largely to German competition
(see Table 4). On the other hand, after 1903 the German
companies appear to have lost ground in both cabin and
steerage traffic to non-British lines. A more detailed company
breakdown of the North European westbound traffic to
New York and Canada is given in Table 5.

TABLE 4: *Division of Westbound North Atlantic Passenger Traffic Between British and German Lines (All Traffic Including Mediterranean)*

	1883		1903		1913	
	Cabin	Steerage	Cabin	Steerage	Cabin	Steerage
British and Canadian Lines	39,838	160,634	113,553	303,769	230,071	476,119
Per cent of total	67.9	41.4	53.7	33.9	50.8	33.9
German Lines	10,934	119,531	62,859	321,342	111,253	393,704
Per cent of total	18.7	30.8	29.7	35.9	24.6	28.0
Total (All Lines)	58,596	388,267	211,321	394,926	452,956	1,405,649

Sources: *Glasgow Herald* (31 January 1884) and Murken, op cit

From this it can be seen that the two German lines increased their share of the total traffic substantially between 1883 and 1903 but failed to maintain this lead up to 1913. But by that date their share of the North European passenger trade was larger (33.9 per cent) than their share of the total Atlantic passenger traffic (28.0 per cent) including the Mediterranean traffic. Of the British lines Anchor and White Star declined in relative importance after 1891. Cunard, on the other hand, managed to maintain its relative position fairly well, and in fact even increased its share of the traffic up to 1903. Thus, despite its rather wavering attitude towards the conference system, Cunard did not do at all badly. Overall, one might say that although the British lines lost the predominant position that they held in the Atlantic trade in the 1870s and early 1880s, they were by no means crushed by the force of foreign competition. In fact, in the early twentieth century, when the conference system was fully in operation, they maintained their relative position better than the Germans who lost ground to non-British rivals.

TABLE 5: *Westbound North Atlantic Passenger Traffic (Excluding Mediterranean) of Certain Lines*

	1883		1891		1903		1913	
	Cabin	Steerage	Cabin	Steerage	Cabin	Steerage	Cabin	Steerage
North German Lloyd	7,228	66,474	16,629	68,239	34,908	161,946	50,738	195,718
Per cent of total	12.3	17.1	11.1	15.3	17.4	23.9	12.9	19.3
Hamburg-American	3,706	53,057	11,016	75,835	22,941	109,523	45,377	148,523
Per cent of total	6.3	13.7	7.3	17.0	11.4	16.2	11.6	14.6
Cunard	9,153	11,647	14,769	27,341	23,686	61,528	43,812	86,176
Per cent of total	15.6	3.0	9.8	6.1	11.8	9.0	11.2	8.5
Anchor	6,380	24,545	7,323	15,082	8,820	11,909	16,970	16,190
Per cent of total	10.9	6.3	4.9	3.4	4.3	1.8	4.3	1.6
White Star	5,842	27,994	13,193	35,502	27,712	45,957	42,095	61,970
Per cent of total	9.9	7.2	8.8	7.9	11.3	6.8	10.8	6.1
Total (All Lines)	58,596	388,267	15,023	445,290	200,972	677,403	391,148	1,016,356

Source: *Glasgow Herald* (31 January 1884) and Murken, op cit

V

Finally, a few comments must be made about the general organisation and services of German shipping. The structure of the industry was in some respects different from that of Great Britain. The bulk of German shipping was employed in the great liner trades and tramp tonnage formed a very small proportion of the total fleet. Britain too, of course, had a large volume of tonnage engaged in liner services, but at the same time a fairly high proportion of her mercantile marine (probably in the region of 40 per cent) consisted of tramp tonnage. This structural difference resulted in a higher degree of concentration of German shipping in the hands of a few companies. Most firms of any importance were joint stock undertakings, and in 1905 the seven largest owned 60 per cent of the total German tonnage whilst three-quarters of the fleet was owned or controlled by nineteen companies.[66] British shipping was much less highly concentrated, largely because of the existence of many small tramp companies. Even after the massive amalgamation movement of the early twentieth century, only one-quarter of the UK fleet was owned and controlled by one of the 'Big Five' groups, though it should be stressed that by the early 1920s about three-quarters of the British liner tonnage was in the hands of seven large shipping companies.[67]

The compactness of the German mercantile marine was, no doubt, facilitated by the fact that there was only one main shore line and two major ports from which German ship-owners operated, as against three different coasts and at least six major ports in Britain. Concentration of and co-operation between German shipowners was, therefore, a simple affair geographically. This appears to have resulted in a fairly tight-knit community of interests within the ports of Bremen and Hamburg. The main lines worked closely with one another, despite a certain amount of inter-port rivalry, and many of the lines which were outside the main group were either controlled by some member of it or worked in close relation with it, the major exception being the German Levant line. It was rare, moreover, to find the German companies competing fiercely with each other as the English lines sometimes did.[68] A series of complex and intricate agreements between companies plying in the same area acted as a safeguard against internal competition. And even when internal differences did occur they were usually resolved quite rapidly in the event of any attack from foreign lines. Indeed, German shipowners were invariably prepared to support each other against competition from foreign flags, and in the early twentieth century the ten largest lines established a *Rheederei-Vereinigung* or Shipping Union which had at its disposal some 23,000 tons of shipping which could be chartered by its members for use as a fighting force against external aggressors.[69]

This is not meant to imply that the German shipping industry was any more efficient than the British because of its compact organisation, but rather to suggest that it was in a better position to meet competition from outside lines. At times, however, one does get the impression that German shipping companies were somewhat better adapted to meeting the conditions of the period. The organisation and direction of the larger companies at least appear to have been rather more dynamic than that of many British companies. Men like Woermann, Ballin (Hamburg-American) and Lohmann and Wiegand of the North German Lloyd were directors or managers of outstanding ability and drive, who built up large and flourishing companies from almost nothing.[70] They were prepared to risk everything to ferret out openings for German ships, and part of their success lay in the way in which they developed trade openings in areas which had hitherto been neglected. Perhaps these men were exceptions, and no doubt they had their counterparts on the British side, but if Sturmey is correct one cannot help feeling that they contrasted sharply with some of the old family cliques who featured so prominently in British shipping.[71]

Such comments are largely impressionistic and the author would be at pains to counter any suggestion that British shipowners were, in general, less efficient than their German

rivals. Occasionally German shipowners were more enterprising;
a case in point being the Woermann line in the West African
trade. Here two British lines had originally held a virtual monopoly until the Woermann line entered the area in the early
1880s.[72] From then onwards British ships were faced with
increasing competition, and if tonnage employed in the West
African service is anything to go by, it appears that the
Germans increased their relative share of the trade substantially
in the late nineteenth and early twentieth centuries *(see Table
6 below)*.

TABLE 6: *Tonnage Employed in the West African Trade*

	1892−3	1906−07
Woermann Line	15,741	71,957
British and African Steam Navig. Co and the African Steamship Co	67,125	97,646

Source: *Royal Commission on Shipping Rings*, Evidence, Vol III, 175

Although British shipowners still continued to exert a dominant influence in the area, a fact which was reflected in the
terms of the first West African conference of 1894,[73] shippers
were becoming increasingly dissatisfied with the services they
offered and many were transferring their custom to the
German line. The reason for this was explained by John Holt
(West African merchant) to the Royal Commission:

> They (the British) have lost it through lack of attention to
> detail and concentration of effort which has characterised
> German action once a common basis of freight was fixed
> between them; it then became a matter of which could most
> attract shippers, and in this the German line has clearly proved
> itself superior. It is the common opinion of shippers that the
> German line is more obliging, more helpful, more pushing,
> more ready to adapt itself to altered conditions of trade, more
> reliable as to time and fulfilment of promise — in other words,

more earnest, thorough and business-like.

Apparently the two British lines had fallen into the hands of the prominent shipowner, Sir Alfred Jones, who, according to Holt, had tended to neglect the West African side of his many business interests.[74]

One swallow does not, of course, make a summer and it would be a gross distortion of the facts to conclude from this single example that German shipowners were more enterprising than their British counterparts. In fact, apart from the case of the West African trade, there is practically no other evidence which would support such a hypothesis. One cannot do anything, therefore, but conclude that British shipowners were, taken as a whole, as efficient and as enterprising as their German counterparts.

There is no doubt that in the period in question German shipowners presented a serious challenge to the British shipping industry. German shipowners had few marked economic advantages over their rivals, however, and their competitive strength lay in the skill and persistence with which they tried to penetrate the established trades. By the late nineteenth century the Germans had gained a firm foothold in many of the major trade routes, though it was only in the North Atlantic passenger trade that they played a dominant role. Although at times British shipowners might be criticised for appearing reluctant to fight the German challenge, one can hardly criticise them for being inefficient. But foreign competition did help to keep British shipowners on their toes. Nor could it be argued that British shipping suffered heavy losses through foreign competition. On one or two routes, especially the North Atlantic and West African, Germany increased her share of the traffic substantially, but apart from the short haul European trades, German shipping only had a fairly marginal influence in most other areas albeit an increasingly important one. British shipbuilders had even less to fear from foreign competition. Although by the early twentieth century there were indications that in some respects foreign

shipbuilders were gaining ground,[75] there was little evidence
to suggest that Britain's monopoly in the shipbuilding field
was in danger of being broken in the near future. In short, the
British maritime industries remained overwhelmingly predominant up to 1914, and whatever criticisms might be made
about them in later years these certainly had no relevant
application in the period prior to World War I. In these years
Britain's competitive position remained virtually unassailable
and, in Pollard's words, if ever there was a class of entrepreneurs
capable of standing on their own legs it was the British shipbuilders and owners.[76]

NOTES

1   Around the turn of the century Japanese competition in Chinese
    waters increased sharply at Britain's expense. See Chi-ming Hou,
    Foreign Investment and Economic Development in China
    (Harvard, 1965), 61

2   *Shipping World* (1 April 1891), 372

3   In a letter dated 23 June 1902 to the Board of Trade the Bucknall
    Brothers commenting on the importance of maintaining the
    conference system in the South African Trade wrote: 'It would
    obviously be impolitic for English lines to recede from this
    mutually beneficial system in connection with the maintenance
    of regular lines, only to give greater opportunity to the Germans
    to accelerate and make greater inroads upon the English mercan-
    tile shipping.' PRO, MT9/734/M11869, 12390, 1900

4   Full details can be found in the *Report on Bounties and Subsidies
    in respect of Shipbuilding, Shipping and Navigation in Foreign
    Countries,* Cd 6899 (1913)

5   *Economist*, Shipping Supplement (21 June 1911), 4. For similar
    opinions see *Shipping World* (1 January 1890), 266, and *Royal
    Commission on the Dominions*: Evidence taken in London during
    October and November 1912, Cd 6517 (1912-13), Q 4611. One
    shipowner even went so far as to suggest that subsidies had
    enabled the Germans to gain the Atlantic blue ribbon. This, of

course, was nonsense since the German fleet employed on the North Atlantic was *not* subsidised. See *Annual Report of the Chamber of Shipping of the UK* (1901), 73-4

6   R.S.J. Hoffman, *Great Britain and the German Trade Rivalry, 1875-1914* (1933), 215

7   These figures are for 1901

8   Entrances and clearances of German shipping in East Asian ports rose from 57,740 net tons in 1883 to 512,369 in 1903, and in the Australian service from 56,717 to 386,115 net tons. G. Jaensch, *Die deutschen Postdampfersubventionen, ihre Entstehung, Begründung und ihre Volkswirtschaftlichen Wirkungen* (Berlin, 1907), 84

9   Jaensch, op cit, 111-12

10   *Fairplay* (20 August 1903), 283, and *Select Committee on Steamship Subsidies,* H of C 385 (1902), Evidence 1 August 1901, para 4236

11   This was later raised to £67,500

12   K. Brackmann, *Fünfzig Jahre deutscher Afrikaschiffahrt* (Berlin, 1935), 36-9

13   Brackmann, op cit, 26

14   A discussion of this will be deferred until later since it involves the question of special through rates

15   *Select Committee on Steamship Subsidies,* H of C 385 (1902), Evidence 15 July 1902, paras 2652-3

16   R. Meeker, *History of Shipping Subsidies* (1905), 94

17   For the French position see Appendix 24 to the *Select Committee on Steamship Subsidies;* and M.A. Raffalovich, 'The Effects of Shipping Bounties', *Journal of Royal Statistical Society* (1888), 141-54. Although France subsidised her mercantile marine more lavishly than any other country, the results achieved were very disappointing indeed. Under the subsidy law of 1881 French shipowners received from the state no less than £1.4 million

annually and from 1892 this was raised to £1.7 million. The main disadvantage of the subsidies was that they tended to favour the building of inexpensive sailing vessels rather than large ocean-going steamers. Thus at a time when most countries were scrapping their sailing fleets France continued to build sailing vessels on a considerable scale and the French sailing fleet actually increased from 1890 to 1912. Moreover, throughout the period the growth of the French mercantile marine was very modest indeed, rising from 919,298 net tons in 1880 to 1,462,639 in 1911, and in fact after the turn of the century it hardly rose at all. Japan, on the other hand, was much more successful in this respect. Subsidies were first paid in 1896 but initially they were fairly moderate and it was not until 1908 that they were paid on a scale comparable with the French bounties. The results were quite favourable. Between 1895 and 1911 the Japanese fleet rose from 386,163 to 1,838,054 gross tons and after 1900 the bulk of the increase consisted of steamships. Thus after making allowance for the differences in tonnage measurement, the Japanese fleet had, by the second decade of the twentieth century, surpassed that of the French

18   Ibid, *Report,* para 7, for other examples

19   Ibid, Evidence 17 June 1902, para 856

20   Union-Castle records (24 August 1894)

21   Brackmann, op cit, 35-6

22   Ibid, 45

23   *Shipping World* (14 February 1906), 180

24   The position is unclear here, but witnesses before the *Royal Commission on Shipping Rings* did mention the existence of through rates to this area. See Vol III, Evidence, QQ 9394-405, 9554-67

25   See *Stahl und Eisen* (22 January 1914), 157

26   S. Pollard, 'British and World Shipbuilding, 1890-1914; A Study in Comparative Costs', *Journal of Economic History,* XVII (3) (1957), 429, 443-4

27 *Select Committee on Steamship Subsidies*, Evidence 3 July 1902, para 1774

28 See *Annual Report of the Chamber of Shipping of the UK* (1895), 64-5; *Annual Report of the Liverpool Steamship Owners' Association* (1906), 3-4; *Fairplay* (25 January 1900), 127

29 *Fairplay* (23 May 1901), 838

30 The application of such regulations had the effect of reducing the cargo-carrying space in ships

31 See PRO MT9/809/M384/1907, Memo by Board of Trade

32 *Annual Report of the Liverpool Steamship Owners' Association* (1913), 20

33 See *Select Committee on Steamship Subsidies*, Evidence 18 July 1901, QQ 3482-7, 2594; *Shipping World* (13 December 1899), 584, and (30 June 1909), 685

34 It is probable, for instance, that British vessels were on average technically more efficient and this would tend to offset the higher wage costs. *Shipping World* (30 June 1909), 685, suggested that the difference in running costs between German and British vessels was fairly small

35 See *Royal Commission on Shipping Rings*, Vol III, QQ 926, 1108, 1116-17

36 *Report of the Departmental Committee on Shipping and Shipbuilding after the War*, Cd 9092 (1918), 103

37 P & O, British India, the City, Clan and Anchor Lines

38 *Fairplay* (8 March 1906), 308, and (13 December 1906), 875; *Royal Commission on Shipping Rings*, Vol III, Evidence, 298, Vol IV, Evidence, QQ 19678-86, 20501

39 *The Times* (12 and 22 January and 5 February 1913); Brackmann, op cit, 94-5

40 A.H. John, *A Liverpool Merchant House: Being the History of*

Alfred Booth and Company, 1863-1958 (1959), 102; *Royal Commission on Shipping Rings*, Evidence, Vol IV, 242-3 and 312

41   *Royal Commission on Shipping Rings*, Evidence, Vol III, QQ 9344-9

42   *Fairplay* (19 September 1907), 434

43   *Royal Commission on Shipping Rings*, Evidence, Vol IV, QQ 18447-8

44   Mr Tredwen, speaking at a Conference with Representatives of the Associated Chambers of Commerce (May 1911), PRO, MT9/926/M12174/1911

45   See Hans Otto von Borcke and Hugo Heeckt, *Entwicklung und Aussichten der deutschen Passagierschiffahrt auf dem Nordatlantik* (Kiel, 1956), 3 and 31; O. Mathies, *Hamburgs Reederei, 1814-1914* (Hamburg, 1924)

46   M.A. Jones, *American Immigration* (1960), 179. These figures do not, of course, include Canadian immigrants

47   These were sanitary control stations established along the Russian frontier by the Prussian Government in the early 1890s. The operation of these inspection posts was entrusted by the Government to the Hamburg-American and North German Lloyd who acted jointly as concessionnaires. It has been alleged that this gave the German shipowners an unfair advantage, since because many of the emigrants had to pass through Germany on their way to the States, they were forced to travel by German lines or risk the penalty of being refused transit permits. Moreover, it is said that this control over the emigrant traffic was used by the German lines as a weapon for dividing their competitors and forcing unfavourable agreements on them

48   B. Huldermann, *Albert Ballin* (1922), 21-3; P.F. Stubmann, *Albert Ballin: Ein Deutscher Reeder auf Internationalen Feld* (Hamburg, 1957), 12

49   A fairly full treatment of most of the agreements can be found in E. Murken, *Die grossen transatlantischen Linienreederei Verbände, Pools und Interessentengemeinschaften bis zum Ausbruch des*

Weltkrieges. Ihre Entstehung, Organization und Wirksamkeit (1922); there are few good accounts in English though some useful details may be found in the *Report of the Committee on the Merchant Marine and Fisheries on Steamship Agreements and Affiliations in the American, Foreign and Domestic Trade*, US Congressional Documents No 805 (Washington, 1914) and E.R. Johnson and G.G. Huebner, *Principles of Ocean Transportation* (New York, 1918), 293-5 and 290 (chart)

50   Even the companies themselves cannot provide the relevant data. The Cunard Company, for example, have no records of the passengers they carried before 1914

51   Some of the relevant documents are now held in this country by the Secretary of the present North Atlantic Conference. The author tried unsuccessfully to gain access to this material

52   *Shipping World* (16 April 1913), 421

53   The French lines had also refused to join

54   The Allan, Allan and State, Anchor, Beaver, Cunard, Dominion and White Star lines

55   Murken, op cit, 51-68

56   Although at least one company, the Beaver line, withdrew from the conference before the end of the century

57   This was the large American shipping combine formed in 1902 when a number of British shipping companies were transferred to American ownership but continued to fly the British flag. The companies involved in the merger were the American, Red Star, Atlantic Transport, Leyland, White Star and Dominion lines

58   *Shipping World* (19 April 1905), 405

59   Ibid, (25 May 1904), 490, and (18 January 1905), 78. *Fairplay* (23 June 1904), 1017-18. Herschel suggests that Cunard would not have been prepared to carry on such a fight had she not been subsidised heavily by the British Government. This, of course, is incorrect. True, Cunard had recently negotiated a subsidy contract with the Government, but this was specifically for the

building of two crack liners and none of the subsidy had been paid to the Company before the rate war broke out. Cunard was paid for carrying the mail, but the profit on this was hardly sufficient to support a costly rate war. See F.B. Herschel, *Entwicklung und Bedeutung der Hamburg-Amerika Linie* (Berlin, 1912), 115

60   D.H. Aldcroft, 'The Depression in British Shipping, 1901-1911', *The Journal of Transport History* (May 1965), 20

61   Murken, op cit, 331

62   Herschel, op cit, 99

63   The Pool was revised and renewed in 1911

64   *The Times* (25 July 1913) and (22 January 1914)

65   These include those transferred to the Morgan Combine in 1902

66   P. Lenz, *Die Konzentration im Seeschiffahrtsgewerbe* (Jena 1913), 61-2

67   Aldcroft, loc cit, 22

68   See particularly J. Russell Smith, 'Ocean Freight Rates and their Control through Combination', *Political Science Quarterly*, xxi(2) (1906), 261. Competition from tramp shipping was much less common in Germany of course

69   *Fairplay* (25 November 1909), 755, and (16 December 1909), 863

70   For an appreciation of Lohmann and Wiegand see P. Neubar, *Der Nord-deutsche Lloyd: 50 Jahre der Entwicklung, 1857-1907*, Vol 1 (Leipzig, 1907), especially pp 46-52 and 91-110

71   Professor S.G. Sturmey in a recent book, *British Shipping and World Competition* (1962), has suggested that many British firms were dominated by family groups which had an adverse effect on their competitive ability in later years, ie in the inter-war period

72   The Woermann family had been traders and shippers since the

1830s. See T. Bohner, *Die Woermanns* (Berlin, 1935)

73   C. Leubuscher, *The West African Shipping Trade, 1909-1959* (1963), 15.

74   *Royal Commission on Shipping Rings*, Evidence, Vol III, 178, Q 5201

75   It has been said that some of the most important technical improvements were taking place abroad, that some foreign yards were better equipped than ours and that the Germans could build cheaper liners. See *Report of the Tariff Commission*, Vol 4, *The Engineering Trades* (1909), paras 90-2; S.J. Chapman, *Work and Wages*, Vol I (1904), 103, and I. Svennilson, *Growth and Stagnation in the European Economy* (1954), 155

76   S. Pollard, *The Economic History of British Shipbuilding*, University of London, PhD thesis (1951), 298

4 The Depression in British Shipping, 1901-11

First published in The Journal of Transport History, 7 (1965)

I

Few industries have been subject to such violent fluctuations in fortune as the shipping industry. One year's trading has never been a very satisfactory guide to the next, and on balance the bad years have outnumbered the good. In the 45 years before 1914 the number of poor years exceeded the prosperous ones by two to one.[1] This may not at first seem surprising, as the period includes the years of the Great Depression (1873-96) when trade and industry were relatively depressed. The fact is, however, that nearly one-third of the bad years occurred in the early twentieth century, a time when the rest of the British economy was by all accounts fairly buoyant. Between 1901 and 1911 the shipping industry remained in a depressed state[2] — so depressed in fact that it has been referred to as the first major international shipping depression.[3] That the industry should display contrary tendencies to the rest of the economy is interesting and requires further examination and elucidation.

Freight rates began to decline towards the end of 1900, and by 1901 many rates had fallen to 50 per cent below those ruling in the autumn of the previous year. During the next few years freights remained heavily depressed, though a very slight recovery seems to have occurred in 1906 and the early part of 1907. Then between 1907 and 1908 freights fell again, this time to the lowest level for over fifty years, and according to Angier 1908 was a year of 'unexampled depression in all freights both outwards and homewards'.[4] By the end of 1909 the worst was over, but in the following years freights only recovered slowly, and it was not until 1912 that they again reached the level of 1900.[5]

It is dangerous, of course, to attach too much importance to the tramp index as a measure of prosperity of the shipping industry as a whole. For one thing the Isserlis freight index, which is the only comprehensive index available for this period, does not include liner rates (both passenger and cargo) which for various reasons tended to be more stable, nor does it differentiate between outward and homeward trades. Cairncross has broken down and reworked the available indexes (namely those of Hobson, Isserlis, and the Board of Trade) so as to take some account of liner rates. It is clear from his calculations that outward freights were maintained at a much higher level than inward freights throughout these years.[6] This is largely what one would expect. The inward trades were always highly competitive, since the cargoes moved in this direction have been particularly suited to the tramp vessel.[7] As a consequence liner conferences, which helped to maintain rates in the outward trades, have made little headway in the opposite direction. Secondly, it should be remembered that freight rates generally were falling almost continuously throughout the latter half of the nineteenth century, and it is not always possible to determine how far this was due to changes in the supply of and demand for tonnage and how far it merely reflected changes in the cost of transport due to technical progress. If anything, however, costs of operation seem to have been rising in the first decade of the twentieth century. Finally, it is as well to point out that freight rates had been severely depressed for most of the 1890s, so that the boom of 1899-1900 can be regarded merely as an interruption to a long period of depression. On the other hand, it is easy to explain the setback of the 1890s in terms of the general recession in the economy as a whole, whereas for the period 1901 to 1911 there is no such obvious explanation.

Shipowning was still far from being a profitable occupation in these years, even when allowance is made for the limitations of the freight index and account is taken of the fact that

outward freights were fairly well maintained. The profitable
operation of shipping is very much dependent upon adequate
cargoes in both directions, and it is abundantly clear that a
sufficient volume of cargo of a remunerative character was
not forthcoming in the homeward trades at this time. Indeed,
contemporaries were in no doubt as to the severity of the
depression. Angier's report for 1902 noted that 'the result
of the past year's trade, as far as 80 per cent of British
shipping is concerned, is an absolute loss to the vast majority
of ships, or at best the bare covering of out-of-pocket expenses.
Of the remaining 20 per cent of the tonnage, consisting of
"liners" proper, only the few most favoured companies have
done well — viz., those with good mail contracts . . . and the
small "set" in the run of Government transport work. The
balance has shown but small profits, and many are in a far
from strong financial position.'[8] The next two or three years
were as bad, if not worse. Losses continued to be made in
many trades, and in some cases freights failed to cover even
operating expenses, as a result of which 'the financial position
of a vast number of fleets of liners as well as cargo boats is
at present very weak'.[9] The slight revival in 1906 proved
transitory. By 1908 shipowners all over the world were said
to be making losses, and much tonnage was laid up. At the
end of the year between 1½ to 2 million tons gross tonnage
lay idle, over half of which belonged to Britain. One German
company, the Hamburg-Amerika, had an average of
136,000 tons gross laid up during 1908. Sir Walter Runciman
estimated that in 1908 dividends of British shipping companies dropped by £25 to £30 million and that shipowners were
short of a living freight by £23.5 million.[10] As one shipowner
put it: 'The prevailing depression in shipping has reached so
acute a pitch as to become a grave menace to the national
prosperity, and shipowners are face to face with a serious
crisis. Unless something can be done to restore a more
healthy tone to trade generally, nothing can avert ruin to
many.'[11]

   Those who hoped for a quick revival were to be disappointed.

1909 was another disastrous year, according to Sir Christopher Furness without precedent in the past twenty years.[12] Even by the autumn of that year 738,000 tons gross of shipping were still laid up at the principal ports of the United Kingdom.[13] For many cargo-boat companies it was the worst year ever experienced. The profits of the Nitrate Producers' Steamship Company were the lowest on record, 79 per cent down on 1900.[14] Forty-five of the chief cargo-boat companies paid no dividend and set nothing aside for depreciation,[15] and few companies made sufficient to cover both and make a profit. By this time the rapid fall in earning power of steamers meant that much of the tonnage was over-valued in relation to market value, up to 50 per cent or more in some cases. Second-hand tonnage was selling for a quarter of its former value in many cases, and vessels over 15 years old were now difficult to sell except to the shipbreakers. *Fairplay* maintained that if all the cargo-boat companies had been wound up and the vessels disposed of at the current market price, most companies would have incurred a heavy deficit and shareholders' capital would have been lost.[16]

The following year brought only slight improvement. In July *Fairplay* reported that freights were still not covering working expenses in all cases and that 90 per cent of the cargo boats were not worth more than half their book value, though by this time some companies had already written down their capital assets.[17] Though conditions continued to improve slowly, Angier's report for 1911 struck a dismal note: 'it is very doubtful whether the industry taken as a whole has, even in the last year when freights have been on a level higher than in any year since 1900, done more than make by hard work and constant vigilance such a return on capital as could have been made by the investing of a like amount in first class securities, involving no labour or attention'.[18] The period of unremunerative freights was finally broken in 1912, when they rose sufficiently to allow shipowners to make a real profit for the first time for more than a decade.

Unfortunately comprehensive profit figures for shipping companies are not available to substantiate the statements above. Many companies did not publish accounts, and those that did often framed them in such a way as to render them almost incomprehensible.[19] Figures in the published accounts require therefore to be handled with a great deal of care. The best data available are those for the earnings (before depreciation) of the principal cargo-boat companies collected by *Fairplay* from 1904 onwards. Nearly 100 companies, owning in all about 1.67 million tons gross (average of the years 1904-14), were covered in the survey. It was found that when allowance was made for depreciation at 5 per cent and dividends these companies were running at a loss in every year between 1904 and 1911. Even in 1911 over a third of the companies were paying no dividend and setting aside nothing for depreciation. If the analysis is extended to the years 1912 and 1913 the effect of the improvement in freights is at once apparent. In the ten years 1904-13 these companies earned a total of £15,944,843, nearly two-thirds of which was made in the last two years when depreciation was being written off at more than twice the normal rate. Even so, by the end of 1913 there was still a deficiency of over £1 million on the depreciation account of these companies, and on this basis *Fairplay* estimated that the deficiency for the whole of the cargo-boat fleet was in the region of £7.3 million.[20] If anything, therefore, the selection taken represents the best companies.

No sample analysis has been made for liner-company earnings, but data for six companies have been extracted from the published accounts and presented in Table 1 *(see opposite)*. As might be expected, profits (before depreciation) of liner companies were maintained somewhat better than those for cargo boats, though it is quite evident that earnings were depressed during the period in question. Powers of resilience, however, varied a great deal from company to company, as the profit figures show. Whilst the P & O and Cunard to a lesser extent showed fairly high profits, other

TABLE 1: *Earnings of Selected Liner Companies (£)*

	Houlder Line	Indo-China Steam Navigation Company	Cunard	Orient Steam Navigation Co	P & O[b]	Prince Line[c]
1898				102,283		111,074
1899		112,400	249,406			147,893
1900	82,419	104,792	279,554	51,730	900,411	155,886
1901	97,194	188,816	538,080	134,429	520,537	81,604
1902	62,094	148,061	195,849	50,905	848,345	51,189
1903	64,480	59,912	247,150	48,314	828,545	82,435
1904	23,964	38,017	248,563	59,371	758,242	82,287
1905	23,079	120,492	61,588	60,327	808,251	80,267
1906	30,458	106,051	308,182	75,305	733,034	102,569
1907	12,163	5,500	553,193	90,542	738,655	90,037
1908	−5,155	24,226	554,794	69,780[a]	686,239	77,478
1909	9,357	7,489	172,971		655,780	74,362
1910	21,236	66,565	649,416		783,244	135,073
1911	16,702	88,852	958,158		831,776	225,646
1912	18,500	82,469	815,724		798,685	443,281
1913	91,238	107,177	1,154,197		1,014,661	

(a) Basis of calculation changed after 1908
(b) Year ending 30 September
(c) Year ending 30 June

liner concerns, particularly the Indo-China and the Houlder
Line, experienced a dramatic slump in profits. In fact the
latter's profits fell continuously from 1900, and in 1907 the
company made an absolute loss of £5,155. The financial
position of the company was so poor that for six consecutive
years (1906-11) it failed to pay a dividend or transfer anything to depreciation.

   Total earnings of course tend to give an unduly favourable
picture of the shipping companies' fortunes, since they take
no account of the expansion in the size of fleets. This is
particularly so in the case of liner companies, whose fleets
expanded rapidly in this period. The P & O, for example,
increased its tonnage by about 150,000 tons in the years
1900 to 1911, and if earnings are divided by the tonnage
employed the profitability of the company is much reduced.
Earnings per gross ton of the P & O fell continuously from
the turn of the century until 1909, and even in 1913 they
only reached 80 per cent of the 1900 figure. Table 2 (*see
opposite*) gives an index of earnings per ton for four companies, two liner and two cargo-boat. It will be seen that
none of the companies managed to regain their base-year
earnings, and in two cases, White Star and the Mercantile
Steamship Company, earnings in 1908 were less than 20 per
cent of the 1900 level.

   Despite the absence of complete profit data, there seems
little doubt that shipping was seriously depressed in this
period. As one might expect, the problem was most acute in
the cargo section of the industry though some of the passen-
ger-liner companies did not escape unscathed. The depression
was not confined to this country; as pointed out earlier, it
was international in scope. However, the evidence, meagre as
it is, does suggest that other countries fared less badly and
that Britain bore the brunt of the burden. This is by no means
an unreasonable assumption, since as she owned the largest
mercantile marine it can be argued that Britain had more to
lose. Moreover, Britain had a greater proportion of tramp
tonnage than other countries, and this section of the

TABLE 2

Index of earnings per ton of four companies
(1900-01 = 100)

	P & O Co (a)	White Star Line	Nitrate Producers' Steamship Company (b)	Mercantile S S Co
1898	64.07	96.65	47.58	78.80
1899	76.34	51.12	66.37	81.42
1900	100	100	53.24	100
1901	62.87	46.08	100	78.14
1902	100.29	53.34	56.20	40.14
1903	87.29	47.89	38.27	21.14
1904	82.63	34.60	25.34	25.41
1905	78.44	49.71	29.82	29.66
1906	69.91	57.74	25.24	29.21
1907	70.80	57.83	22.75	29.92
1908	64.22	18.35	24.82	14.03
1909	60.32	37.57	21.03	16.38
1910	65.12	64.81	25.34	27.55
1911	67.21	58.60	30.00	37.29
1912	64.07	48.08	36.72	75.77
1913	80.09	57.64	78.79	84.80
1914	57.03	45.31	71.55	

Note: P & O and White Star per ton gross;
         Mercantile and Nitrate Producers' per ton deadweight

(a)   year ending 30 September
(b)   year ending 30 April

Source: *Fairplay* (24 December 1914), 1040, and F.C. James, *Cyclical Fluctuations in the Shipping and Shipbuilding Industries* (1927), 78, Table 1

industry came off the worst. Finally, it is important to note that British trade, particularly the import component, was growing less rapidly than that of other countries, particularly Germany, the second largest shipowner.

Basically the depression in shipping was due to an imbalance between the available carrying capacity and the volume of world trade. The most pertinent question to answer is how this situation arose.

In the first decade of the twentieth century world tonnage increased at a faster rate than in any decade of the nineteenth century, from 29 million tons gross in 1900 to 41.9 in 1910, an increase of 45 per cent. By 1914 the world fleet was 70 per cent greater than in 1900, compared with an increase of 62 per cent in the volume of world trade. Two factors account for this. First, the Spanish-American and Boer Wars gave an artificial stimulus to the industry. Large amounts of shipping were chartered for Government transport service — some two million tons gross by the British Government alone — and this greatly stimulated the demand for new orders. But the extraordinary demands of war had already passed away by the time the new tonnage was completed. As so often happens, 'overproduction of tonnage, started in the years of prosperous trade, retains the impetus given to it long after the reaction of the boom has set in, and the effect of the continued overproduction is greatly exaggerated by the ever slow and gradual restriction of trade following the booming times'.[21] The net additions to world tonnage continued at a high level during the next few years, since it was at this time that Germany and Japan were rapidly building up their fleets and Britain was renewing her own. Thus the world was already overstocked with tonnage when the crisis of 1907-8 brought an appreciable drop in the volume of trade and passenger traffic. The latter suffered the more severe decline. Between 1907 and 1908 the number of passengers crossing the Atlantic from British and European ports fell from 1,725,736 to 688,885.[22] This was particularly serious for the large liner companies such as Cunard, White Star, and Hamburg-Amerika, which concentrated on the North Atlantic passenger trade. Passenger traffic of the Hamburg-Amerika company dropped from 470,290 to 280,404, and its profits were halved.[23] Cunard lost nearly half its passengers, with an even greater reduction in total earnings.

The crisis did at least bring a halt to the shipbuilding boom, and until 1911 net additions to new tonnage were comparatively moderate. But the damage had already been done. The new tonnage in itself might not have been so bad had it not been for the fact that much of it was far superior to anything which had been built before. The couple of decades before 1914 had seen the completion of the technological revolution in shipping. During that time the bulk of the British fleet was rebuilt. Of the tonnage on the register in 1913, 85 per cent had been built since 1895 and 44 per cent since 1905. These vessels consisted of the largest and most efficient types of ships and were capable of carrying more per ton than the ones they replaced. Hence there would still have been an increase in total carrying capacity had the size of the fleet remained constant. For the fifteen years ending in 1908, Sir Norman Hill estimated the increase in carrying power of the net ton to be in the region of 14 per cent.[24] A rough estimate would suggest therefore that the total carrying capacity of the British fleet was 38 to 40 per cent greater in 1908 compared with 1900, whilst during the same period the volume of British trade increased by only about 21 per cent.[25]

It can of course be argued that it was the demand rather than the supply side of the equation which was the crucial factor. The imbalance between the carrying capacity and the volume of cargo to be carried was partly a reflection of the uneven growth in British trade. Though trade expanded fairly rapidly, imports increased much more slowly than exports; by 1910 the volume of British imports was only 15 per cent greater than in 1900, compared with a rise of about 50 per cent for British exports.[26] In other words outward cargoes were growing far more rapidly than inward ones, a point which is reflected in the index of freight rates. Hence the deficiency in the volume of inward cargoes depressed profit margins. Moreover, there is a further point to bear in mind. The relative ease with which outward cargoes could be obtained encouraged shipowners to keep their vessels running in the hope of acquiring homeward cargoes. This of course only served to worsen the situation by depressing the market even further.

The crisis was aggravated by a number of minor, though not unimportant, factors. For one thing profit margins were squeezed because costs of operating vessels, which had risen sharply at the turn of the century, did not decline with the fall in freights. No satisfactory data are available on costs, but by all accounts coal prices, wages and insurance premiums remained at a high level compared with freights throughout this period.[27] Intermittent rate wars also reduced earnings in some cases. Despite the existence of freight conferences and passenger pools, rate wars were not uncommon, and according to one author they 'sprang up with renewed vigour' in the early twentieth century.[28] Some of them were disastrous to the profits of the companies concerned. The Union-Castle company's profits were seriously depleted when a rate war lasting 18 months broke out in the South African trade in July 1902.[29] One of the most serious of all rate wars occurred in the North Atlantic passenger trade in May 1903 as a result of Cunard's withdrawal from the passenger pool. By 1904 steerage rates had been reduced by two-thirds. Peace was eventually restored in October 1904, though not before the companies concerned had sacrificed most of their profits for that year: Cunard's earnings, for example, dropped from £248,563 to £61,588 in 1904. Altogether it has been estimated that the crisis cost the participant companies nearly £1 million.[30]

Finally the revision of the *Freeboard Rules and Tables* in 1906 added some 1½ million tons of shipping to an already depressed market, though in 1909 it was counter-balanced to some extent by the withdrawal from the market of a certain amount of tonnage due to the adoption of an international load line.[31]

II

Shipowners burned their fingers badly in the depression,

yet few lessons were learnt. Certainly after the depth of the crisis (1908) investment in ships was checked and shipowners adopted a more cautious financial policy. The book values of fleets were reduced drastically — up to half in some cases — and the fancy dividends of the boom years 1899-1900 were slashed. Moreover, it seems probable that owners paid more attention to building up depreciation funds in later years. Yet the experience was soon forgotten. Even by the end of 1910 it was said that some were 'at the old game of paying dividends which, regard being had to the depreciation of the property, most certainly have not been earned'.[32] During and shortly after the First World War speculation was again rife, and excessive optimism in the boom of 1919-20 produced disastrous results once again.[33] As Gregg observed: 'Shipping men, it seems, have never been able to persuade themselves in periods of prosperity that good times would not last always. Overbuilding of tonnage has continually recurred, sometimes coincident with a falling off of the amount of cargo shipped.'[34]

One good result of the depression was that it strengthened the inclination of shipping concerns everywhere to compromise and eliminate competition.[35] Sir Christopher Furness, speaking at the annual meeting of Manchester Liners Ltd in October 1909, felt the time had arrived 'when cut-throat competition shall come to an end and reasonable freights be earned on the large amount of capital employed in ships flying the British flag'.[36] Other important shipowners such as Booth of Cunard and Ballin of the Hamburg-Amerika endorsed this view, but few were prepared to take positive action on the matter. A strengthening of the conference system is all that seems to have taken place, for attempts to extend the boundaries of co-operation failed. Numerous suggestions were put forward to regulate freights and tonnage, but none were implemented. In October 1907 suggestions for a freight union among tramp owners failed to get widespread support, partly because many tramp owners were also merchants and freight contractors which resulted in a certain conflict of interests in the dual capacity.[37] The most ambitious scheme for regulating tonnage on an international basis was drawn up by J.H. Welsford, a member of the Liverpool Steam Ship Owners' Association. Briefly the proposal was that all surplus tonnage be laid up and financed out of a levy on shipping in full work.[38] Welsford's scheme was of necessity based on voluntary action, and in the absence of general support from shipowners in this country and elsewhere the Association recommended that no action be taken.[39]

One of the most notable features of this period was the number of combinations or mergers which took place among shipping companies. How far this was due to the depression is difficult to say, but there is no doubt that the unfavourable conditions encouraged firms to combine, and Sturmey attributes the numerous mergers of 1912-14 to the lagged responses to the depression.[40]   The amalgamation movement seems to have begun in earnest around the turn of the century when two well-established lines, the Union Steamship Company and the Castle Line, merged their interests after a period of intense rivalry. Two years later Blue Funnel acquired a controlling interest in China Mutual, their former competitors in the Eastern trade. During the next few years most of the larger liner companies such as P & O, Cunard, Royal Mail, and Furness Withy were rapidly absorbing other companies. Cunard acquired a large interest in the Anchor Line (1911), Furness Withy secured Houlder Brothers (1911) and the Warren Line (1912), whilst in 1914 P & O made a still larger catch when it absorbed the British India Steam Navigation Company. The combined group had a capital of £15 million and controlled nearly 1¼ million tons gross of shipping. Perhaps most spectacular of all however was the Royal Mail grouping. In 1903 Sir Owen Philipps, already an established figure in British shipping, became chairman of the Royal Mail Steam Packet Company, the oldest British steamship line trading to South America. He rapidly raised the line to pre-eminence in the shipping world and brought many other companies within the Royal Mail group. His acquisitions included such notable concerns as Elder Dempster, the Pacific Steam Navigation Company, Union-Castle, and the Glen, Shire and Nelson lines. By 1914 Philipps, who by then was known in shipping circles as the 'Colossus of the Seas', controlled one of the largest shipping groups in the world. The amalgamation movement accelerated during and early after the First World War, when many firms were acquired at inflated prices. By the early 1920s about one-quarter of the UK tonnage was owned and controlled by one of the 'Big Five' groups — P & O, Royal Mail, Cunard, Ellerman, and Furness Withy — whilst about three-quarters of the British liner tonnage was owned by seven large shipping companies.

III

In concluding, perhaps two points might be raised. In the author's opinion the material presented in this paper casts some doubt on the relative severity of the Great Depression (1873-96), at least as far as shipping is concerned. During the first decade of the twentieth century British shipping was more depressed than at any time during the last quarter of the nineteenth century. Admittedly the statistical data on which this conclusion is based are very weak, but what evidence there is does suggest that shipping fared better before 1900 than afterwards. The second point arises from this. As regards the profitability of ship operation, either before or after 1900, we are still groping in the dark, and until more case studies of individual firms are produced we shall continue to do so. So far only one really first-class study of a shipping firm has been produced, namely Professor Hyde's *Blue Funnel*.[41] Surely Britain's nineteenth-century mercantile supremacy deserves a larger contribution than this?

NOTES

1   E.S. Gregg, 'Vicissitudes in the Shipping Trade, 1870-1920',

Quarterly Journal of Economics (August 1921)

2   Cf F.C. James, *Cyclical Fluctuations in the Shipping and Ship-building Industries* (Philadelphia, 1927), 24

3   Sturmey refers to the period 1904 to 1911: S.G. Sturmey, *British Shipping and World Competition* (1962), 50, n 1

4   E.A.V. Angier, *Fifty Years' Freights, 1869-1919* (1920), 126

5   This summary is based on the tramp index constructed by Isserlis: L. Isserlis, 'Tramp Shipping Cargoes and Freights', *Journal of the Royal Statistical Society*, Part I (1938), 122

6   A.K. Cairncross, *Home and Foreign Investment, 1870-1913* (1953), 174-6

7   If the figures of vessels sailing in ballast are anything to go by, it would appear that cargo was much easier to obtain in the outward direction. In 1913 the proportion of British vessels clearing in ballast was only half that for those entering: H. Leak, 'The Carrying Trade of British Shipping', *Journal of the Royal Statistical Society*, Pt II (1939), 233

8   Angier, op cit, 107

9   Ibid, 111

10   *Fairplay* (21 January 1909), 91

11   Ibid (3 September 1908), 324

12   Ibid (21 October 1909), 564-5

13   Ibid (21 October 1909), 564

14   Ibid (24 December 1914), 1040

15   Ibid (30 December 1909), 927-98

16   Ibid (30 December 1909), 927-32

17   Ibid (28 July 1910), 109

18 Angier, op cit, 132

19 *Fairplay* maintained that it surpassed the wit of man to arrive at the profit and loss account on shipping: ibid (13 January 1910), 34

20 *Fairplay* (26 December 1912), 1022, and (24 December 1914), 1041

21 Angier, op cit, 107

22 E. Murken, *Die grossen transatlantischen Linienreederei-Verbände, Pools und Interessengemeinschaften bis zum Ausbruch des Weltkrieges — ihre Entstehung, Organisation und Wirksamkeit* (Jena, 1922), 693-7

23 F.B. Herschel, *Entwicklung und Bedeutung der Hamburg-Amerika-Linie* (Berlin, 1912), 99; cf P. Lenz, *Die Konzentration im Seeschiffahrtsgewerbe* (Jena, 1913), 91

24 *Annual Report of the Liverpool Steam Ship Owners' Association for 1909*, 5-6; *Shipping World* (30 October 1909), 377

25 Compiled on the basis of information given in *Fairplay* (25 December 1913), 1066-9. The calculation does not of course include passenger traffic

26 See A.H. Imlah, *Economic Elements in the Pax Britannica* (1958), 97-8

27 Angier, op cit, 124 and 129

28 E.A. Saliers, 'Some Financial Aspects of the International Mercantile Marine Company', *Journal of Political Economy* (November 1915), 921

29 M. Murray, *Union-Castle Chronicle 1853-1953* (1953), 148

30 Murken, op cit, 278

31 D.H. Robertson, *A Study of Industrial Fluctuations* (1915), 34, n 4

32 *Fairplay* (29 December 1910), 909

33   See the author's 'Port Congestion and the Shipping Boom of 1919-20', *Business History* (June 1961)

34   Gregg, loc cit, 617

35   B. Huldermann, *Albert Ballin* (1922), 112

36   *Fairplay* (21 October 1909), 565

37   Ibid (3 October 1907), 485

38   *Annual Report of the Liverpool Steam Ship Owners' Association for 1909*, 3-5

39   *Minutes of the General Meeting of the Liverpool Steam Ship Owners' Association* (16 November 1909)

40   Sturmey, op cit, 365

41   Since this was written Professor Hyde has completed further such studies *(see page 11, note 27 above)*

5 The Decontrol of Shipping and Railways after the First World War

First published in The Journal of Transport History, 5 *(1961)*

I

Before 1914 the degree of State interference in railways and shipping in Great Britain differed markedly. In the latter half of the nineteenth century it was felt that the freedom given to our shipowners as to the ships they built and as to the trades in which they engaged them was the foundation of British mercantile supremacy.[1] With rare exceptions the State had given little direct financial assistance whatever to British shipowners[2] and the industry was practically free from State control except for the control that was needed to secure the safety of life and property at sea.[3] In contrast an important feature of British railway history in the nineteenth and early twentieth centuries was the amount of Parliamentary legislation passed to regulate the activities of the railway companies. A series of general Acts from the 1830s to the Railway and Canal Traffic Act of 1913 laid the basis of a solid foundation of railway law[4] and provision had already been made for the Government to assume control of the railways in the event of war by the Act of 1871.[5]

For the exacting criteria of war conditions, however, the free economic system 'produced too little, it produced the wrong things and it distributed them to the wrong people'.[6] Immediately the war broke out, therefore, the Government commandeered the railway network, actual control of the railways being vested in the Railway Executive Committee composed of the general managers of the chief railway companies.[7] Under the Act of 1871 the Government undertook to assume complete responsibility for compensating the railway owners whilst the

undertakings were under Government control. This requirement was met by agreements between the Government and railway companies by which the latter were guaranteed their net
income based on 1913.[8] Thus the Government undertook to pay
the Railway Executive Committee, on the basis of provisional
estimates, monthly instalments of compensation to the companies, and, as the Government met all the expenses of the
railways out of the receipts, the prosperity of the undertakings
naturally became a matter of some importance to the State.

On the other hand, the control of shipping was performed
in a very sketchy manner until 1917 despite the fact that by
early 1916 some form of control had been imposed on nearly
all shipping.[9] It was left, therefore, to the new Ministry of
Shipping (created at the end of 1916) and its Controller to
inaugurate the universal requisitioning of ships and initiate
a national shipbuilding programme; in the course of a few
months the new Ministry brought practically the whole of
the British ocean-going mercantile marine, liners as well as
tramps, under requisition at fixed (Blue Book) rates of hire.[10]
This was followed by what was probably the most revolutionary innovation of all — the national shipbuilding programme
— the ships built being operated entirely on Government
account. The control of shipping was finally completed at
the end of 1917 by its international extension through the
formation of the Allied Maritime Transport Council which
was to supervise the distribution of tonnage for the Allies.[11]
By the end of the war this international authority was controlling 90 per cent of the sea-going tonnage of the world.[12]

There is little doubt that in both spheres Government
control proved fairly successful during the war. The war
record of British shipping was, in the words of Fayle,[13] 'one
of extraordinary achievement'. Likewise the railways achieved
a similar degree of success. The amount of work they had to
cope with in the war was phenomenal, and it was to the
credit of the Railway Executive Committee that so much
was done under such trying conditions.[14] Operating expenses
were cut to a minimum where possible, and a revolution in

co-operation and economic handling took place on the British railway system at this period, particularly by pooling of wagons between the companies. It was to the credit of the administration that the number of passengers annually injured on the railways in the years of war was (barring 1915) among the lowest on record.[15]

II

The question what was to be done with the railway and shipping industries after the war was a difficult one which exercised the Government's ingenuity to the full, and even by the time of the Armistice the Government's intention as to their future was far from clear. Essentially the structure of these industries, their outlooks and problems differed radically, and the manner in which they were dealt with in the transitional or decontrol period was partly an outcome of these differences. The shipping industry relied heavily on international carrying trade. By 1913 British ships carried some 50 per cent of the entire sea-borne trade of the world,[16] and at that time the British possessed a semi-monopoly in the shipping and shipbuilding world.[17] The war brought untold disaster to mercantile shipping, the destruction of shipping amounting to more than one quarter of the world tonnage afloat in 1913,[18] whilst Britain alone suffered a net loss of nearly 3.5 million gross tons.[19] On the other hand, an enormous fillip was given to world shipbuilding so that by the time hostilities ended the total world tonnage in existence was slightly larger than that of 1913; yet at the same time Britain's existing tonnage was less by some 14 per cent and her proportion of world tonnage had fallen by 5 per cent. Many countries had greatly expanded their merchant fleets and extended their shipbuilding capacity, a notable example being that of the USA, which had increased its tonnage by 144 per cent and expanded its shipbuilding output by 14 times that of the pre-war period.[20] Furthermore, the end of the war saw a serious reduction in international trade and there was hardly a single important item in our export trade in which the volume of shipments was not well below the level of 1917.[21] Nevertheless, though the Booth Committee had envisaged a world-wide tonnage shortage after the war,[22] partly because of the need for relief supplies and troop repatriation, it appeared, if anything, that a surplus of tonnage was more likely to occur in the first few months after the Armistice in view of the international dislocation of trade. Thus the eagerness with which British shipowners demanded a free rein in order to re-establish their position in the troubled post-war era and the success with which they had built up their supremacy before 1914 under a regime of *laissez-faire* was to a large extent reflected in the method and early rapidity with which the Government decontrolled the industry.

In contrast, the railways had far less reliance on the international economy for their market. The physical losses in the war had not been terribly disastrous though there had been a severe depreciation and running down of rolling stock and equipment. Their monopoly of internal transport in Great Britain was as yet still fairly complete and there was little doubt that they would be able to meet most of the demands for passenger and freight space in the period of transition.[23] But it was clear to many that the railways could not return to the pre-war competitive position. The acting chairman of the REC was known to be in favour of a large measure of co-ordination for the system;[24] and in 1918 a Select Committee on Transport came to a similar conclusion. This committee agreed that some sort of unification should and could take place, though here the members were not sure whether it should take place through public or private ownership.[25] 'From a purely technical view, it appears, therefore, to be desirable that there should be unification of ownership', for 'so long as the companies remain as separate corporations, it will be difficult to apply either method of securing economies to the fullest possible extent'.[26]

Partly to gain time to think about the future of the railways, though more in order to avoid trouble on the railways when wage advances were conceded, the Government in 1916 had finally resolved to extend the period of control and guarantee of net receipts of the companies for two years after the termination of the war.[27] This undertaking was to prove financially embarrassing to the Government: for, whereas during the war the State on the whole did quite well out of the railways financially,[28] because of the various wage increases and the institution of the eight-hour day in 1919, *inter alia*, this fine state of affairs rapidly disappeared and in the years 1919, 1920 and 1921 it was necessary to award Government compensation to the railways at the rate of £34, £41 and £51 million respectively.[29]

Thus the structure of the two industries, their histories, their types of market and the forms of war control necessarily implied that their post-war problems would be different and that the method by which they were decontrolled would also be different. The one, railways, involved difficulties of finance and form of organisation and they ended up by receiving a large dose of regulation and rationalisation; the other, shipping, was allowed to revert to its original free competitive surroundings of the nineteenth century with little thought for the industry's future.

To appreciate the problems involved and the method in which they were dealt with we must now examine the industries separately.

III

By the time the Armistice arrived there was some doubt as to what the Government's intentions were on the future of the railways. On more than one occasion both Lloyd George and Winston Churchill had intimated that nationalisation was a possible remedy[30] and it was known that other members of the Government hoped that the benefits of unified control in the war would not be allowed to lapse in time of peace.[31] In view of this uncertainty it was perhaps in some ways fortunate that the Government was forced into action early in 1919 by the rapidly worsening financial position of the railways.

Through the Government's concessions of war wages and the institution of the eight-hour day without any comparable increase in rates charged, the railways were placed in a position in which it was impossible for them to resume profitable operations[32] for by that time it was estimated that the railways were spending £17 or £18 for every £14 or £15 they earned.[33] In the light of this the Government confirmed its two-year extension of the guarantee made in 1916 and brought in a Bill to establish a Ministry of Transport.

That this Bill got through (though in a greatly modified form) was in large part due to the feeling in many quarters that it was a reasonable compromise until something better could be arranged and that to have rejected it would have left the Coalition Ministry in a quandary.[34] To return to pre-war conditions would be casting valuable experience to the winds, whilst nationalisation might imply a reliance on Government control out of all proportion to the true necessities of the situation, which few people desired. The Bill became law on 15 August 1919[35] and transferred to the new Ministry considerable powers and duties relating to the railways and other forms of internal transport. The Minister was to retain control of the railways for a further two years (that is, until 15 August 1921) and the former financial guarantees were to remain for that period. The most important clauses of the Bill were those conferring on the Minister power to alter railway rates and charges after reference to a Rates Advisory Committee.

If many of the powers conferred by the Act were not used, the clauses relating to the fixing of new charges, rates and dues were worked to exhaustion in an effort to establish the pricing policy of the railways on an economic basis: 'Never before in railway history was any question of rates and classification tackled so systematically and so thoroughly.'[36] During the war only two main increases had been made in passenger fares and none at all in freight rates,[37] with the result that wage advances had been conceded out of all proportion to the increase in rates and charges.[38]

Pessimistic estimates on the losses that the railways were likely to incur were put forth early in 1919,[39] but a later and more reliable estimate reckoned that the net income of the railways for the year ending 31 March 1920 would be a mere £3 million which meant that on the basis of the guarantee the net deficit falling to the Exchequer would be in the region of £45 million.[40] Whereupon the Minister immediately made reference to the new Rates Advisory Committee for the revision of charges and as a result of their report freight rates were increased in January 1920.[41]

These revised rates were expected to yield nearly £50 million, thus wiping out the anticipated deficit, but any real effect that might have been gained was mitigated by the additional wage advances that had been made in 1919[42] with the result that the net receipts continued to decline in 1920. Not that the railways were actually making a loss on a year-to-year basis at this time — at least not until 1921. What seems to be a proper statement of the position is that the railways did not lose £50 million in 1919 or any other amount but that, whilst still making a profit, their net earnings fell below those of 1913 by some millions of pounds which the Government had to make good under the guarantee. From an analysis of the figures it appears that falling net revenue was a direct function of increased costs[43] which was in the main part due to wage advances.[44] The only practical thing to do, therefore, was either to reduce wages or raise charges and as the latter seemed to be the easier solution it was adopted.[45]

And so the Rates Advisory Committee got to work once again.

This time they had the task of covering an estimated annual liability of £54.5 million which was expected to accrue from 1 April 1920.[46] As a result the Committee recommended in two reports[47] increases both in passenger fares and in the rates for various classes of merchandise. These revised charges were promptly put into effect in August and September of 1920. Yet even these increases did not improve the financial position of the railways, for total

net receipts fell from £12.8 million in 1919 to £5.7 million in
1920 and in 1921 a real loss was recorded of £10.3 million.[48]
In spite of a fall in wages and the downward movement in
prices revenue was adversely affected by a stoppage in the
coal trade in October 1920 and a rather longer strike in 1921,
by the general trade recession which set in during the closing
months of 1920 and by the amount of maintenance expenditure which was on an abnormal scale largely because arrears
from previous years were being undertaken.[49] With regard to
the last factor it appears that the railways were spending
something to the equivalent of 1913 prices on maintenance
and renewal of rolling stock and equipment. Moreover, it
appears that by early 1921 a number of companies had not
only overtaken all the arrears of maintenance accumulated
from the war, but had carried out, and charged to the
Government, a greater quantity of maintenance work than
was represented by the expenditure and provision of 1913,
and were continuing to spend in excess of the 1913 figure.[50]

It was quite evident that piecemeal increases in railway
charges were of little assistance in checking falling revenue.
Not that any aspersions can be cast on the Rates Advisory
Committee, for it had undoubtedly worked hard and diligently
in the course of its inquiries, but there is reason to believe
that it had far too much work to do in too short a time. It
should never have been encumbered with the task of making
interim revisions in railway rates but it should have been
allowed to concentrate its attention on the primary reference
of holding an inquiry into the main principles or details of a
new scheme of classification.[51] The result was that no report
was issued on this most important subject until late in 1920.

Meanwhile the Government had been considering the
second major question: that of reorganisation of the railway
system. It was not until the summer of 1920, however, that
nationalisation was finally rejected as an unsuitable solution.[52]
Whereupon the Government produced its plan for the future
of the railways in a White Paper.[53] The main proposal was
the organisation of more than one hundred railway companies

into a few major groups the object of which was to ensure that 'direct competition between the groups would be as far as possible eliminated'. A most important clause was that relating to the financial side of the new system: 'The rates and fares shall be fixed at such a level as, with efficient and economical management, will in the opinion of a prescribed authority enable the railway companies to earn a net revenue substantially equivalent, on some pre-war basis to be settled in the Act, to the combined net revenue of all the companies absorbed in the group.'[54] Under the new plan the Government was to have a fairly large measure of control over the railway system of Great Britain.

The time between the issue of the White Paper at the end of June 1920 and the introduction of the Railways Bill in May 1921 was utilised in conducting lengthy discussions between railway and trade interests and the railway trade unions in order to secure a substantial measure of agreement on the proposed new policy, and as a result of opposition from many quarters the original plan was considerably modified.[55] Furthermore, the Government was awaiting the report of the Rates Advisory Committee on the general revision of rates and charges which came out in December 1920[56] and whose recommendations were embodied for the most part in Part III of the 1921 Act.

All was now set for the introduction of the famous Railways Bill in May 1921. After long and heated debates it became law on 19 August 1921,[57] four days after the Government had ceased to control the railways. In many ways the Railways Act of 1921 was the most constructive measure of domestic legislation of the whole post-war era,[58] and was probably the most important piece of railway legislation since the Act of 1844. The Act introduced for the first time in British railway history a serious attempt to grapple with the problem of scientific planning of the railway system and swept up masses of un-coordinated legislation.[59]

The Act amalgamated nearly all the existing railway companies into the four groups which remained until

nationalisation. This amalgamation was effected with great
rapidity indeed, and for all practical purposes the most
important achievements had been accomplished by the end
of 1922.[60] In order to achieve the best possible results from
the new system the Minister was given important regulatory
powers over the railways and provided with facilities to
require them gradually to standardise their equipment and
participate in co-operative working.[61] In return the railway
companies received £60 million as 'a full discharge and in
satisfaction of all claims'.[62]

That part of the Act dealing with railway charges was the
longest and the most interesting; it gave effect to the Rates
Advisory Committee's report on the general revision of rates
and charges and provided for the appointment of a new
permanent charging body, the Railway Rates Tribunal. This
Tribunal was to approve a new schedule of rates submitted
by the amalgamated companies (it eventually came into force
on 1 January 1928). Although the Act of 1921 in no way
guaranteed railway earnings by the standard revenue theory,
it did initiate a new policy in that charges to be fixed in the
first instance would be such that, together with other sources
of revenue, they would yield, with efficient and economical
working and management, an annual net revenue equivalent
to that of 1913.[63]

This part of the Act was very important because charging
powers were made much more flexible and scientific than
was previously the case.[64] Under the old procedure, once
rates were increased they tended to become static and in
effect new maximum rates whereas under the Act of 1921
far greater facilities were provided for a reduction in charges
if conditions warranted it. In fact the Act was framed on the
clear assumption that railway rates would be lowered, though
this was not actually written into the text of the Act.[65]
One might go so far as to say that this flexibility in rate
charging was the key to the whole situation, for at the time
of the passing of the Act the railways were faced with a deficit
of over £19 million[66] and the only course possible in view of

the economic situation was to reduce rates in the hope that demand elasticity would be great enough to increase total returns. This course was followed in 1921, 1922 and 1923 but with disappointing results. Only in 1922 was a figure anywhere near the standard revenue of £50 million, as fixed by the Rates Tribunal, attained, and in 1926 the net earnings of the companies fell as low as £19 million.[67] This was of course an exceptional year owing to the General Strike, but even in 1924 and 1925 the net earnings had failed to reach £40 million.

IV

The method adopted for decontrolling the shipping industry differed considerably from the method applied for decontrolling the railways. The State had no financial obligation towards the shipping industry and little attention was paid to the future of the industry as a whole. The Government was merely concerned with securing adequate shipping space at reasonable rates of hire for the carriage of its own cargo and other essential supplies in the transitional period. Release from control was, therefore, on a piecemeal and *ad hoc* basis as and when the tonnage supply became sufficient to meet requirements.

One factor common to both railways and shipping was the question of nationalisation. Discussion on the subject had been going on long before the end of the war, Sir Leo Chiozza Money being the major advocate of State acquisition of the industry partly on the grounds that it had made large profits during the war and partly because by such a policy a thorough overhaul of the British mercantile marine could be effected.[68] But for a number of reasons the idea attracted little enthusiasm; even the Labour Party was lukewarm towards it[69] and the National Seamen's and Firemen's Union definitely rejected it.[70] The prevailing opinion was against Government control in any shape or form: 'We believe', said the Booth report,[71] 'that the continuance of Government operation and control is bound to extinguish private enterprise and lead to

State ownership', and any departure from private enterprise in this sphere 'would be a dangerous experiment and a blunder of the worst kind'. Any fears which the shipowners might have had as to the possibility of a State-owned fleet being permanently operated were partly dissipated on 23 October 1918 when it was announced by the Ministry of Shipping that they were prepared to consider tenders, from owners who had lost ships through enemy action, for the purchase of a limited number of standard steamers.[72] A few days later it was announced that the Government had no intention of nationalising the shipping industry.[73]

Within a few days of the Armistice being declared it may be said that the whole principle of State ownership and construction of ships was abandoned.[74] Directly the cease fire was announced telegrams were sent to shipbuilders in all parts of the country telling them to cease work on standard ships[75] and at the same time the application of the convoy system was suspended.[76] The following day the Government's intentions were made clear in an announcement by the Shipping Controller to the effect that: 'It is not contemplated that the control of merchant shipping should continue for any longer period than is necessary to provide for the extraordinary conditions arising out of the war. It is the intention that privately owned ships now under requisition should be released from control as soon as the tonnage available is considered clearly sufficient to provide reasonably for such essential services as may be necessary in the national interest.'[77]

Various considerations, however, delayed the beginning of general release of ships from requisition right away. First of all there were a large number of troops to be repatriated and the relief of Europe which had to be undertaken. Then there were the enormous commitments into which Britain had entered with the other Allied governments which necessitated a certain amount of international shipping control. In fact it was expected that in the early post-war period an acute shortage of shipping tonnage would arise not only in Great

Britain but throughout the world in general.[78]

Nevertheless it was possible to begin freeing vessels from control as soon as hostilities ceased, and before the end of November 1918 many steamers had been released for commercial employment. In the tramp section, now that military requirements were relaxed, it was possible to allow greater consideration to commercial enterprise and to break up the North Atlantic concentrations. Rapid progress was made by the Liner Requisition Committee in the redistribution of liner tonnage and the restoration of normal services. The vessels which had been directed from the Australian, Far Eastern and other long-distance routes to the North Atlantic were returned to their normal employment. Pending the subsequent release of requisitioned vessels, the lines were instructed to give preference to shipments of foodstuffs and essential raw materials. On the North Atlantic run a certain proportion of space was released to the lines for bookings at their own discretion with a view to reviving normal commercial intercourse,[79] and the Allied Maritime Transport Executive was able to cancel almost at once the allocation of a large block of British tonnage for American military supply.[80] In December the French steel service from the United States ended, together with the special liner service to France and Italy and, in the same month, the Chilean nitrate service was suspended and several of the cargoes in transit were diverted to Allied and neutral requirements. Furthermore, most of the limited control which had been exercised over coastal shipping was abandoned with the issue of a general licence[81] and preparations were made for the general release of tankers from requisition.

The approximate result of this early release was a reduction of 184 in the ocean-going steamers on full government service (exclusive of tankers) and an increase of 264 in the number of free ships.[82] This of course was only a small proportion of the total vessels under government control at the time of the Armistice when about 2,800 British ships of over 1,600 tons and 1,400 ships of lesser tonnage were under some form of requisition.[83] Yet the immediate effect of this early relaxation and transfer of tonnage from munition and troop movement was quite extraordinary, amounting to an increase of some 10 million tons in the importing capacity of the country.[84] The net result was a glut of tonnage and a falling freight market;[85] on the North Atlantic run liner freights fell in some cases to one-sixth of the rates in force just before the Armistice.[86] This situation was not to last for very long, however, for in the spring of 1919 peculiar conditions translated this glut of tonnage into a shortage and the freight market commenced an upward swing to a hitherto unprecedented level.

In view of this favourable effect the Shipping Controller in January 1919 issued a notice which stated that all privately-owned ships, other than those needed for naval and military purposes, would be released from requisition as fast as they returned to their ports of redelivery in the United Kingdom and that owners would be free to make arrangements through their own agents or brokers for the subsequent employment of their ships;[87] but the Shipping Controller emphasised that: 'With a view to safeguarding the essential imports and exports of the United Kingdom and of the Allies, it will be necessary for some time to come to maintain a system of direction as to employment and a limitation of freight rates for the carriage of such essential commodities.'[88] In addition, the right to requisition should an emergency arise was retained.[89]

The date for general release was set for 1 March 1919[90] and within a few months the process of releasing shipping from requisition was, apart from the ships still on naval and military service, very nearly complete.[91] By the end of October 1919 only 109 vessels remained on full requisition.[92] But if we include Government-owned and prize ships there were probably 159 together with 47 smaller vessels on full Government service by the end of the year.[93]

These figures, however, convey a false impression of the position and it has to be remembered that certain modifications were applied to the freedom of most ships even though they were released from requisition. It was clearly recognised that during the period of transition a modified form of control had to be retained. A completely free market was not desirable from the Government's point of view since it was still importing large quantities of food and other commodities.[94] The licensing system was adopted as the main instrument of control and this was supplemented by the direction of individual vessels into specified employment and by the fixing of limitation rates for government cargoes. Thus every ship, whether in the foreign or coasting trade, was still subject to licence; all liners were subject to space agreement and nearly all large tramps not on time charter were run on directed voyages.

Most tramp vessels were liable to be 'directed' into certain trades to load imports at limitation rates. Throughout 1919 direction coupled with freight rate limitation was applied in regard to the carriage of wheat from Canada, Australia, America and the River Plate, maize from the Plate and South Africa, sugar from Cuba, the British West Indies and Mauritius, and timber from Canada. In addition, outward coal freights to France, Italy and the chief bunker ports abroad were controlled until July when the limitation orders were rescinded.[95] In fact during 1919 the tramp section had little freedom at all on the directed routes, for the Government usually took up about 80 per cent of the space in each directed vessel.[96]

The second method of control was mainly applied to the liner companies. The Government reserved the right to requisition at fixed rates a certain proportion of the cargo space on the companies' vessels. The percentage of space actually taken up by the Government during the year varied considerably from route to route and from month to month. The proportion acquired in the North Atlantic trade averaged approximately 50 per cent for the whole of 1919[97] though up to August 1919 as much as 75 per cent was taken over.[98] This amount was probably equalled in the Australian and South African trades and, when account is taken of the special Board of Trade contract for insulated space, in the Plate trade as well.[99] Furthermore, the Government had at its disposal a large proportion of the inward voyages of passenger liners for troop transport.[100]

Altogether, during the twelve months from the date of general release, approximately 25 per cent of the imports into the United Kingdom were brought in at Government-controlled rates which were roughly at bare cost, if not below, and another 25 per cent were carried at rates far below the world market level.[101] In fact, speaking generally, the freedom of British shipping during 1919 was somewhat restricted, and free chartering was reduced to a small number of transactions.[102]

From the Government's point of view the situation proved very favourable, for the general rise in free market shipping freights coincided with the release of shipping from requisition, producing a boom almost without parallel in the annals of the industry. The factors causing the boom of 1919-20 are outside the scope of this essay, but it needs to be recorded that it was not caused by a real shortage of tonnage as such, since just after the Armistice the world's mercantile marine was slightly above that of 1913 whilst the volume of international trade was much diminished. The shortage therefore was rather a 'paper' one caused by a number of peculiar factors, the chief of which was the chronic port congestion, which impaired the efficiency of the existing British merchant tonnage by some 30 per cent or more.[103] Had the Government not been able to requisition space at limitation rates it would have been forced to pay the highly inflated free market values. For example, British tonnage was directed to convey grain from the River Plate at 62s 6d per ton, whilst 200s or upwards per ton was the prevailing free tonnage rate to Continental ports.[104] In the case of liner companies the rate paid per ton of Government cargo carried was often less than half that paid by private merchants.[105] That many of these controlled rates were uneconomic is evident from the fact that early in 1920 some of them were raised by appreciable amounts.[106]

Early in 1920 the 'paper' tonnage shortage showed signs of improvement and the freight market appeared to be less firm.[107] In February it was discovered that the Government could have secured space in the open market at rates below those agreed with the liner companies[108] and as the liner agreement was coming to an end it was allowed to lapse in the March of that year.[109] The end of the boom in freight rates occurred between March and April 1920[110] and from that date the bottom dropped out of the freight market. In these changed circumstances the reason for control disappeared for the Government was able to meet its requirements by open market chartering.[111] Applications for licences became more and more a mere formality so that in July 1920 the Shipping Controller announced that they would be issued for all voyages[112] and on 15 July all limitation rates were abolished.[113] With the issue of a general licence on 4 September 1920, permitting all ships to engage freely in any trade, nearly all vestiges of control were swept away.[114] The powers of the Shipping Controller were not suspended, however, and in the coal strike of October 1920 he used them again for the last time. The only restrictions remaining were those on the transfer of ships abroad and the obligations of the lines regarding insulated space under the Board of Trade's meat contracts, both of which came to an end in 1921. The Ministry of Shipping itself remained in existence until March 1921 as it was involved in certain winding-up operations.[115]

V

This brief essay has attempted to outline the reconstruction problems involved in decontrolling the railway and shipping industries and the different manner in which the Government dealt with them in the period 1918-21. Before handing back the railways to the private owners there was a definite though abortive attempt to restore their financial solvency. Moreover, the Government was convinced that the experience gained through the war operation of the railway system should not be neglected. The result was, as we have seen, the Act of 1921. In the case of shipping the State had a vested interest in control in so far as it served its purpose in securing adequate tonnage at reasonable rates to meet the Government's requirements in the transitional period. As Government trading operations diminished and the free freight market registered levels below the controlled freight rates, all justification for the retention of control disappeared and the industry was freed. At no time was there ever any question of the Government effecting a reorganisation of the shipping industry as in the case of the railways.

The question how far the policy of decontrol can be said to have been successful is not difficult to answer. Undoubtedly the reorganisation of the railways under the 1921 Act was highly beneficial. But the attempts to grapple with the financial side of the railways proved a total failure in the early post-war years, though the declining profitability of the British railway system in the subsequent years cannot be attributed to this failure. To a great extent the evidence suggests that the decontrol of the shipping industry was not well handled.   Had the Government retained a more complete control over the industry during the boom of 1919-20 and had there been some concrete attempt to deal with the port congestion, the eagerness with which shipowners invested in the new tonnage might have been restrained, thereby relieving the industry, to some extent, of the burden of excess tonnage in later years. Taken as a whole the Government was unable to cope with the transport problems in these critical years and the disaster and chaos which took place in transport services, both internal and external, at this time is probably unparalleled in British history.

NOTES

1   See N. Hill, *The British Mercantile Marine and State Control* (based on a paper read before the Manchester Statistical Society on 11 February 1918), 6

2   C.E.Fayle, *The War and the Shipping Industry* (1927), 20-2; W. Ashworth, *An Economic History of England, 1870-1939*

(1960), 154-5. This view is perhaps subject to some modification in the light of recent research; see S. Pollard, *'Laissez-Faire* and Shipbuilding', *Economic History Review* (1952-3), 111. I must express my thanks for a private communication from Dr S. Pollard on this matter

3   A. W. Kirkaldy, *British Shipping* (1914), Ch V; N. Hill, 'The British Mercantile Marine in its Relation in the Past to the State', in *Trans of the Manchester Stats Soc* (1917-18), 107-30; C.E. Fayle, *A Short History of the World's Shipping Industry* (1933), 374-5; cf Pollard, loc cit, 115

4   For the history of railway legislation see E. Cleveland-Stevens, *English Railways — Their Development and Their Relation to the State* (1915); E.A. Pratt, *The Rise of Rail Power in War and Conquest, 1833-1914* (1915); there is a good summary in the *Railway Gazette* (23 May 1919), 882-4

5   *Regulation of the Forces Act* (1871), 34 and 35 Vict cap 86, sect 16

6   J.A. Salter, *Allied Shipping Control* (1921), 17

7   It was made clear at the time that there was no intention of super-seding the existing management of the railways by a permanent body of control; see E.A. Pratt, *British Railways and the Great War,* Vol 1 (1921), 37

8   F.H. Dixon and J.H. Parmelee, *War Administration of the Railways in the United States and Great Britain* (1918), 82-4; *Railway Gazette* (18 September 1914), 323

9   E. Crammond, *The British Shipping Industry* (1917), 43. The standard works on shipping in the war are C.E. Fayle, *The War and the Shipping Industry* (1927); Salter, op cit, and J. Russel Smith, *Influence of the Great War upon Shipping* (1919)

10   See Fayle, op cit, 234-7. Little control was exercised over the coasting trade

11   Salter, op cit, 175

12   Alfred Zimmern, *The League of Nations and the Rule of Law 1918-1935* (1939), 146; *Brassey's Naval and Shipping Annual*

for 1919, 161-2

13   Fayle, op cit, 314; for statistical evidence see *War Cabinet Report for 1918*, Cd 325 (1919), 166-7

14   For the work of the Railway Executive Committee see *Railway Gazette* (5, 12, 19 and 26 April and 3 May 1919); also *Board of Trade Journal* (28 March 1918), 367-8

15   See *Report to the Ministry of Transport upon the Accidents for the Railways of the United Kingdom during 1920*, Cd 1366 (1921), 5

16   *Report of the Departmental Committee on the Shipping and Shipbuilding Industries after the War*, Cd 9092 (1918), *Third Report*, 74

17   See L. Jones, *Shipbuilding in Britain* (1957), 61

18   A.L. Bowley, *Some Economic Consequences of the Great War* (1930), 181

19   *Merchant Tonnage and the Submarine: Supplementary Statement for the United Kingdom and the World for the Period August 1914 to October 1918*, Cd 9221 (1918), 2

20   *Committee on Industry and Trade: Survey of Metal Industries* (HMSO, 1928), Pt IV, 378; see also Sir Wescott Abell, 'American Shipbuilding During the War', in *Brassey's Naval and Shipping Annual* (1920-1), 194-202

21   C.E. Fayle, *Seaborne Trade*, Vol III (1924), 413

22   Cd 9092, *Third Report*, para 73

23   Though there was a serious shortage of suitable railway wagons. See A.W. Kirkaldy and A.D. Evans, *The History and Economics of Transport* (1924 ed), 202; *Shipbuilding and Shipping Record* (25 December 1919), 731; *The Times* (11 December 1919)

24   Sir Herbert Walker in an interview with the *Daily Dispatch* said: 'I cannot think that our railways will ever again revert to the independent and foolish competitive system (of before the war). . .

if we are to prove that the experience gained has been beneficial there must be vastly more co-ordination between the various lines and companies.' See *Railway Gazette* (22 June 1917), 726

25 *Select Committee on Transport*, H of C 130 and 136 (1918), *Second Report*, xii

26 Ibid, vii

27 *Statement as to Railways in connection with the Ministry of Transport Estimates 1920-21*, Cd 654 (1920), 4. This was for two years longer than had been intended originally

28 It is extremely difficult to ascertain how much the Government benefited financially but it was probably in the region of £17 million or more; see *Statement Showing the Cost of Running the Railways in Great Britain during the Period of Government Control of the Railways (1914-1918)*, Cd 147 (1919), and *Statement Showing the Results of Working the Railways During the Periods of Government Control of the Railways in Great Britain (5 August 1914-31 August 1919) and Ireland (1 January 1917-31 August 1919)*, Cd 402 (1919). Contemporary interpretations are apt to be misleading; cf *Railway Gazette* (17 December 1920), 784-5, and *The Times Trade Supplement* (15 January 1921), 417

29 Figures from the *Railway Returns* for 1919, 1920 and 1921

30 *The Times* (5 and 11 December 1918)

31 See *H of C Deb*, cvi (15 May 1918), 393

32 *Railway Gazette* (3 January 1919), 4; A.E. Davies, *The Case for Nationalisation* (1920), 106-7

33 *Economist* (8 March 1919), 400

34 Bonar Law threatened to resign if the Bill was not passed

35 *Ministry of Transport Act* (1919), 9 and 10 Geo, Ch 50

36 Kirkaldy and Evans, op cit (1931 ed), 137

37   *First Annual Report of the Railway Rates Tribunal for the Year 1922* (under the Railways Act of 1921) (HMSO, 1923), 3

38   By January 1920 the weekly wage rates of railway workers were about 140 per cent above the pre-war average; A.L. Bowley, *Prices and Wages in the United Kingdom 1914-1920* (1921), 164

39   It was estimated by *The Economist* (19 April 1919), 640, that the future loss on the railways would be in the region of £90 million

40   Cd 402 (1919), 3

41   See *Report of the Rates Advisory Committee on the Rates for Conveyance of Goods, Minerals and Merchandise*, Cd 525 (1920), for full details

42   Kirkaldy and Evans, op cit (1931 ed), 203. The increases in freight rates were already months too late, for the great authority on railway affairs, W.M. Acworth, had written in the October of 1919 that the 'need for an immediate increase in goods rates had been evident for many months'. See his article 'The Problem of Railway Reconstruction' in the *National Review* (October 1919), 256-64

43   It cannot be attributed to a fall in traffic carried by the railways, for even though the volume of goods traffic did fall off in 1919 the increase in passenger traffic more than compensated for this. See *Railway Returns for 1923* (HMSO, 1924), 22; *Economist* (17 April 1920), 812

44   Whereas expenditure had more than doubled since 1913 freight rates were at the pre-war level throughout 1919 and ordinary passenger fares had been increased by 50 per cent only. Wages accounted for nearly 75 per cent of the increase in total costs; see *Railway Returns for 1919*, Cd 1160 (1921), 4

45   See W.M. Acworth in the *Contemporary Review*, cxvi (1919), 504-10

46   *Statement Showing the Results of Railway Working in the Financial Year 1919-20, with an Estimate of the Receipts and Expenditure for the Financial Year 1920-21*, Cd 815 (1920), 2

47   *Report of the Rates Advisory Committee on the Interim Revision of Railway Rates, Tolls, Fares and Charges,* Cd 857 (1920), and ibid, Pt II — *Goods,* Cd 886 (1920)

48   See *Railway Returns for 1919,* Cd 1160 (1921), 4; *for 1920,* Cd 1430 (1921), 7; and *for 1921* (HMSO, 1922), 7. These figures are for the UK and they exclude miscellaneous receipts amounting to some £4 million or more a year. Under the guarantee therefore these net receipts had to be made up by the Government to around £46 million a year

49   *First Annual Report of the Railway Rates Tribunal for the Year 1922* (under the Railways Act of 1921) (HMSO, 1923), 7

50   This is a complicated problem which cannot be gone into fully here; for full details see *Select Committee on National Expenditure, Second Report,* H of C 118 (1920), v, and *Report of the Departmental Committee on Railway Agreements,* Cd 1132 (1921), 20; also *Railway Gazette* (19 December 1919 and 20 and 27 February 1920); *Economist* (29 May 1920), 1193-4

51   See *The Times Trade Supplement* (4 September 1920), 458

52   *H of C Deb,* cxxx (24 June 1920), 2455, and cxxxii (19 July 1920), 36

53   *Outline of Proposals as to the Future Organisation of Transport Undertakings in Great Britain and their Relation to the State,* Cd 787 (1920)

54   Ibid, 3

55   As one writer put it, 'These "outlines", if ever adopted in legislative form, would constitute an attempt to combine private ownership and responsibility with public control in a bastardised scheme of quasi-nationalisation fatal to railway progress': H.J. Jennings, 'Our Insolvent Railways', in *Fortnightly Review,* ns, cviii (1920), 477. For the views of various interests see *Railway Gazette* (10 December 1920), 754-6; (1 October 1920), 417; (29 October 1920), 564-5 and (15 April 1921), 569; *The Times* (29 June 1921); *Economist* (20 November 1920), 903

56   *Report of the Rates Advisory Committee on General Revision of*

Railway Rates and Charges, Cd 1098 (1920)

57   *Railways Act* (1921), 11 and 12 Geo 5, Ch 55

58   Cf *Railway Gazette* (26 August 1921), 337

59   For a fuller discussion of the Act see W.M. Acworth, 'Grouping under the Railways Act 1921' in *Economic Journal* (March 1923), 19-38; K.G. Fenelon, *Railway Economics* (1932), 107-17; W.E. Simnett, *Railway Amalgamation in Great Britain* (1923); probably the best account especially with a view to later events is in H.C. Kidd, *A New Era for British Railways* (1929)

60   See *The Times* (28 and 29 December 1922). Full details of the schemes of the amalgamation were not complete until the end of 1923; Kidd, op cit, 78

61   Parts I and II of the Act

62   *Railways Act* (1921), 11 (2); £9 million of this sum was returned in tax

63   *Railways Act* (1921), 58 (1)

64   Cf C.I. Savage, *An Economic History of Transport* (1959), 105

65   Kidd, op cit, 43; see Geddes (Minister of Transport) in *H of C Deb*,cxlii (26 May 1921), 356, 359

66   Kidd, op cit, 52

67   Ibid, 53

68   *The People's Year Book for 1920*, 205; *Economist* (28 December 1918), 875

69   Fayle, *The War and the Shipping Industry*, 336

70   Father Hopkins, *'National Service' of British Merchant Seamen, 1914-1919* (1920), 85; *Shipping World* (13 October 1920), 320

71   *Report of the Departmental Committee on the Shipping and Shipbuilding Industries after the War*, Cd 9092 (1918), *Third*

Report, paras 71 and 73

72   *The Times* (23 October 1918)

73   Bonar Law, *H of C Deb*, cx (28 October 1918), 1116-17

74   Fayle, *The War and the Shipping Industry*, 341

75   *Fairplay* (14 November 1918), 747; *The Times* (12 and 13 November 1918)

76   *Shipping World* (20 November 1918), 389; C.E. Fayle, *Seaborne Trade*, Vol III (1924), 417. For details of the convoy system see Sir Norman Leslie, 'The Convoy System in 1917-18' in *Brassey's Naval and Shipping Annual* (1919), 147-60; Salter, op cit, 124-5; S.J. Hurwitz, *State Intervention in Great Britain* (1949). 193

77   *Manchester Guardian* (12 November 1918)

78   Fayle, *Seaborne Trade*, Vol III, 416

79   As much as 30 per cent of the cargo space had been released for commercial purposes by the end of 1918; *Fairplay* (6 February 1919), 313

80   Fayle, *Seaborne Trade*, Vol III, 417-18

81   N.B. Dearle, *An Economic Chronicle of the Great War, 1914-1919* (1929), 235-6

82   Fayle, *The War and the Shipping Industry*, 365

83   *Select Committee on National Expenditure, Fifth Report*, H of C Paper 245 (1919), para 18

84   *Fairplay* (9 January 1919), 155

85   Ibid (12 December 1918), 855-6; *Shipbuilding and Shipping Record* (9 January 1919), 52

86   A.C. Pigou, *Aspects of British Economic History, 1918-1925* (1947), 79

87   *Fairplay* (16 January 1919), 198-9; *The Times* (15 January 1919)

88   J.L. Garvin, *The Economic Foundations of Peace* (1919), 143

89   *Economist* (18 January 1919), 71

90   *H of C Deb*, cxiii (18 March 1919), 1911

91   Ibid, cxviii (29 July 1919), 1960

92   Ibid, cxxi (17 November 1919), 121

93   Fayle, *The War and the Shipping Industry*, 369

94   It was estimated that early in 1920, 30-50 per cent of our imports were still under State control: *Shipping World* (11 February 1920), 192

95   A. Hurd, 'Paralysis of Shipping', in *Fortnightly Review*, cvii (1920), 593-4; *Chamber of Shipping Annual Report (UK)* (1919-20), 18

96   *H of C Deb*, cxxi (17 November 1919), 662

97   *The Times* (2 March 1920); Hurd, 549

98   D.H. Robertson, *Economic Fragments* (1931), 124

99   On the other hand the percentage taken up in the Far East trade was quite small

100   *The Times* (30 August and 19 September 1919)

101   Hurd, 549

102   *Shipping World* (7 January 1920), 21-2

103   See *Select Committee on National Expenditure, Fourth Report*, H of C Paper 150 (1920), para 32. This aspect is dealt with more fully in the author's article, 'Port Congestion and the Shipping Boom of 1919-20', in *Business History* (June 1961)

104   *The Times Annual Financial and Commercial Review* (23 January 1920), 31; *Shipping World* (10 September 1919), 220

105   *The Times* (2 March 1920)

106   Eg the Plate rate was raised from 62s 6d to 107s 6d. See *Shipbuilding and Shipping Record* (29 January 1920), 126, and (4 March 1920), 294

107   *Fairplay* (24 February 1921), 682

108   *Shipbuilding and Shipping Record* (4 March 1920), 294; *H of C Deb*, cxxvi (10 March 1920), 1428

109   *Fairplay* (11 March 1920), 842

110   Ibid (8 April 1920), 90; see also *Shipping World* (24 March 1920), 330

111   *Chamber of Shipping Annual Report* (1920-1), 22

112   *Shipping World* (14 July 1920), 23 and 71

113   *The Times* (8 July 1920)

114   *Chamber of Shipping Annual Report* (1920-1), 22; *Shipping World* (5 January 1921), 17

115   *Shipping World* (16 December 1920), 720

6 The Eclipse of the Coastal Shipping Trade, 1913-21

First published in The Journal of Transport History, *6 (1963)*

During the nineteenth century the development of the railways, together with the steady increase in the size of ships, produced a growing concentration of the general trade of Great Britain into the larger ports. By the early twentieth century the 12 major British ports had secured about 75 per cent of the import and export trade, exclusive of iron and coal.[1] These big ports were ideally equipped for handling the large ships and tonnages of the time, and they also provided facilities for the secondary channels of distribution and collection which completed the flow mechanism. Hundreds of little coastal vessels played a vital role in this work; they collected cargoes from the large ports and distributed them to the many small ports dotted around the British Isles, or brought cargoes into the principal ports for trans-shipment abroad.[2]

The importance of coastal shipping in the British system of transport can be judged from the fact that for much of the nineteenth century the tonnage of coastal traffic was substantially greater than that of ocean shipping: only from the 1890s onwards did the latter tonnage exceed the former.[3] Yet despite a steady expansion in the coastal trade up to 1913 it was quite clear well before this date that the employment of sea transport in the coastal trade was not keeping pace either with the growth of traffic passing through the major ports or with the needs of the population and industries grouped around the smaller ports. Furthermore, coastal shipping was expanding more slowly than other forms of transport. In the 50 years or so before 1914 the shipping employed in our foreign trade had increased more than five-fold whilst that in our coasting trade had only doubled.[4]

I

[The year 1914 proved to be a turning point in the history of British coastal shipping. During the next three or four years the trade experienced a dramatic — in fact a catas-trophic — decline from which it took a very long time to recover. The volume of coastwise shipping of the United Kingdom dropped by 50 per cent or more, both in the number of ships and the tonnage they represented *(see Table 1 below)*.

TABLE 1

Number and Net Tonnage of British and Foreign Sailing and Steam Vessels, including their repeated voyages, that arrived and departed with cargoes, coastwise at principal ports in the United Kingdom

	ARRIVED		DEPARTED	
	Vessels	Tons	Vessels	Tons
1913	168,877	34,759,156	165,237	34,282,349
1914	156,823	36,001,235	153,571	35,782,797
1915	125,101	27,468,449	123,151	27,277,911
1916	104,492	22,360,123	103,332	22,292,055
1917	89,798	19,201,463	88,019	19,200,863
1918	82,007	16,780,401	80,037	16,309,061
1919	88,514	19,900,605	86,368	19,829,765
1920	99,905	24,176,450	98,325	24,003,964
1921	83,697	20,949,163	82,439	20,847,242

Source: *Annual Statements of the Navigation and Shipping of the United Kingdom*

NOTE. The proportion of foreign tonnage engaged in the British coastal trade was less than 1 per cent

If intercourse with Ireland is excluded the collapse is even more marked, for by late 1918 and early 1919 the volume of coasting trade was barely one-third that of 1913 *(see Table 2, page 146)*.[5] Detailed figures for individual ports tell a simi-lar story. The coastal traffic of the big ports such as London, Liverpool, and Glasgow declined by one half or more, whilst from some of the smaller ports such as Blyth, Grimsby,

TABLE 2

Arrivals and Departures of vessels with cargoes in the General Coasting Trade of the United Kingdom (excluding intercourse with Ireland)

	ARRIVALS 000 net tons	DEPARTURES 000 net tons
1913	22,723	22,343
1918	7,328	7,005
1919	10,152	10,115
1920	12,953	12,867
1921	10,553	10,520

Source: *Annual Report of the Chamber of Shipping of the United Kingdom* (1922-3), 116, Table 20

Poole, Dartmouth, and Weymouth it disappeared almost completely. Probably the most spectacular collapse was that of Weymouth, where in 1918 exactly six vessels, with a total tonnage of 224 net tons, arrived and departed compared with 496 vessels of 149,194 net tons in 1913 *(see Table 3 opposite)*. Only one or two ports, notably Fleetwood and Beaumaris including Holyhead, recorded a net increase in their coastal traffic during these critical years. The above figures refer, of course, to the net tonnage of vessels with cargoes and not to the total amount of cargo carried coastwise, but they nevertheless give a fair indication of the extent of the decline. Indeed they may even understate it, for many of the vessels were probably running with considerably more unoccupied space than in pre-war years.

Concurrently with this heavy fall in the volume of coastal traffic there occurred a similar decline in the number of ships and services of the various coastal shipping lines. Unfortunately it is impossible to give an accurate estimate of the number of ships employed in Britain's coastal services, but one authoritative source estimated that the 41 principal coastal shipping lines owned 378 ships in 1914 whereas by 1919 they owned only 238. Some lines were affected seriously. For example, the number of ships operated by the General Steam Navigation Company of London fell from 49 in 1914 to 27

TABLE 3

Number and Net Tonnage of Vessels that arrived and departed with cargoes at selected Principal Ports in the Coastwise Trade of the United Kingdom

ARRIVALS (A) AND DEPARTURES (D)

Name of Port		1913 No of vessels	1913 Net tonnage	1918 No of vessels	1918 Net tonnage	1919 No of vessels	1919 Net tonnage
Glasgow	A	7,593	1,513,870	3,495	753,727	3,774	834,317
	D	7,748	1,431,508	3,616	764,275	4,112	846,157
London	A	11,845	5,725,607	3,878	1,961,711	5,214	3,193,055
	D	9,525	2,340,148	3,075	691,384	3,606	884,275
Liverpool	A	11,256	2,184,493	4,888	1,120,722	5,608	1,508,902
(including Birkenhead)	D	12,904	2,325,952	7,407	1,386,263	7,517	1,609,926
Belfast	A	8,723	2,329,950	7,833	1,880,095	8,201	1,987,512
	D	5,876	1,915,055	3,572	1,263,431	3,583	1,332,415
Beaumaris	A	2,887	1,059,485	1,913	1,288,741	1,880	1,207,591
(including Holyhead)	D	5,332	1,340,584	3,498	1,505,935	3,272	1,442,001
Bristol	A	6,173	759,934	3,377	364,318	3,480	417,922
	D	3,760	453,726	2,213	220,543	2,758	326,655
Portsmouth	A	7,266	808,891	2,487	171,356	2,897	277,946
	D	7,503	564,046	2,720	161,440	2,662	187,020
Blyth	A	42	4,237	1	56	2	169
	D	597	178,744	85	46,385	291	156,352
Weymouth	A	283	128,050	4	72	45	21,332
	D	213	21,144	2	152	10	848

Source: *Annual Statements of the Navigation and Shipping of the United Kingdom*

in 1919; the fleet of the Leith, Hull & Hamburg Steam Packet
Company was reduced by one-half, whilst the Clyde Steam
Ship Company of Glasgow was reported to be operating 14
ships in 1919 as against 26 in 1914. Many of the smaller companies, which had once been dependent on the earnings of a
single vessel, must surely have perished altogether; it therefore
seems reasonable to assume that roughly one-half of the ships
engaged in the home water trade in 1913 had disappeared
from it by the end of the war.[6]

Many bulky commodities which had once been carried by
water now went by rail. Wool was no longer sent by sea from
London to Goole, and tin-plates no longer took the sea trip
from South Wales to Liverpool. China clay was now sent from
Fowey direct to the Potteries instead of *via* the Manchester
Ship Canal.[7] Most serious of all, coal had ceased to be the
staple cargo of the coastwise carriers. As a result of this fall
in commodity traffic the coastal lines were forced to suspend
or discontinue many of their pre-war services. Some of these
were curtailed more than others. On the whole the Irish
services seem to have been fairly well maintained, but those
of the western seaboard suffered badly. None probably suffered
more severely than those to and from the port of Liverpool;
The Times stated in August 1919 that 15 ownerships which
had maintained services from the port in 1914 had ceased to
be represented in the coasting trade.[8] Similarly, the amount
of cargo consigned between Manchester and Liverpool fell
appreciably; early in 1919 coastal services carried an average
of 17 tons of cargo per week between these two points compared with 1,000 tons in 1914.[9] Frequent complaints were
made after the cessation of hostilities from the towns and
villages on the west coast of Scotland and from the neigh-
bouring islands of the inadequacy of the steamboat services
to these places. Even the daily mail-boat service to the island
of Lewis, which had been carried on for the past 30 years,
was suspended.[10]

Enough has been said to indicate the declining fortunes of
coastal shipping in this period. Perhaps the most pertinent

questions which suggest themselves are: Why did Britain's coastal shipping services decline so dramatically? What action did the Government take to arrest the decline or to revive the industry? And lastly, what were the consequences?

II

Judging from the complaints made at this time by shipping interests, and by coastal shipowners in particular, the most important causal factor in the situation was the unfair and indiscriminate competition of the railways. Whilst admitting the fact that railway competition provided a legitimate source of grievance, and that basically this was the chief factor causing the decline, it must be pointed out that the emphasis placed on this factor by contemporaries tends to be misleading; it overlooked the fact that there were a variety of reasons which accounted for the industry's misfortunes in these years.

During the nineteenth century it was generally cheaper to transport goods by water in spite of increasing competition from the railways.[11] The latter, however, not only offered a more convenient and quicker service than the ships, but they made their rate structure more competitive especially from the 1890s onwards. Between 1892 and 1914 there was practically no change in the nominal freight rates in force; but a downward adjustment had been achieved by the creation of many exceptional rates. By 1914 probably 75 per cent of the total railway traffic, other than coal and coke, was being carried either at scale rates (those rates fixed with reference to private scales, below the class rates) or at exceptional rates, the number of which ran into many millions.[12] In some cases, particularly port-to-port destinations, the class rates were often cut by 40 per cent or more.

War conditions greatly accelerated this tendency. In 1914 the Government took control of the railways and froze the rate structure. Between 1914 and January 1920 railway rates for merchandise remained unchanged whilst general expenses increased by at least 200 per cent.[13] Comparative figures for the coasting trade show that their expenses rose by more than 200 per cent and in general, unlike the railways', their charges were adjusted accordingly.[14] By the end of the war, therefore, many coastal rates were from 50 to 200 per cent in excess of the comparable railway rates.[15] Thus the coasting trade could not now compete with the railways and in many cases it was unprofitable to resume operations, particularly where the railways ran a service at a loss.

Several examples might illustrate this point more clearly. In November 1918 the lowest coastal rate for the carriage of tin-plates from Swansea to Liverpool was 25s per ton compared with a through raiiway rate from works to destination of 13s per ton. In pre-war days, when the tin-plate traffic had gone almost entirely by sea, the coastal rate ranged from 7s 6d to 10s per ton.[16] Before the war shipowners had carried cocoa from London to Bristol for 16s 7d (made up of a shipping rate of 8s 4d and expenses at terminals of 8s 3d). By 1920 the terminal expenses alone had risen by 23s 11d to 32s 2d. In view of the fact that the railways were quoting an exceptional rate of 38s 8d (a 40 per cent reduction on the class rate) for the same cargo, it was impossible for the coastal trade to compete profitably. Moreover, this was the position after railway charges had been increased in 1920. Prior to this revision, the exceptional rate was a mere 17s 4d, little more than half what the shippers had to pay for their post-war terminal charges.[17]

Exceptional rates of this magnitude were by no means uncommon. Copper, soap, and earthenware were carried from London to Leeds at rates of between 41 and 47 per cent below the class rates, whilst biscuits and margarine went from London to Scottish ports at a reduction of 42 per cent.[18] In many cases it was quite obvious that railway pricing policy discriminated in favour of port-to-port traffic. For example, the special rate from London to Hull (221 miles) for the Groceries List No 1 was 41s 6d per ton; from London to Leicester (99 miles) for the same commodity it was 40s and from London to Birmingham (112 miles) 41s 6d.[19] Thus a town which could be reached from the sea was granted the same railway rate as a town almost exactly half the distance away but which was not a port.

Many of the railway rates, especially the port-to-port exceptional charges, had ceased to be economic. In 1919 groceries were being carried from Bristol to Barry and Newport at 8s 8d per ton; this was 4d less than the actual cost of collection and delivery, quite apart from the cost of carriage of the goods over distances of 49¾ and 26½ miles respectively.[20] To take another example, it was estimated that the general cost of carriage alone between industrial districts in Lancashire and Yorkshire was around 10s per ton; yet in 1919 the entire railway charge for collection, transportation, and delivery was 6s 6d per ton, a loss of at least 3s 6d.[21]

The result was that coastal shipowners were unable to compete with railway rates which were little different from those prevailing in 1892, and in many cases (particularly the port-to-port exceptional charges) represented a loss. As one coastal shipowner bluntly put it: 'How can we keep running in face of railway rates that, between ports, can hardly pay for wear and tear on rolling stock and permanent way?'[22] Under these conditions it was not surprising that a large part — perhaps as much as 35 million tons — of cargo formerly carried in coastwise vessels was, by the end of the war, being moved by the railways.[23]

As we have previously intimated, however, railway competition was only one, albeit a very important one, of a number of factors which tended to reduce the volume of coastwise shipping and inhibit its revival. In part, of course, the decline was an inevitable outcome of changes wrought by the war. At times strategic reasons had occasioned the suspension of some services, whilst during the war coastal vessels were frequently either requisitioned by the Government for Admiralty and collier service or were employed in the near Continental waters to relieve the shortage of overseas tonnage.[24] Naturally, therefore, services had to be suspended or sailings reduced. Before the war there were 49 regular services

of coasting vessels to 39 destinations from the north-eastern
ports of Hull, Goole, West Hartlepool, Middlesbrough,
Stockton, Sunderland, and Newcastle-on-Tyne. Under war-
time conditions there were only 7 sailings to 13 destinations.
Similarly, at one point during the war, Liverpool had coasting
services to only 10 ports compared with 64 in 1914.[25] A
number of these services were, of course, resumed soon after
the war. For example, the Ellerman's Wilson Line resumed its
Liverpool to Hull service in the autumn of 1919, whilst the
Preston to London run operated by the Coast Lines was
revived early in 1921.[26] Furthermore, coastal shipping
suffered heavy physical losses during the period of hostilities.
Unfortunately, it is not possible to give even a rough estimate
of the total number of *bona fide* coastal vessels which were
lost or destroyed, but from an inspection of the official
returns for merchant shipping losses[27] it seems clear that the
losses amongst the smaller class of vessels (that is, those under
2,000 gross tons) were fairly considerable, particularly among
coasting tramps.[28] Specific examples substantiate this conclusion. In the short space of 18 months it was recorded that
22 Irish cattle boats engaged in cross-channel passages to
England had been destroyed by enemy action. Again, the
Cork Steamship Co Ltd lost over half its vessels during the
war, whilst only one of Carron Company's vessels survived to
1918.[29] In so far as war-destroyed vessels could not be
replaced at once, the trade naturally had to operate at a
diminished level commensurate with its reduced capacity.

Equally important, the exigencies of war had reduced the
volume of Britain's trade, external and internal. Imports in
1918 were estimated at about 35,250,000 tons and exports
at about 39,000,000 tons, compared with 56,025,000 and
91,803,000 tons respectively in 1913.[30] The volume of
Britain's international trade recovered only slowly in the
years after the war, and it was not until 1923 that the volume
approached pre-war dimensions.[31] This naturally led to a
reduction in the amount of cargo for coastwise shipment. But
this was not all. Much of the remaining cargo now went by

rail, whilst the volume of internal trade in goods originating in Great Britain had been reduced appreciably. In 1919 the railways, the canals, and the coastal shipping trade were all carrying less in volume than in the years immediately before the war. It is extremely unlikely that motor transport made up for this difference.

In some cases direct control over the economy by the Government had been detrimental to the coasting trade. This was particularly true where the Government chose to direct a large part of water-borne cargo to the railways in an attempt to make the most economical use of the transport facilities available and make it less vulnerable to enemy action. Coal was a typical example. Before the war it was estimated that nearly half the coastwise traffic consisted of coal cargoes. During the years 1914 to 1918 a great change took place; the production of coal fell by some 50 million tons, and immediately after the war there was a severe shortage of this fuel.[32] Not only was there less coal to be carried, but the war-time Coal Transport Reorganisation Scheme involved a great deal of transfer of coal traffic from the sea to the railways, thereby reducing appreciably the work of the coasting trade.[33] Thus, by the end of the war, most of the 23 million tons of coal formerly carried by sea to London and other home centres of consumption from the ports in or bordering on coalfields was being transported by rail.[34] In addition, the coasting trade was at a decided disadvantage with regard to its bunker coal. After 10 May 1919 coastal vessels had to pay the excessive free market prices for their bunkers — prices which were far beyond what the railways and industrial consumers were paying for their coal under official control.[35] Indeed, the coastal shipowners were in the ironical position of having to pay 65s to 70s per ton for their coal whilst under official direction they were freighted to carry it for gas, rail, and factory purposes, for which it was purchased at a controlled price of only 30s per ton.[36]

A topic often neglected in discussions on transport history is that of port and dock facilities; these had an important, though perhaps a more indirect, bearing on the fortunes of the coastal trade in this period. Apart from the fact that most port dues and charges had been increased by 100 per cent or more during the war,[37] the facilities offered by the ports had declined markedly. To some extent the war did nothing more than accelerate a pre-war trend, for it is probable that before 1914 port and dock development did not keep pace with the increase in the volume of ocean and coastal shipping, whilst loading and discharging facilities were not adapted sufficiently to meet the increased size of ships.[38] It was even more significant that many of the smaller ports which catered for the coastwise trade had been neglected, sometimes deliberately through the influence of the railways but more often because various factors had placed a premium on the use of the larger ports and consequently most of the development tended to be concentrated upon the latter.[39] During the war port improvement and development almost came to a standstill and maintenance was rendered very difficult largely because of the enormous rise in capital expenditure costs. In most cases expenditure by port authorities was reduced to a minimum and any development that did occur was usually to provide facilities on a lavish scale for the big liner traffic in contrast to the modest facilities offered to the tramp, coastal, and ordinary traffic.[40] Thus, where in 1913 Barry spent over £67,000 in capital improvements on the docks, thereafter it spent an annual average of only £8,500. Similarly, average annual expenditure at the Bute Docks, Cardiff, during the years 1915-19 was only £6,600 compared with £51,000 in 1914.

Not surprisingly, by the end of the war loading and discharging facilities at many British ports had deteriorated appreciably, there being a particular deficiency at the smaller ports in accommodation facilities for coastwise ships. Many British ports lacked adequate coal-shipping facilities, and bunkering arrangements were far from satisfactory.[41] Some ports were deficient in modern appliances and labour-saving machinery, such as cranes and elevators; and methods of, and equipment for, unloading were often out-dated. At the port of Glasgow it was said that a good deal of the existing equipment for handling goods was obsolete whilst at another port the unloading facilities were so bad that, in the words of Mr A.W. Gattie, it was like 'baling out a cistern with a teaspoon'.[42] In some ports (eg Liverpool) facilities for the transhipment of cargoes from the ocean ship direct to the coastwise vessel scarcely existed.[43] Not only would the wide adoption of this method have reduced costs, it would also have speeded up the turn-round of shipping and thereby increased the employment of coastal vessels. As far as quay accommodation and equipment were concerned the position was no better, and probably it was a great deal worse: 'it is the exception rather than the rule to find Port Authorities providing anything equal to the requirements of the present time; in fact, modern shed accommodation, suitably equipped with mechanical appliances, is conspicuous by its absence. The only sheds upon the quays at one particular port are the wooden structures originally erected in the middle of the last century'.[44] Furthermore, a number of ports, particularly the smaller ones, lacked adequate road and rail facilities to the quays, whilst the improvement of terminal arrangements for the reception and distribution of goods was often 'necessary and even urgently required'.[45]

These inadequacies of Britain's port and dock facilities were inimical to the revival of prosperity in the coasting trade. As the Port and Transit Committee observed in 1919: 'The port authorities in the great ports which deal with nearly 90 per cent of the total imports of the United Kingdom are unanimous that the facilities for distribution by the coasting services as they now exist must be improved before they will be able to deal with anything approaching the volume of imports that pass through those ports under peace conditions.'[46] Generally speaking, it would appear that in the past the port authorities of Great Britain had regarded the coasting trade as the Cinderella of the transport world. A decade after the war this was probably still true. 'The evidence which we have received', said the Royal Commission on Transport,[47] 'regarding the partner of the coastwise trade — the port — shows that many of the ports most used by and most useful to coastwise shipping are in a state of decay. Some have silted up, others lack storage accommodation or adequate equipment for loading and unloading vessels.'

Finally, there were the peculiar conditions obtaining in the period immediately following the war. The great shortage of shipping (albeit largely a paper one) in 1919 and early 1920, and the high freights prevailing in the near Continental trades, attracted a considerable amount of shipping which would otherwise have been available for the coastwise trade had sufficient inducement been offered.[48] Moreover, the extreme congestion prevailing at nearly all the British ports at this time not only deterred many vessels from plying in the home trade but in fact rendered it virtually impossible for them to maintain operations on the pre-war scale even had other things been equal. However, it has already been shown[49] that the chaotic situation prevailing at the ports was more an outcome of the decline in coastal shipping than an *a priori* factor of that decline. Nevertheless, the Chamber of Shipping was convinced that the coasting trade suffered more from congestion at the ports than any other branch of the industry.[50] In so far as congestion reduced the efficiency of shipping and delayed operations it did prevent a revival of the coasting trade. Cargo was often available for transport coastwise but could not readily be moved either because of the non-availability of ships, or because of the impossibility of acquiring berths when needed as a result of the prevailing port congestion.[51]

III

Shipping interests continually pressed the Government to take remedial action. They did not ask for a subsidy or any special privileges. Their main request was that the Government should reform the railway rate structure in order to allow fair competition.[52] The Government, well aware of the seriousness of the situation, delayed dealing with the railway rates and chose instead to introduce a temporary stop-gap measure in the form of a subsidy to coastal shippers.

During most of the war coastal shipping had operated almost free from Government control, though a number of vessels had been requisitioned. The increasing congestion on the railways and at the ports, however, forced the Government to take some action in 1918. A loose form of control (namely ship licensing and rate limitation for some principal commodities) was imposed on the coasting trade and, in April 1918, the Board of Trade was given power under the Defence of the Realm Regulations to make an Order enabling the railway companies to refuse to accept goods for carriage by rail in cases where other means of transport existed.[53] Nevertheless, the Board of Trade did not exercise its newly acquired power but preferred to place reliance on the Port and Transit Committee and the Home Trade Transport (Control) Committee which, through their local committees, were seeking to divert traffic from the railways wherever alternative water routes were available.[54] This voluntary control left much to be desired. Though a certain amount of cargo was diverted from the railways, the complete success of the scheme was inhibited by the fact that the local committees had no power to enforce their arrangements, and traders often refused, especially when the war had ended, to make use of coastal services.

After the Armistice, action became even more imperative as conditions were rapidly deteriorating. The ports and railways became increasingly congested as pre-war coastal traffic continued to be diverted to the railways. Three solutions appeared possible: the reform of the railway rate structure; the use of the Board of Trade's power under the Defence Regulations; and a subsidy. The first two solutions proved unacceptable. The Government maintained that a detailed enquiry would have to be made before railway rates could be altered, whilst it was considered unconstitutional in peace-time for the Board of Trade to exercise its powers under Defence Regulations expressly designed for war purposes. Consequently, the third

remedy was adopted. In August 1919 the War Cabinet gave
directions to the railway companies 'that no goods which have
been imported foreign, or which are intended for export
foreign, shall be carried by rail between points which can be
effectively served, in whole or part, by coastwise carriage'.
For this purpose schedules of traffic were prepared by the
Home Trade Transport Committees, and all goods included in
such schedules were to be carried in whole or in part coastwise at current rates of freight; the difference between the
rate paid and the equivalent railway rate was to be refunded
to the trader in the form of a subsidy. Initially the subsidy
gave a fillip to the coastwise trade and attracted many vessels
which had been engaged in the more lucrative near-Continental
trades. Even then traders did not take advantage of the subsidy scheme to the extent which might have been expected.
As time went on the subsidised traffic gradually diminished.
Up to May 1920, one month before the subsidy was discontinued, the total volume of goods carried under the scheme
amounted to only 1.2 million tons.[55]

The subsidy apart, little attempt was made by the Government during 1919 to facilitate the revival of the industry. It
is true that the Ministry of Shipping directed certain vessels
from the foreign to the home coasting trade to lift coal cargoes,
and the Government encouraged the use of motor transport
(lending 1,200 of its own lorries to the railways to help
relieve the congestion at certain terminal stations);[56] at the
end of the year, moreover, it permitted coastwise vessels to
secure bunker coal at the same limitation prices as industrial
consumers.[57] But, in general, the direct effect of these actions,
including the subsidy, was small. Ironically, the railway strike
of October 1919 probably gave a greater stimulus to the
trade than any of the measures the Government took to
revive it. As one contemporary journal remarked: 'Who would
have foreseen that in the month of October 1919, two of the
King's sons would have returned from Balmoral by the sea
route from Aberdeen to Charing Cross Pier and that coasting
shipping would have again been accorded a highly important

place in the feeding of the nation?'[58]

The relative ineffectiveness of these measures encouraged the Chamber of Shipping, the Shipowners' Parliamentary Committee, and the Liverpool Steam Ship Owners' Association to press more vigorously for the reform of the railway rate structure. The Government's initial response was slow, partly because it was occupied with the general problem of reorganising the railways and partly because it was already conducting lengthy enquiries, through its newly formed Rates Advisory Committee, concerning the best method of adjusting railway rates.[59] Moreover, although it was realised that the railway rate structure would have to be revised if ever the coasting trade were again to compete successfully, it would appear that both the Government and the Rates Advisory Committee were in doubt how this could be achieved. In fact, the Rates Advisory Committee openly admitted that 'we do not see in what manner this can be done at the present moment'.[60]

Eventually, on the advice of the Rates Advisory Committee, railway freight rates were raised twice in 1920. For two important reasons this proved to be no complete solution to the problem. First, the railways continued to be heavily subsidised: the revised charges only brought goods rates up to 112 per cent above the pre-war level, whereas the rise in costs was more than double this figure, and the costs and charges of coastal shipping had risen by 200 per cent or more.[61] Second, although certain flat-rate additions were made, the general method was to raise railway rates percentage-wise, which served only to accentuate further the differences between the class and the exceptional rates. An example will make this point clear. An addition of 60 per cent to a class rate of 40s and to an exceptional rate of 30s raised the first to 64s and the second to 48s, thus increasing the differential by 6s. To have maintained the original differential at 10s an increase of 80 per cent in the exceptional rate would have been required.

A final though abortive attempt was made to deal with the problem in the Railways Act of 1921. The Government was thereby relieved of the subsidy payments to the railways, and it was laid down that railway charges had to be fixed at a level which would yield an annual net revenue equivalent to the aggregate net revenue of 1913. Special provision was made for the newly created Railway Rates Tribunal to revise any rates which could be shown to be unfairly competitive with coasting traffic. The abolition of the subsidy undoubtedly removed one of the main grievances of the coasting shipowners, but, apart from this, most of the other amendments proposed by the Chamber of Shipping were 'kangarooed' in Committee. Even the question of exceptional rates was not dealt with satisfactorily. Though the intention of the Act was to get rid of as many exceptional rates as possible, the companies were still allowed to continue to quote new exceptional rates down to 40 per cent below the standard rates without the consent of the Railway Rates Tribunal.[62]

IV

Coastwise shipping received a set' ick in the years 1914-19 from which it took more than a ₁eneration to recover. The few measures taken by the Government to assist the trade were largely ineffective, and in 1921 it was recorded that half the ships in the trade were laid up.[63] The attempt to assimilate railway rates with coastal charges was only partially successful. Railway competition continued throughout the inter-war years partly because, contrary to expectations, the number of exceptional rates and the volume of traffic moving at these rates increased rather than diminished. By 1935, 68 per cent of the railway receipts from freight traffic came from freight carried at exceptional rates, compared with 50 per cent in 1928.[64] In addition, the generally depressed conditions in trade and industry in these years and the increasing competition of road transport added to the coastal shipowners' difficulties. Even by 1938 the coastwise trade had not recovered to its former level, and soon afterwards it was dealt another severe blow by the Second World War. After 1945 recovery was somewhat more rapid, and in 1949 the trade belatedly assumed pre-1914 proportions.[65]

The crisis had an important effect on the industry; it encouraged a fusion of interests and forced many independent concerns out of business. One by one the old-established coastal shipping firms were obliged to abandon their vessels or to surrender their identity to more dynamic rivals, who constantly added to their fleets by a series of absorptions and amalgamations. Behind this movement stood the famous Coast Lines Syndicate, formed in 1917 with the clear intention of absorbing as many British coastal lines as possible, and two prominent shipowners, Sir Alfred Read and Sir Owen Philipps.[66] During this period a large number of hitherto independent shipping lines were taken over by Coast Lines,[67] and the coastal shipping of many ports became increasingly dominated by this combine. By the autumn of 1919 it was estimated that, together with its chief subsidiaries, it controlled some four-fifths of the tonnage in the coasting trade.[68] This must surely have placed coastal shipping among one of the most highly concentrated industries of the period.

What impact did the decline in coastal services have on the British economy in general? The severe disruption which took place in Britain's transport facilities in the early years after the war can in part be attributed to the deficiency in coastal shipping services (though it is not always easy to distinguish clearly between cause and effect in this matter). One of the chief causes of congestion both on the railways and at the ports was the fact that a large volume of traffic, which before the war would have gone by water, now went by rail.[69] Although the full repercussions of this breakdown in communications have still to be examined in detail, it is abundantly clear that it had a severe effect on trade and industry in the immediate post-war years. Time and again industrialists were held up by the lack of transport facilities to move raw materials or finished goods. Commodities piled up at the ports or terminal stations and at the works of firms, awaiting delivery for weeks and even months. At one point the firm of Brunner Mond of Swansea was compelled to close down three-quarters of its nickel works because of the delay in deliveries of raw materials, and nearly every large manufacturing centre was suffering similar difficulties. Delays in transit of between three and five days were not uncommon,[70] and in some cases they were much longer. In this respect the north-east coast appears to have suffered the worst. The average time taken by the majority of goods trains for short-distance traffic was three times that taken before the war, whilst in one or two exceptional instances the delivery of goods from Sheffield, Leeds, and Glasgow to the Tyne area took from 55 to 60 days.[71]

Furthermore, the dislocation in communications played a significant part in raising industrial costs and prices at this time. The prices of many commodities and the cost of finished goods were enhanced by the delay. It was estimated, for instance, that congestion at the docks was costing £10 a standard for timber in freights and charges.[72] This is by no means an isolated example, and it is probable that at least 25-35 per cent of the increase in costs and prices at this period was due to transport difficulties. As the *Economist* pointed out: 'The tinplate trade, like others, has been greatly handicapped by the scandalous inefficiency of transport facilities, and it seems doubtful whether it is generally realised to what a preponderating degree this question is at the root of most of our commercial difficulties.'[73]

NOTES

1   *The Times Trade Supplement* (10 July 1920), 467

2   See J.A. Todd, *The Shipping World* (1934), 209

3   W.G. Hoffmann, *British Industry, 1700-1950* (trans by W.O. Henderson and W.H. Chaloner, 1955), 47; C.J. Fuchs, *The Trade Policy of Great Britain and Her Colonies since 1860* (1905), 121-4

4   N. Hill, 'The Importance of Coastal Shipping', *Brassey's Naval*

and Shipping Annual (1921-2), 263

5   A comparable, though less dramatic, decline in the traffic on
    British canals took place in this period; see C. Hadfield, *British
    Canals* (1959), 260

6   *Shipbuilding and Shipping Record* (28 August 1919), 236;
    Fairplay (8 July 1919), 236

7   Ibid (17 July), 238; *The Times* (19 July 1919)

8   Ibid (25 August 1919)

9   *Annual Report of the Chamber of Shipping (UK)* (1918-19), 138

10 *Shipbuilding and Shipping Record* (1 January 1920), 1; *Glasgow
    Herald* (1, 14 and 22 November, 11 December 1919)

11 Cf Sel Comm on Transport, H of C 130/136 (1918), Evidence,
    16 October 1918, Q 1159

12 *Report of the Rates Advisory Committee on the General Revision
    of Railway Rates and Charges,* Cd 1098 (1920), 13

13 For further details and the implications of this stabilisation policy
    see D.H. Aldcroft, 'The Decontrol of British Shipping and
    Railways after the First World War', *Journal of Transport History*,
    5 (1961-2), 92-3

14 *The Times Trade Supplement* (31 January 1920), 527;
    Shipbuilding and Shipping Record (17 November 1921), 642-4

15 *The Times* (16 December 1919)

16 E.A. Pratt, *British Railways and the Great War,* Vol I (1921), 277

17 *Report of the Rates Advisory Committee on Coastwise Shipping
    and Exceptional Rates,* Cd 1372 (1921), 2

18 *Railway Gazette* (16 May 1919), 825-7

19 *Shipping World* (23 June 1920), 675

20   *Railway Gazette* (16 May 1919), 825

21   *The Times* (18 March 1919)

22   *Shipping World* (18 August 1920), 165

23   This is a rough estimate given in *H of C Deb*, cxvi (19 May 1919), Col 5

24   Pratt, Vol I, 272; C.E. Fayle, *Seaborne Trade*, Vol II (1923), 63

25   Pratt, Vol I, 273

26   *Shipbuilding and Shipping Record* (16 October 1919), 444; *The Times Trade Supplement* (4 December 1920), 286

27   *Merchant Shipping (Losses) Return* (4 August 1914 - 11 November 1918), H of C, 199 (1919)

28   Cf *Final Report of the Departmental Committee on the Shipping and Shipbuilding Industries After the War*, Cd 9092 (1918), 111

29   *The Times* (27 January 1919); *Shipbuilding and Shipping Record* (19 February 1920), 244; R.H. Campbell, *Carron Company* (1961), 322

30   N.B. Dearle, *An Economic Chronicle of the Great War for Great Britain and Ireland, 1914-1919* (1922), 240

31   *Fairplay* (17 February 1921), 608; E.V. Morgan, *Studies in British Financial Policy, 1914-25* (1952), 306

32   *Board of Trade Journal* (21 November 1918), 634; *Economist* (28 December 1918), 878

33   *Shipbuilding and Shipping Record* (17 November 1921), 642-3; *Annual Report of the Chamber of Shipping (UK)* (1921-2), 61. The scheme was not abolished until August 1919: *Iron and Coal Trades Review* (5 September 1919), 303

34   Pratt, II, 728-31. The policy was not confined to coal, of course

35   *Shipbuilding and Shipping Record* (4 December 1919), 664; *The*

Times (22 November 1919)

36 *Fairplay* (Bunkering Suppl) (20 November 1919), 48-9; (11 December 1919), 1393

37 *Fairplay* (3 July 1919), 10. Many port authorities would have been rendered insolvent had they not been allowed to increase their charges. See *Select Committee on Transport*, H of C 130-136, Evidence, 5 November 1918, QQ 3391 and 3471-4; *Shipbuilding and Shipping Record* (24 October 1918), 402

38 This was especially true of some of the older ports. See *Final Report of the Departmental Committee on Shipping and Shipbuilding after the War*, Cd 9092 (1918), 119; D.J. Owen, *The Port of London Yesterday and Today* (1927), 23 et seq; *Shipping World* (21 February 1900), 202. Fletcher attributes the relative stagnation of Britain's entrepôt trade in the late nineteenth and early twentieth centuries to the slower rate of improvement and development of port facilities in Great Britain compared with that on the Continent. M.E. Fletcher, 'The Suez Canal and World Shipping, 1869-1914', *Journal of Economic History* (1958), 567

39 Anon, *The Coastwise Trade of the United Kingdom Past and Present and its Possibilities* (1925), 63-5; *Fairplay* (19 February 1920), 614; *Shipbuilding and Shipping Record* (10 June 1920), 774

40 F.W. Lewis, 'Port Facilities of Great Britain', *Brassey's Naval and Shipping Annual* (1925), 228; L.H. Savile, 'Harbours, Docks and Inland Waterways, 1910-1935', *Engineering* (Silver Jubilee Edition, 3 May 1935), 40; *Fairplay* (20 May 1924), 502

41 *Fairplay* (22 April 1920), 269; (29 April 1920), 358 and (29 May 1924), 502

42 *Minutes of Proceedings before the Departmental Committee Appointed to Investigate Mr A.W. Gattie's Proposals for Improving the Method of Handling Goods and Traffic*, Cd 580 (1920), 26 August 1919, Q 74

43 Anon, *The Coastwise Trade of the United Kingdom Past and Present and its Possibilities* (1925), 86-7

44   Ibid, 91

45   *Fairplay* (22 April 1920), 269; *Report of the Departmental Committee Appointed to Investigate Mr A.W. Gattie's Proposals for Improving the Method of Handling Goods and Traffic*, Cd 492 (1919), 4

46   *The Times* (1 September 1919)

47   *Final Report of the Royal Commission on Transport*, Cd 3751 (1931), 138

48   *Shipbuilding and Shipping Record* (9 October 1919), 400

49   D.H. Aldcroft, 'Port Congestion and the Shipping Boom of 1919-20', *Business History* (June 1961), esp pp 101-5

50   *Annual Report of the Chamber of Shipping (UK)* (1919-20), 28

51   *Shipbuilding and Shipping Record* (31 July 1919), 119

52   *Annual Report of the Chamber of Shipping (UK)* (1918-19), 37, and (1919-20), 116

53   C.E. Fayle, *The War and the Shipping Industry* (1927), 222-4; Pratt, Vol I, 275

54   C.E. Fayle, *Seaborne Trade*, Vol III, 340; Pratt, Vol I, 275

55   *Shipbuilding and Shipping Record* (28 August 1919), 235 and (24 June 1920), 822, 844; *The Times Trade Supplement* (19 June 1919), 384; (27 March 1920), 20

56   *Shipbuilding and Shipping Record* (25 September 1919), 358 *Report of the Committee on Road Conveyance of Goods by Railway Companies*, Cd 1228 (1921), 3

57   *The Times Annual, Financial and Commercial Review* (23 January 1920)

58   *The Times Trade Supplement* (11 October 1919), 99

59   D.H. Aldcroft, *Journal of Transport History*, 5 (1961-2), 92-4

60   *Report of the Rates Advisory Committee on the Interim Revision of Railway Rates, Tolls, Fares and Charges*, Pt 2: *Goods*, Cd 886 (1920), 13

61   Cd 1098 (1920), 4, 9; *Shipbuilding and Shipping Record* (17 November 1920), 642-3

62   Railways Act (1921), 11 and 12 Geo 5, ch 55, sect 37-9, 59 (1)

63   Cd 1372 (1921), 2

64   A.A. Harrison, 'Railway Freight Charges', *Journal of the Institute of Transport* (July 1957), 146; G. Walker, *Road and Rail* (1947 ed), 67-8; J.R. Sargent, *British Transport Policy* (1958), 43

65   P. Ford and J.A. Bound, *Coastwise Shipping and the Small Ports* (1951), 3

66   G. Chandler, *Liverpool Shipping* (1960), 53. Practically the whole capital of Coast Lines was held by the Royal Mail Steam Packet Co, the Union-Castle Co, Elder Dempster & Co, Lamport & Holt Ltd, the Glen Line and the Moss Line, with individual holdings by Read and Philipps. *Shipping World* (12 November 1919), 383

67   For examples of the take-overs see *Shipbuilding and Shipping Record* (6 November 1919), 529, 534, and *Shipping World* (22 October 1919), 331

68   *Shipbuilding and Shipping Record* (28 October 1919), 471-2

69   It is true that the railways were carrying less merchandise in 1919 than in 1913, but one should not assume from this that the resources of the railways were commensurate with the demands made upon them. There are three reasons for this: (1) railway rolling-stock and equipment had been depleted during the war; (2) there was a greater concentration of traffic at main-line terminal stations, causing marked congestion; (3) an increase in passenger traffic had taken place on the railways

70   Ibid (26 June 1919), 820; *Fairplay* (25 March 1920), 1029-30

71   Ibid (1 April 1920), 13

72   *Report of the Building Materials Sub-Committee on Timber*, Cd 985 (1920), 6

73   *Economist, Commercial History and Review of 1919* (21 February 1920), 431

7 Port Congestion and the Shipping Boom of 1919-20

First published in Business History, *3 (1961)*

I

Though fluctuations in freight rates and shipping booms were a common feature of the nineteenth century, the boom which occurred just after the First World War in Great Britain and the world in general had certain unusual features. Not only was it unparalleled in its intensity but it was peculiar in view of the fact that it took place in a world already overstocked with tonnage[1] and at a time when international trade had not returned to its pre-war level.[2]

Even more notable was the extremely short duration of this boom. In May 1919 the shipping freight market was reported to be firm.[3] A partial index of freight rates constructed by Dr Isserlis stood at 87 in February and rose to 157 in August after which it fell back to 126 in January 1920.[4] From this date the more reliable Chamber of Shipping freight index is available. This shows that the end of the boom in freights took place between the months of March and April of 1920, though the time-charter rate turned down nearly a month before.[5] *Fairplay* stated[6] that the last two weeks in March and the first two in April marked the beginning of the end of the boom in freights; two months later the demand for tonnage in some markets had almost 'dried-up' and charterers were even wanting to cancel their charters.[7] From its peak of 141 in March 1920 the Chamber's freight index fell to 58 by the end of the year[8] and its time-charter index fell from 149 in February to 60 by December 1920.[9]

Not all freight rates were high in the boom of roughly a year, for a number were still under war-time control, but the

general rise in freight-rate levels did correspond with the
general release of shipping from requisition in March 1919.
Nevertheless it was sufficient to stimulate activity among shipowners, shipbuilders and speculators alike. Despite the greatly
enhanced costs of construction[10] and operation the shipowners
were not deterred from adding new ships to their fleets, nor
were the shipbuilders deterred from building them, for an air
of optimism reigned over the industry. Thus the appreciation
in shipping values, which was 24 per cent in the first half of
1919, was 42 per cent for the whole of 1919.[11] An idea of
the enormous increase in values is given by *Fairplay*'s calculation of the price of a new ready cargo steamer of 7,500 tons
which they publish half-yearly:[12]

Year		Price £
mid 1908		36,000
end 1912		58,000
end 1914		60,000
end 1916		187,750
end 1917		165,000
mid 1918		180,500
end 1918		169,000
mid 1919		195,000
end 1919		232,500
March 1920 (peak) ..		259,000
mid 1920		180,000
end 1920		105,000

This phenomenal rise was in no way confined to new tonnage for, if anything, the prices of second-hand tonnage
increased even more. For example, the *Scatwell*, of 8,140
tons dead weight, built in 1911, was disposed of for £125,000
in November 1917, in May 1919 for £164,000 and in
December 1919 for £197,000, showing an appreciation of 31
per cent in twelve months.[13] The *Vermont*, of 6,800 tons
dead weight, built in 1900, was sold in 1916 for £110,000
and resold in May 1919 for £170,000.[14] Many of the older
vessels appreciated by 100 per cent or more: the *Annandale*,

built in 1878, sold for £10,000 in January 1920 and was resold in the May for £25,000, a profit of 150 per cent.[15] These examples are by no means isolated cases as a glance at *Fairplay's* pages will show.

Until the budget of 1919[16] the market was fairly quiet: whereupon the Cardiff owners rushed in and started the price spiral.[17] The flotations of shipping companies and issues of fresh capital, of which there were few in 1918 and for most of the first half of 1919, became almost a daily event in the third quarter of 1919, and, in one week alone, the *Economist* recorded no less than five new issues.[18] Amongst the recent creations was the Western Counties Steamship Company which in March 1920 invited subscriptions for £1,000,000 of ordinary shares on the acquisition of the Sutherland Steamship Company: the issue was heavily over-subscribed.[19] This line then went on to buy up the Moor Line in 1920 from Walter Runciman at the rate of £22 per ton for 82,000 tons.[20] The following year they had to sell 8 of these ships for £4 per ton.

This shipping boom was reflected slightly later in the order books of the shipbuilders. Owing to the slower rate of production the total tonnage launched in the United Kingdom in 1919 was only 1,620,442 tons compared with 1,932,153 in the last year before the war.[21] However, the tonnage under construction during 1919 in British shipyards increased from 2,254,845 tons in the first quarter to 2,944,249 in the fourth quarter and reached 3,394,425 in the first quarter of 1920[22] which was over a million tons more than at any other time in the previous six years. The tonnage under construction continued to increase at a diminishing rate to reach a peak of 3,798,593 tons in the first quarter of 1921.[23] The peak of the launchings came in 1920 with just over 2 million tons.[24]

Many shipbuilders greatly expanded their yards in the early post-war period; the classic case was of Palmer's at Jarrow who spent £2 million on extensions including the acquisition of the Hebburn shipyard, graving dock, and other properties of Robert Stephens, Amble Shipbuilding Co, Hebburn, Ransome Machinery Co and Palmer's (Swansea)

Dry Dock.[25] Another notable example was the meteoric rise
of the Northumberland Shipbuilding Company, Hawden-on-
Tyne, which though relatively insignificant in 1919, was by
1923 the largest company of its kind. In 1924 its fate was
sealed by forced liquidation because of its attempts to secure
control by share exchange, obtaining advances from subsidiaries,
pledging assets and using the funds so provided to extend its
interests.[26] As Ellen Wilkinson so rightly observed: 'Such
speculative transactions, the dissipation of cash reserves, and
the handicap of increased interest liabilities consequent on
the issue of bonus shares and the heavy watering of shipping
capital, left the British shipping and shipbuilding industry
without the reserves necessary to meet the post-war
problems.'[27]

II

The question this paper endeavours to answer is why such
a shipping (and of course shipbuilding) boom occurred at all
at this time. On the international side three main factors were
responsible for the increase in net tonnage. First, the desire
to replace war losses and the rapidity with which they were
made good. Second, the emergency shipbuilding programmes
of the various countries in the later years of the war which
came to fruition after the war had ended. The United States
showed the most spectacular increase; between 1914 and
1921 she was responsible for 86 per cent of the net increase
in world tonnage, over half of which was completed after the
Armistice.[28] Before the war America had rarely launched
more than 200,000 gross tons of shipping a year and even in
1917 the amount only reached 821,115 tons. The following
year showed a tremendous absolute increase, the tonnage
launched being 2,602,153, and in 1919 a record was set up
with 3,579,826[29] tons — never to be repeated in the following
decade. Third, all nations realised in the war that self-sufficiency
in shipping was a thing to be coveted. The thanks Britain
received for being the shipping servant of the Allies during
the war was a recognition by them that their national fleets

must be built up at all costs so that a greater proportion
of their seaborne trade could be carried by ships under
their respective national flags. This policy was only too
clearly expressed in the preamble to the Jones-White Act of
1920:[30]

> It is necessary for the national defence and for the proper
> growth of its foreign and domestic commerce that the United
> States shall have a merchant marine of the best-equipped and
> most suitable types of vessels sufficient to carry the greater
> proportion of its commerce and serve as a naval and military
> auxiliary in time of war or national emergency.

On the British side the conventional reasons have already
been outlined. As Professor Pigou observed,[31] the recollection
of war profits, the prospect of release from control, the
general expectation of a world-wide boom in trade, the
Chancellor of the Exchequer's announcement in May 1919
that the Excess Profits Duty would be reduced from 80 to
40 per cent, the natural desire to restore the United Kingdom's
share of the world shipping which had dropped from 41.6
per cent in June 1914 to 34.1 per cent in June 1919 all acted
together to stimulate British shipping and shipbuilding.

That these were important causal factors in the boom of
1919 is no doubt true but they are by no means sufficient by
themselves in explaining the intensity of the boom at this
period when there was actually only an apparent shortage of
shipping space. How could there possibly be a shortage, even
allowing for troop repatriation and the feeding of Europe,
when world tonnage capacity was above the pre-war level and
when the tonnage available to Britain was by 1920 almost
equal to that of 1913, whilst the volume of trade was so
much reduced?[32] Obviously the reason for the tremendous
boom must be sought in one or two abnormal factors which
tended to reduce the effective capacity of our shipping below
the level of demand potential. Shortly after the Armistice
there had been a glut of shipping but by the end of March
1919 peculiar conditions had translated this excess supply

into a shortage and it is to these conditions which we must now turn.

III

By far the most important factor in the situation was the terrible port-congestion which *Fairplay*[33]   so well described as the 'swollen lethargic snake of congestion which lies stifling the life of Britain'. A few examples will not be out of place here. The time taken to discharge five vessels of an important line in 1913, in London, amounted to 32 days; the time taken to discharge the same vessels in 1919 amounted to 165 days.[34] At Manchester, in December 1919, steamers were delayed as much as fourteen days waiting to discharge cotton and general cargo and there were as many as seven ships waiting their turn for berths and unable to get alongside the wharf.[35] The case of the *Greleden* was not untypical. This vessel of 7,500 tons deadweight arrived in London from Bombay on 17 November 1919; she waited ten days before obtaining a berth from the Port of London Authority, she then discharged slowly into the warehouse and lightered up till 11 January 1920. She was then turned out of her berth owing to the shortage of lighters and from 11 to 16 January lay idle; she recommenced discharging on 16 January and finally completed this process on 24 January having taken 68 days in all.[36]

The delay experienced in the coal ports, due partly to the insufficient coal output, was particularly bad.[37] The principal ports were the worst affected by such delays[38] whilst in contrast many of the smaller ports remained relatively idle. The tonnage entering British ports with cargoes in 1919 was only 60 per cent of pre-war and 75 per cent in 1920 and 1921 and not until 1923 was the pre-war tonnage figure of ships with cargoes entering British ports exceeded.[39] In all it was estimated that the ports were bringing in no more than 75 per cent of their pre-war imports at this time,[40] and tonnage clearances from UK ports were probably not much more than 50 per cent.[41] The effect of port congestion on the efficiency of shipping was disastrous. Sir Norman Hill estimated that the average number of voyages per year of vessels employed in overseas trade had been reduced from 5 to 4 or 20 per cent which represented a loss of some 10 million tons carrying capacity a year.[42] Another contemporary estimate believed that it was the major factor in reducing the efficiency of British merchant tonnage by some 30 per cent or more, as compared with before the war,[43] and even this estimate is possibly on the low side. Nor were the delays through port congestion peculiar to Britain for it seems to have been an international phenomenon; in fact the American ports were said to be even worse in this respect and in six European ports the 'turn-round' of 66 vessels averaged 14½ days.[44]

The reason for port congestion and the delays entailed were numerous. Hours of labour at the British docks had been reduced from 52 to 44[45] and also working hours were less on the railways and in the coal-mines. Thus meat in London, which before the war had been delivered out of the stores at night, was now moved by day and as a result the sheds were not clear for the incoming cargoes.[46] Strikes of dock workers, railwaymen and coal-miners added to the difficulties.[47] For instance, when the limitation on coal freight rates ended in July 1919 there was a glut of tonnage in some of the coal ports and owners were unable to benefit from ordinary market rates. For at least a month after the rescinding of the limitation rates many vessels left the UK ports in ballast rather than wait for cargoes. Then came the strike of the Yorkshire miners and by the beginning of September the glut of tonnage had been turned into a shortage.[48]

The Government was partly to blame for the difficulties by virtue of its buying policy and sudden release of wartime restrictions. During 1919 commodities came pouring into the country.[49] The Ministry of Food imported great quantities of food, much of which had to be stored at the port warehouses for long periods though the dock warehouses had been designed merely to facilitate the through transit of merchandise.[50] The lack of co-ordination between Government buying departments resulted in exceptionally heavy cargoes of frozen meat arriving in London which led to the choking of every available cubic foot of cold storage space.[51] Stocks of imported commodities were allowed to pile up in the warehouses at the ports with the result that there was no room for new imports. With the freeing of wool sales in April 1919,[52] great shiploads of wool came in and during the whole of 1919 two million bales of wool were imported into London (as compared with 800,000 bales before the war) with a total disregard of the regulation of its arrival.[53] Many docks became literally choked with bacon and meat[54] for the restoration of free imports in bacon was construed as an invitation to dump.[55] American bacon poured into the ports and due to the lack of accommodation it was left to roll about on the quays[56] and rot with other food lying there.[57] On top of this came great quantities of meat — often of pre-war lineage — to take advantage of the high prices offered by the Ministry.[58] Likewise timber was rushed in from America and Sweden and Bristol became choked with tobacco when Government restrictions were lifted.[59] At Liverpool on 23 August 1919, there were 33 vessels awaiting berths and six others, which were lucky enough to obtain them, could not be unloaded owing to the quays and sheds behind them being piled up with cargo.[60] Another factor here was the quantity of 'shut-out' cargo sent down to the docks, that is more cargo was being sent down to the ports than ships could possibly take away with them and consequently much stuff was left behind to add to the accumulation.[61]

The railways contributed their share to the port chaos. The lack of railway wagons and sheets with which to cover them was the main problem. Latterly in 1919 the deficiency of railway wagons varied between 35,000 and 40,000 compared with pre-war[62] and the position was made worse by the excessive number of wagons standing under demurrage per working day.[63] Early in 1920 the shortage of wagons became so acute that at certain works on the north-east coast stocks had accumulated from a normal 5,000 tons to 29,000 tons owing to the congestion in the sidings.[64] Moreover, the whole railway system, whose facilities for the transport of goods had steadily deteriorated in the war,[65] became even more disorganised when, in August 1919, the restrictions which had been imposed by the war-time Coal Transport Reorganisation Scheme were abolished. In effect the whole scheme, the idea of which was to overcome the congestion on the railways and shortage of rolling-stock and to produce economies in handling, came to an end.[66] Thus to quote one case, it took four days to get cargo from Nottingham to London by rail.[67] Delays in transit of this sort were not un-common and the general effect was that cargoes often arrived at the ports after the vessel for which they were intended had sailed, which meant that either the goods were dumped on to the already congested ports or left in the trucks.

What made things worse was the great concentration of traffic on the major ports to the comparative neglect of the smaller ones which threw an added burden on the railways. The latter ports had been used a great deal before the war but partly because of the heavy loss of smaller vessels in the war and partly because of the stagnation of coasting traffic after the war their services as distributive centres for the main ports had declined. The main cause seems to have been the almost complete extinction of coastal transport by sea which before the war had been cheaper than railway carriage. The Government's policy of conveying merchandise on the rail-ways at pre-war rates, and the enormous rise in the cost of running coastal vessels during the war, resulted in the coastal rates being twice the equivalent railway charges,[68] and of course coastwise shipping found it very difficult to compete with the railways owing to their unlimited number of excep-tional rates. Very little effective control — not enough really in view of the situation — was exercised over coastwise ship-ping but in August 1919 the Government, in order to wipe out the disparity between railway and coastwise rates for the same cargo, agreed to refund the difference in the form of a subsidy.[69]

Another factor adding to the congestion of the ports was the issue of regulations by the Coal Controller which came into force on 1 August 1919, and which restricted the forwarding, from all collieries in Lancashire, Yorkshire and North Wales, of any coal by rail to Liverpool and other Lancashire ports for export and for bunkering purposes. This meant that coal supplies would have to be either brought coastwise to Liverpool or the ships would have to bunker in ports other than the restricted ones thereby adding to the congestion of such ports; as an alternative, of course, ships could bunker abroad for the round trip but in so doing they would lose valuable cargo space. Though the coal regulation was made with good intentions — to conserve domestic coal supplies in the North — it had disastrous effects, for apart from adding to the congestion of the South Wales and Bristol ports, the bunker facilities at Liverpool were intended expressly for rail-borne coal from the northern fields and not water-borne coal from the Bristol Channel.[70]

There were other factors of course which tended to magnify the apparent shortage of tonnage or reduce the efficiency of the British tonnage already in existence. Long after the cessation of hostilities the redirection of trade from shorter to longer routes often continued. For example, sugar formerly imported from Austria and Germany continued to come from more distant sources such as Cuba; likewise much timber and dairy produce had to be carried from more distant sources than the White Sea and Baltic. Above all, the shortage of coal in the United Kingdom and the high prices charged meant that our Allies drew large quantities of fuel from the United States which involved a far longer haul.[71]

Though cargo vessels constructed in the post-war period had an average speed of two knots more than similar vessels built in 1913[72] this only helped to increase the port congestion rather than relieve it. One 'bear' point[73] in the situation, however, lay in the fact that many passenger liners lost in the war were replaced by cargo liners thus increasing overall cargo capacity. On the other hand, the effective rate of completion

of vessels in the shipbuilding yards was greatly reduced; in
1913 the output of tonnage in the United Kingdom was 99
per cent of the tonnage under construction at the beginning
of the year; by 1919 and 1920 the average time required to
complete a ship was sixteen or seventeen months.[74] Moreover,
the restriction on sales of ships abroad increased the average age
of the British mercantile marine at a time when nearly 12 per
cent of the available ocean-going tonnage was in the hands of
the ship repairers.[75]

IV

If we have been inclined to overstress the factor of port
congestion in the boom of 1919-20 it is partly because its
significance has been somewhat neglected in the past by
economic historians and partly because of its importance in
explaining the suddenness, intensity and possibly the short
duration of the boom. That the efficiency of the British
mercantile marine was reduced by 30 per cent and probably
even 40 per cent at this time cannot but have had a tremendous effect upon the actions of the shipowners. That shipowners were willing to purchase second-hand tonnage at vastly
inflated prices is evidence enough that they were eager to
take advantage of the unrealistically high freight rates engen-
dered by the artificial conditions which prevailed.[76] We
cannot of course subscribe to the theory that there would
have been no shipping boom had there been no port congestion for there were other factors in the situation which have
already been outlined. But what we might say is that there
need have been no shortage of tonnage nor such high freight
rates if there had been no port congestion since there was
more tonnage afloat in the world than ever before,[77] and in
some cases the effective carrying capacity of ships was greater
than before the war. Thus it was in fact the relative inefficiency
of shipping, brought about by a sharp drop in the velocity of
circulation of the existing tonnage mainly because of the
severe port congestion, which gave rise to the 'apparent'
shortage of carrying capacity of the British (and even the

world's) mercantile marine.[78] In so far as this was the major causal factor of the shipping boom of this period it was unique in the history of the mercantile marine.

The fact that the boom broke when it did (early in the spring of 1920) cannot be attributed to the complete disappearance of the factors that caused it. They did however tend to diminish in importance and the beginning of improvement in the state of the ports[79] did coincide with the end of the boom, though as late as August 1920 port congestion might still have been a major factor contributing to the inefficiency of shipping.[80] The boom collapsed largely because it was at last realised that the 'paper' tonnage scarcity was unreal. It was abundantly clear even to people of limited intelligence that, with one and a half million tons of new shipping taking the water every three months in a world whose existing service tonnage was some 4 million tons more than immediately before the war,[81] a slump was inevitable.[82] As the *Shipping World* so wisely remarked:[83] 'The truth of the matter seems to be that the fact is at least being driven home that there is more than enough tonnage to go round and whilst this dominating factor prevails freights must inevitably continue on their downward course.'

In conclusion we might add the well-known fact that the boom was disastrous to British shipping and shipbuilding alike. Not only did it denude the industries of their war-accumulated reserves in a frivolous manner but the blind policy of speculation called into existence enough tonnage to last a decade or so. Early in 1921 there was over 10 million tons more shipping in existence than before the war and over 5 million tons were laid up in various ports of the world. Of this some 2 million tons belonged to Great Britain.[84]

NOTES

1   Just after the Armistice the total world tonnage in existence was

slightly greater than before the war; by June 1919 the world's mercantile marine was greater than that of June 1913 by 8.4 per cent but shipbuilding capacity was greater by 114 per cent. D.H. Robertson, *Economic Fragments* (1931), 112

2   In 1920 it was estimated that the overseas commerce of the UK, taking imports and exports in bulk, worked out at 19 per cent and 56 per cent respectively below the levels of 1913. *Fairplay* (17 February 1921), 608. C.E. Fayle, *The War and the Shipping Industry* (1927), 382, estimates a total reduction in the volume of British trade of about 42 per cent

3   *Shipping World* (14 May 1919), 494

4   A.C. Pigou, *Aspects of British Economic History, 1918-25* (1947). 82-3

5   Ibid, 238, Table vii

6   *Fairplay* (8 April 1920), 90; see also *Shipping World* (24 March 1920), 330

7   *Fairplay* (17 June 1920), 881

8   1920=100 on a geometric basis

9   A.C. Pigou, op cit, 238. In February 1920 freights were some 500 per cent above the level of July 1914 whilst general wholesale prices were only some 200 per cent greater. G.C. Allen, *British Industries and their Organization* (1935), 152

10   It was calculated that a cargo vessel of the refrigerated type cost something like £135,000 to build before the war whereas by the middle of 1919 it cost around £500,000. C. Maughan, 'Shipping Prospects', *Quarterly Review*, 232 (October 1919), 479

11   *Fairplay* (6 January 1921), 151, only to be paralleled by an equivalent drop in 1920

12   *Fairplay* (7 July 1921), 65-6. *Fairplay* also publish a very useful graph based on the price of this steamer

13   *Fairplay* (3 July 1919), 46, and (1 January 1920), 139

14   Ibid (7 July 1921), 67

15   Ibid (15 July 1920), 225-6

16   In which the Excess Profits Duty was reduced from 80 to 40 per cent

17   *Fairplay* (3 July 1919), 46

18   *Economist* (19 July 1919), 98; two more followed the week after: ibid (26 July 1919), 140

19   C.E. Fayle, op cit, 380-1

20   E. Wilkinson, *The Town That Was Murdered* (1939), 129

21   *Lloyd's Register of Shipping — Annual Summary of the Mercantile Shipbuilding of the World for the year 1930*, 10, Table X. These figures include vessels of 100 tons gross and upwards. The total launchings for the whole world reached a peak in 1919 of 7,144,549 tons compared with 3,332,882 in 1913

22   *Chamber of Shipping Annual Report* (1923-4), 112

23   Ibid, 112

24   L. Jones, *Shipbuilding in Britain* (1957), 132

25   Lloyd's Annual Summary for 1930, op cit, 10, Table X

26   Ibid

27   E. Wilkinson, op cit, 129

28   L. Jones, op cit, 28

29   Figures from Lloyd's Annual Summary for 1930, op cit, 10, Table X

30   A. Hurd, *The Eclipse of British Sea Power* (1933), 26

31   A.C. Pigou, op cit, 83

32   By the middle of 1920 the British mercantile marine was only
      some 700,000 tons below the level of 1914 and over 400,000 tons
      down on 1913. *The Times* (20 September 1920), and *Chamber of
      Shipping Annual Report* (1921-2), 114-15, Table 19

33   *Fairplay* (25 March 1920), 1029

34   Ibid (25 March 1920), 1028

35   Ibid

36   Ibid. She experienced another memorable delay at the Bristol
      Channel on reloading

37   *Shipbuilding and Shipping Record* (22 April 1920), 540; *Shipping
      World* (20 August 1919), 166; *Fairplay* (25 March 1920),
      1028-30

38   The position in the Bristol Channel was serious beyond words.
      A. Hurd, 'Paralysis of Shipping', *Fortnightly Review*, 107 (April
      1920), 593

39   *Chamber of Shipping Annual Reports*

40   *The Times* (21 November 1919), and (6 January 1920); also
      Shipping World (11 February 1920), 129

41   *Chamber of Shipping Annual Reports*

42   *The Times Trade Supplement* (5 June 1920), 323

43   *Select Committee on National Expenditure, Fourth Report,*
      H of C Paper 150 (1920), para 32

44   *Fairplay* (2 September 1920), 699

45   *Shipbuilding and Shipping Record* (First Shipping Exhibition
      Number) (25 September 1919), 9

46   *Fairplay* (25 March 1920), 1029

47   *The Times* (28 June 1919)

48   *Shipbuilding and Shipping Record* (7 January 1920), 58

49   *The Times* (17 June 1919)

50   *The Times* (27 June 1919)

51   *The Times* (10 and 12 January 1920); see also *Shipbuilding and Shipping Record* (29 January 1920), 126

52   L.C. Money, *The Triumph of Nationalization* (1920), 154

53   *The Times* (8 March 1920)

54   The title of an article in *The Times* (23 February 1920) read 'Glut of Meat . . . Docks choked with Meat'

55   F.H. Coller, *A State Trading Adventure* (1925), 248

56   *The Grocer* (13 September 1919), 506-7, 509 and 519; see letters to *The Times* (9, 10 and 11 September 1919); cf L.C. Money, op cit, 151-2. According to F.H. Coller, op cit, 248, the Ministry had been letting bacon rot on the quays for years

57   *Shipping World* (24 September 1919), 257

58   *Board of Trade Journal* (18 March 1920), 422

59   *Shipbuilding and Shipping Record* (25 September 1919), 10

60   *Shipping World* (3 September 1919), 202

61   *Fairplay* (25 March 1920), 1029

62   *Shipbuilding and Shipping Record* (25 December 1919), 731; *Economist* (27 December 1919), 1180; A.W. Kirkaldy and A.D. Evans, *The History and Economics of Transport* (1924), 202. The Barry Roads suffered acutely from the shortage of railway trucks, for where 102 trucks were required only 2 daily could be provided. *Fairplay* (25 March 1920), 1029

63   This to some extent was mitigated by an increase in demurrage charges in January 1920 as a result of recommendations from the Rates Advisory Committee. *See Report of the Rates Advisory*

Committee — Recommendations as to Demurrage, Cd 526 (1920); *Railway Gazette* (2 January 1920), 8-9 and *H of C Deb*, cxxix (10 May 1920), Col 64

64 *Economist* (27 March 1920), 685

65 *Fairplay* (22 April 1920), 257

66 *Iron and Coal Trades Review* (15 September 1919), 303

67 *Fairplay* (25 March 1920), 1029-30

68 See *Report of the Rates Advisory Committee on Coastwise Shipping and Exceptional Rates*, Cd 1372 (1921)

69 This subsidy was continued until 30 June 1920, see A.C. Pigou, op cit, 81; *Shipping World* (25 June 1920), 625

70 See *Shipping World* (23 July 1919), 91. This unjust order, with some modifications, was actually renewed in December 1920. *Fairplay* (2 December 1920), 605-6

71 C.E. Fayle, op cit, 371

72 *Fairplay* (15 January 1920), 260

73 That is with regard to the freight market

74 D.H. Robertson, op cit, 116

75 A.C. Pigou, op cit, 80; C.E. Fayle, *Seaborne Trade*, Vol III (1924), 421, puts the percentage at 10 per cent for the first three months of 1919

76 We must of course remember that many freight rates were controlled during 1919. This, however, substantiates our argument even more so for it means that shipowners were not solely influenced by high free market rates but were acquiring or ordering tonnage to meet a 'paper' tonnage shortage in the controlled market

77 Cf *Fairplay* (11 March 1920), 834

78   To what extent shipping efficiency was impaired by congested ports abroad requires further investigation. There is, however, plenty of evidence to suggest that it was not an unimportant factor especially in the United States, cf supra, 175

79   The measures taken to relieve port congestion such as the use of motor lorries, the revival of coastal shipping services and the schemes of dock extension and enlargement of shed and ware-house accommodation at the ports, fall outside the scope of this essay

80   *Fairplay* (5 August 1920), 400-1

81   *The Times* (19 April 1920)

82   C.E. Fayle, *The War and the Shipping Industry*, 382

83   *Shipping World* (7 April 1920), 400

84   *Fairplay* (3 March 1921), 768

The virtually uncontrolled development of road transport in
the decade following the First World War was brought to an
abrupt halt in the early 1930s by the Road Traffic Act of
1930 and the Road and Rail Traffic Act of 1933. This legislation created a licensing system for both public passenger
transport and road haulage which was designed to control
entry into and regulate conditions in the separate branches of
the industry. The institution of control and its operation have
been criticised on several counts by various writers and quite
recently the whole system has been subject to considerable
modification. However, the intention here is to look more
closely at the working of the licensing process relating to
passenger transport in the 1930s to see what benefits it
produced and in the light of some of the main criticisms
expressed about it.

Local authorities had powers to regulate passenger transport undertakings under the Town Police (Clauses) Acts of
the nineteenth century but these were infrequently used and
even when they were the degree of control was often mini-
mal. The result was that the industry was left to develop
almost unhindered and during the 1920s, when motor transport got going in a big way, thousands of companies and
individuals set up in business to run bus and coach services.
The whole process of development was little short of chaotic.
Severe competition led to a great deal of duplication of
facilities, fare cutting and undesirable operating practices.
Though some large groups emerged the industry was
characterised by a proliferation of very small operators (often

the one-man-one-bus variety) with few business scruples. The practices adopted to gain traffic were not only unethical from a business point of view but they often constituted a source of inconvenience and danger to the public. Time and fare tables were conspicuous by their absence, while dangerous driving and badly maintained vehicles were common and provided much cause for anxiety. The Royal Commission on Transport (1928-31) expressed concern about the state of the industry and urged the introduction of a more up-to-date system of regulation. Before it had finished its deliberations the Road Traffic Act was on the Statute Book.

This Act divided the country into 13 Traffic Areas (11 for England and Wales and 2 for Scotland)[1] each of which was presided over by Traffic Commissioners. The latter were empowered to control, through a licensing system, the vehicles to be used, the services run and the conditions of employment. In other words, no public services could be operated without the consent of the Commissioners and all applications for licences were heard and disposed of at public sittings of the Traffic Courts.

Before any service could be operated the company or individual had to satisfy the Commissioners on several counts. Each vehicle used had to possess a certificate of fitness and these were only granted provided the vehicles passed a test of inspection carried out by a qualified examiner. Secondly, the operator or owner had to obtain a public service vehicle licence for each vehicle which could be withheld if it was considered that the person concerned was not fit to hold one. Thirdly, all drivers and conductors of public service vehicles had to obtain licences to prove their technical competence as transport personnel. All three licences were designed to protect the safety of the travelling public. The conditions attached were fairly stringent but they constituted a barrier to entry only insofar as the applicants could not satisfy the specifications laid down.

The more controversial feature of the legislation was the road service licence which could be used to regulate entry into the industry. Apart from contract work, each individual service had to be licensed. In considering applications for service licences the Commissioners were to pay particular regard to the suitability of the route, the extent to which it was adequately served, whether the proposed service was necessary in the public interest and the transport needs of the area as a whole. This latter requirement embraced the provision of adequate, suitable and efficient services including unremunerative services, and the coordination of all forms of transport. The Area Commissioners were also given wide powers to attach conditions to the licences such that fares should not be unreasonable nor fixed at a level likely to produce wasteful competition, that passengers were to be taken on and set down at recognised stopping places, and that copies of time and fare tables should be available for public inspection. The requirements attached could be varied at the Commissioners' discretion but the prime objective was to secure the safety and convenience of the public at large.

In short, therefore, the road passenger transport industry was rigidly controlled by the Act of 1930 and it was evident that the free-for-all competition of the previous decade would no longer be allowed to continue. Apart from the Thesiger Committee of 1953, which waxed almost lyrical about the system,[2] most commentators have been rather critical of the operation of the licensing system. Lacking any precedent to fall back upon the Commissioners from the start tended to base their judgements on three principles: priority, protection and public need; that is the existing operator was given priority over the new applicant and that once licensed an operator was afforded protection from competitive road services, while alternative transport operators were protected from road competition. Thus the question of public need, it is argued, was passed over in favour of the first two principles.[3] Furthermore, by restricting entry and protecting the existing operator it discouraged development and stifled enterprise within the industry and 'put a premium upon inefficiency by linking most operators in a pricing system based upon those with the highest costs'.[4] The large territorial bus companies, which tended to have the highest overhead costs, steadily expanded their fleets at the expense of the smaller independent concerns. This, it is alleged, meant the loss of some competitive thrust and led to a certain amount of inertia within the industry. Finally, the railways were unduly protected by the system from road competition and 'there was no sign of a determined counter-attack by the railways with services adapted to meet the growing competition'.[5]

While not wishing to deny that the legislation was far from perfect nor that existing operators were treated more favourably under the new system, it is the belief that the licensing procedure as applied in the 1930s brought the public more benefits than losses and that some of the alleged detrimental effects were either insubstantial or non-existent.

There can be little doubt that in terms of the general nature of service facilities the public benefited considerably from inspection and control exercised by the Traffic Commissioners. In their early reports all the Area Commissioners reported upon the greater reliability of passenger transport facilities especially as regards time-keeping and the regularity of services. There was also a marked improvement in the standard of equipment and maintenance of public service vehicles generally, especially among small operators. Vehicles were no longer worked to a standstill before repair and 'dirty interiors, unhealthy fumes, bad springing and noisy machinery, are now of rare occurrence in Public Service Vehicles, while the safety of the Public is increased by constant supervision of the maintenance of steering, brake gear, and general improvement'.[6] Vehicle inspection was very rigorous indeed and some operators known for their poor facilities were obliged to have their vehicles tested several times before the Commissioners were satisfied with their condition.[7] Many small operators lacked proper facilities for carrying out maintenance work with the result that in some cases the condition of their vehicles was nothing short of appalling.[8] The comfort and cleanliness of the interiors was of no lesser concern than the mechanical fitness of the vehicles. A number of the Area Commissioners even went so far as to impress upon operators the need for a daily disinfection of their vehicles, a practice which is no doubt absent from routine operations nowadays.

But perhaps the greatest benefit arose from the improvement in the standard of conduct of road service operators. Before the Act unbridled competition had led to chaotic conditions in many parts of the country. Many services were run irregularly with no proper time-schedules or fare specifications and there was virtually no attempt at coordination and cooperation among operators. In an effort to attract custom some operators adopted such dubious practices as 'chasing', 'hanging back' and running only at peak hours or on special occasions, thereby creaming the best traffic off the road. This intensive form of competition was not only unduly wasteful in terms of resources but it also constituted a serious threat to public safety.[9] One of the worst areas was in the Potteries where before 1930 some 90 omnibuses had been licensed by Stoke-upon-Trent Council to run on the main route 7 miles long through the 5 towns of the Potteries, Longton, Stoke, Hanley, Burslem and Tunstall. The vehicles were owned by 25 different companies which were organised into two rival groups, the Association and the Alliance. The result was anything but a public service as the West Midland Commissioners described in their first report:

> No time-table existed, and the vehicles shuttled up and down in a continuous game of leap-frog, with an average frequency of less than a minute at peak times. Coupons giving cheap fares all day long were instituted by the Association and adopted subsequently by the Alliance. As each group only accepted its own coupons, the habit of a vehicle of one group running close to the vehicle of another group was acquired in order to cater for its coupon holders. Competition between individual omnibuses accordingly became general, and convictions of both drivers and conductors for dangerous driving or obstruction were frequent.[10]

The advent of control brought a considerable measure of improvement. Time-table working, with one minute frequencies at peak times and two minutes during the rest of the day, was established, service and fare schedules were coordinated and the coupons of either group were accepted on any vehicle.

The situation in the Potteries was by no means unique. Most regions experienced the same sort of practices and it was often the small concerns which were responsible for the unsavoury aspects of the industry. In the Western Traffic Area, for example, a large number of small independent companies had never operated to a regular time-table, and even where time-tabling did exist it was usually arranged to suit the convenience of the operators and not the public.[11] Once control was instituted many of the worst practices quickly disappeared. Cut-throat competition of a type detrimental to the public interest was banned and service schedules were improved by coordinating time and fare tables. In the first year of the Act some 600 time and fare tables were coordinated in the East Midlands Area alone, to the benefit of both the public and operators alike. One operator, for instance, found that after time-table coordination he required only 3 vehicles instead of 4 to perform his services and that his aggregate receipts rose by 30 per cent.[12]

The sense of protection afforded by the licensing system helped to improve relationships among operators during the 1930s with the result that they were much more willing to assist each other in terms of sharing out peak traffic, loaning vehicles and coordinating services. Often the intervention of the Traffic Commissioners brought together a number of rival operators with a view to rationalising their facilities and providing a greater measure of coordination.[13] Working agreements and coordination schemes between private operators and the local authorities and the railways were certainly much more in evidence than in the 1920s, a situation which was facilitated by the greater involvement of the railways in road transport. The Commissioners' reports abound with examples of such schemes.[14] The process was patchy, it is true, but in some areas, notably Lancashire, the coordination of road/ rail facilities made considerable headway in the 1930s.[15]

But if, generally speaking, the public got a better deal in terms of the quality of services offered was this at the expense of consumer choice and the amount of capacity supplied? We know, for instance, that entry into the industry was difficult to secure, that existing operators, especially the municipal authorities, were protected, that many small operators disappeared as the large territorial groups took over their services, and that the Commissioners were anxious to cut out wasteful competition which in some cases meant a reduction of capacity on offer. On the surface it could be argued that consumers of public transport had less choice than previously and that the licensing system tended to restrict rather than encourage the growth of new services.

The statistics of the industry confirm some of these points but they do not offer conclusive proof that the public was adversely affected by such developments. Table 1 *(see page 194)* shows that the number of small concerns (under 50 vehicles) declined sharply between 1931 and 1937 so that their share of the total number of vehicles fell from 44.5 to just over 32 per cent. By contrast, firms with 100 vehicles or more increased their share of the market quite substantially, though a good part of this can be accounted for by the formation of the London Passenger Transport Board in 1933. The data in Table 2 *(see pages 195-7)* suggest that local authorities accounted for most of the growth in passenger transport services after 1931 with the result that their share of the market had increased appreciably by 1937. Private operators experienced only a modest increase, mostly in stage and contract work, the last of which was not controlled by the Traffic Commissioners.

However, none of these figures provides conclusive proof that the operation of the licensing system worked to the detriment of the public. Though local authority transport undertakings were accorded a degree of protection from outside competition within their boundaries their traffic

TABLE 1: *Number of Operators of Public Service Vehicles*

Number of vehicles owned by each	Number of operators		Number of vehicles owned		% of total number of vehicles	
	31 Dec 1931	31 Dec 1937	1931	1937	1931	1937
1-4	5,269	3,763	9,369	7,110	20.27	14.34
5-49	1,052	885	11,200	8,900	24.22	17.95
49-99	53	52	3,732	3,534	8.07	7.13
100 and over	60	77	21,929	30,030	47.44	60.58
Total	6,434	4,798[1]	46,230	49,574		

[1] The total includes 21 concerns owning no vehicles as at 31 December 1937

Source: *Seventh Annual Reports of the Traffic Commissioners, 1937-8*

growth cannot be attributed simply to that measure of protection. Most municipalities were abandoning tramway routes
rapidly in the 1930s so that part of the growth came from the
switch to omnibuses; between 1931 and 1939 some 39 local
authorities dispensed with trams and by the latter date over
half the local transport authorities had given them up.
Moreover, outside one or two large cities most of the remaining tramway systems had only one or two routes left.[16] A
second source of growth came from the rapid suburban development of this period which encouraged the extension of
municipal transport networks over a wider area. Moreover,
municipal transport catered largely for the lower-income, non-
car-owning sector of the population which provided another
source of expansion.

The degree of protection afforded local authority operators
varied from area to area though there is little doubt that it
existed. But it is difficult to argue that protection worked
against the public interest. The data in Table 2 *(on pp 195-7)*
scarcely suggest that they were prevented from meeting the
expanding demand for transport within the cities and, apart
from peak periods, there is little evidence that there was a

TABLE 2
Traffic Statistics of Public Service Vehicles in Great Britain 1932-7

| | 1932 | | |
	Local Authorities	Other Operators	Total
Operators at end of period	100	6,207	6,307
Vehicles at end of period	5,622	40,836	46,458
% of total	12.10	87.90	100.00
Total seating capacity (mn)	0.23	1.24	1.47
% of total	15.42	84.58	100.00
Average seating capacity	40.32	30.45	31.65
Passenger Journeys (mn)			
Stage	1,194.8	4,068.3	5,263.1
Express	0.1	19.2	19.3
Excursions and tours	0.1	15.1	15.2
Contract	4.5	42.8	47.3
All Services	1,199.5	4,145.4	5,344.9
% of total	22.44	77.56	100.00
Vehicle Miles (000s)			
Stage	172,552	1,002,451	1,135,003
Express	42	76,644	76,686
Excursions and tours	69	26,545	26,614
Contract	822	44,597	45,419
All Services	173,484	1,150,237	1,323,721
% of total	13.10	86.90	100.00

continued on next page

TABLE 2
(continued)

1934

	Local Authorities	LPTB	Other Operators	Total
Operators at end of period	96	1	5,649	5,746
Vehicles at end of period	6,160	6,234	33,401	45,795
% of total	13.45	13.61	72.94	100.00
Total seating capacity (mn)	0.26	0.30	0.94	1.46
% of total	17.37	19.84	62.79	100.00
Average seating capacity	42.23	47.68	28.16	32.71
Passenger Journeys (mn)				
Stage	1,408.4	2,048.7	2,178.7	5,635.8
Express	0.1	0.4	14.5	15.1
Excursions and tours	0.2		17.2	17.3
Contract	5.1	1.0	47.8	53.9
All Services	1,413.8	2,050.1	2,258.2	5,722.1
% of total	24.71	35.83	39.46	100.00
Vehicle Miles (000s)				
Stage	195,450	271,270	735,141	1,201,861
Express	45	754	61,256	62,055
Excursions and tours	63		30,186	30,248
Contract	981	497	50,195	51,674
All Services	196,540	272,521	876,778	1,345,839
% of total	14.60	20.25	65.15	100.00

continued on next page

TABLE 2
(*continued*)

1937

	Local Authorities	LPTB	Other Operators	Total
Operators at end of period	95	1	4,702	4,798
Vehicles at end of period	8,431	6,305	34,838	49,574
% of total	17.01	12.72	70.27	100.00
Total seating capacity (mn)	0.39	0.31	1.03	1.74
% of total	22.39	18.05	59.56	100.00
Average seating capacity	46.14	49.75	29.70	35.05
Passenger Journeys (mn)				
Stage	2,032.0	2,003.0	2,520.5	6,555.6
Express	0.2	0.1	17.7	18.0
Excursions and tours	0.2	0.01	19.3	19.5
Contract	7.2	1.1	63.1	71.4
All Services	2,039.6	2,004.3	2,620.6	6,664.5
% of total	30.60	30.08	39.32	100.00
Vehicle Miles (000s)				
Stage	261,562	269,736	756,935	1,297,233
Express	75	149	58,057	58,281
Excursions and tours	85	31	33,745	33,861
Contract	1,362	505	70,334	72,202
All Services	263,085	270,420	928,071	1,461,576
% of total	18.0	18.50	63.50	100.00

Source: *Seventh Annual Reports of the Traffic Commissioners, 1937-8*,
Appendix II

shortage of capacity. Moreover, average fares per passenger journey on local authority undertakings (stage services) declined continuously between 1932 and 1937, and by slightly more than the decline in average fares charged by other operators. In these circumstances there would seem little point to the criticism about the evils of protection. If anything the public probably gained from protection since a more competitive climate would merely have served to cream traffic off the more profitable city routes with the result that local authorities would have been less inclined to maintain 'public' services on some of the less remunerative routes. The issue of cross subsidisation is admittedly a debatable one, but given the acceptance of public need on routes which by their nature could not be self-supporting then cross subsidisation by a monopoly supplier in the form of a local authority would seem to be the best answer to the problem. It is difficult to conceive that the public would have secured a better deal had greater competition been allowed on urban routes.

As for the private sector the trends are quite clear. Many small companies disappeared, the vehicle fleet remained fairly static and there was only a modest growth in the volume of traffic carried. Here there are two points to take into consideration. Private operators tended to concentrate their activities outside large towns (with longer hauls on average than those of municipal operators) and often they catered for the wealthier sections of the community. It was here that the rate of car ownership was growing rapidly and this would tend to limit the scope for further sustained expansion. Indeed, it is quite probable that on some routes traffic growth was beginning to peak out during the 1930s, a not unreasonable assumption in view of the fact that soon after the Second World War public service traffic finally peaked out altogether.[17] It is difficult to believe that the very slow growth in traffic carried by private operators during this period could have been caused simply by capacity restriction arising from the licensing system since this would imply either that some good traffic routes were left unserviced which was not the case, or that vehicle load factors were high from the start which seems unlikely. Secondly, some slowing down in growth, particularly in terms of the number of vehicles and vehicle-miles run, was inevitable following the severe rationalisation of services after the hectic and haphazard growth of the previous decade. The licensing system certainly facilitated this process but it is quite clear that it would have occurred in any case since the growth of services in the 1920s had produced an excessive duplication of facilities many of which were unremunerative. Many operators were unable to maintain regular services and vehicles often ran light; as the Metropolitan Commissioner observed in his second report: 'It was . . . a frequent occurrence for operators to become insolvent as a result of excessive competition.'[18]

It is more than likely therefore that the very slow growth in the number of vehicles owned and the number of vehicle-miles performed by the private sector can be explained in terms of the process of rationalisation, which entailed economies in route servicing and the elimination of many unprofitable services, often as a result of the absorption of small undertakings by the larger groups. This was the logical outcome after a decade of unrestricted, haphazard and often ill-conceived development which had resulted in far too much dead capacity. The Traffic Commissioners were quite justified in assisting the process given the uneconomic nature of much mileage. In East Anglia alone, for example, some 400,000 vehicle-miles per annum were saved by reducing winter express services in 1935-6 because of limited patronage.[19] Similarly, long distance services from the Northern Traffic Area to Scotland, Newcastle and London were rationalised by amalgamation and coordination and as a result considerable economies were effected.[20] One operator in the North Western Traffic Area in applications affecting 98 services showed a saving of 40,000 vehicle-miles per week (only two objections were lodged), while another operator had been able to reduce his vehicle fleet by 12 without detriment to the public.[21] In many cases it was merely a question of reducing the

frequency of services rather than eliminating them altogether.
On some routes in the West Riding, for example, stage carriage
services were passing every three minutes when a 10 minute
service would have amply sufficed.[22] Here and in many other
similar situations drastic reductions in service frequency were
necessary.

The rationalisation process obviously left the public with
less choice than previously though it was still often considerable.[23] But on economic grounds it could easily be defended
and travellers certainly had no right to expect operators to
run services at a loss, though many continued to do so. As
the South Eastern Commissioners remarked: 'The existence
of competition, and to a certain extent, wasteful services in
the past had spoilt them, and they could not expect such a
state of affairs to continue indefinitely.'[24] The argument that
free competition should have been allowed to prevail so that
small operators, with their lower overheads, could provide
services in the sparsely populated areas is vitiated by the fact
that many firms had already gone to the wall in the process.
Larger firms were much better placed to cross subsidise some
of the less trafficked routes; but had there been more competition on the profitable routes they would not have been
able to do this, or else fares on those routes least subject to
competition would have had to be raised. Either way the
public taken as a whole would have lost out on the deal and
hence there are strong grounds for suggesting that more
competition would have entailed worse services in aggregate.

In any case, it is a mistake to imagine that the Commissioners
were bent on reducing services at all costs irrespective of
public needs. In fact, if anything, the Commissioners appear
to have leaned over backwards to ensure that the public was
not adversely affected by rationalisation and amalgamation,
and it could be argued that they pandered too much to
individual demands which meant the retention of some uneconomic services. Though the South Eastern Commissioners
complained about the unreasonable expectations of the
public they proceeded to refuse Maidstone & District

Motor Services permission to withdraw an unprofitable stage
service in the sparsely populated district of Heathfield,
Sussex,[25] because it would have caused inconvenience to a
limited number of inhabitants.[26] A careful reading of the
Commissioners' reports hardly suggests that they placed
priority and protection before public need. The Northern
Commissioners, for example, were very concerned about the
adequacy of services following rationalisation measures and
they insisted that 'mileage should be eliminated only by a
gradual process and then not until it has been ascertained by
experience and careful study of the needs of the area served,
to what extent the service can be reduced without inconvenience
to the travelling public, whose needs must be the first
consideration'.[27] The Metropolitan Commissioner stated from
the outset that his policy was to pursue 'a definite course
with a simple aim, that of the convenience of the travelling
public and welfare of the transport industry . . . '[28]

Nor did the Traffic Commissioners favour large operators
at the expense of the small independents. Indeed, most of
them deplored the passing of the small independent concerns
which they felt had a useful part to play. The Southern Commissioners made a point of trying to protect the small operator
wherever possible though often it had been necessary to
restrict their activities because of the poor condition of their
vehicles and the running of unremunerative services.[29]
Similarly, the South Wales Commissioners had misgivings
about the decline of the one-man business since they had
pioneered many local services and had the personal touch
which many of the larger operators lacked.[30] The Yorkshire
Commissioners also stated quite categorically that 'It has been
our duty, which we have attempted to carry out to the best
of our abilities, jealously to protect the rights of the "small"
operator against the larger undertakings and, at the same time,
to give our decisions without fear or favour'.[31] Nevertheless,
whatever regrets might be expressed, the disappearance of
the small operator by amalgamation often led to an improvement in service, with better vehicles and more reasonable fares

than would otherwise have been the case.[32] Moreover, the
Commissioners were fully aware that the activities of the
large combines might need to be kept in check. The Northern
Commissioners in particular expressed themselves forcibly on
this matter in their report for 1936-7: 'If any road transport
combine made the interests of their shareholders paramount,
to the detriment of the travelling public, the Commissioners
would consider that to that extent the operators concerned,
however financially prosperous they might be, were falling
short of the serious responsibility laid upon them as providers
of an essential public utility.'[33]

Though route protection or monopoly service rights
(especially in the case of local authorities) were often granted,
the Commissioners made it plain that such protection from
competition could not be expected to persist indefinitely if
it was shown to be detrimental to the public interest.[34] The
number of new services and routes opened may have been
small compared with the 1920s but this was only because
most areas with any real traffic prospects had already been
tapped in the previous decade. And as the West Midland
Commissioners observed: 'The highly unremunerative figures
which are produced when it is desired to withdraw some of
these services (that is newly licensed services), subsequently
suggest that there can be no services lacking where there is
a real public need.'[35] There can be no doubt either that the
Commissioners were quite prepared to grant licences for new
services when genuine need arose, especially for those serving
new housing or trading estates even though these might not
at first prove profitable.[36] There was, of course, no lack of
applications to start new services, and though many of them
were turned down after careful vetting (often because they
were not viable or because the operators could not satisfy the
requirements relating to safety etc) the Commissioners were
often prepared to license new services on an experimental
basis. The comments of the South Wales Commissioners leave
little doubt as to their willingness in this respect; referring
to new licences issued during 1937-8 the Commissioners

explained that:

> In some cases such services are experimental and have been
> commenced by enterprising operators in the hope that they
> will attract such traffic as will justify their continuance as
> regular and permanent services. There can be no doubt that
> facilities often create traffic and that need for new services can
> only be demonstrated by experience. We are always anxious to
> encourage the introduction of new services . . . [for which] we
> are prepared to grant a road service licence for an experimental
> period of one year so that the proposed route may be tested.
> The time has now arrived when it can be said that a public road
> service is in operation on practically every road in the Area
> which is suitable for such a service. There is no doubt that
> wherever roads are suitable operators are willing to provide
> new services and that the introduction of new services has the
> effect of making more travel minded the inhabitants of the
> districts which they serve.[37]

Finally, as regards the treatment accorded to rival transport
operators, mainly the railways in this instance, there is little
firm evidence to suggest that the Commissioners protected
them unduly. Indeed, though the railways lodged many pro-
tests to road service applications, the indications are that the
Traffic Commissioners tended to favour road operators rather
than the reverse.[38] For example, in 1934 the railways wanted
the existing duplication of services to be restricted between
Glasgow and Aberdeen and Glasgow and Lancashire but the
Commissioners decided to make no change in the powers to
operate extra vehicle journeys on these routes.[39] As the
railways acquired greater interests in road transport undertakings their opposition tended to dwindle and during the
course of the 1930s there was a much greater inclination,
compared with the previous decade, on the part of road and
rail operators to enter into agreements to coordinate their
respective services both on long distance routes and within
towns.[40] Thus there is little reason to suppose that the
railways were sheltered excessively from road competition,
for if they had been then their passenger traffic figures

would have been much better than they actually were. Between 1929 and 1935 passenger miles travelled by rail were virtually static and thereafter they increased only slowly to reach a level not much higher than in 1920. Finally, the suggestion that protection led to inertia on the part of the railways lacks any real substance. No doubt they could have been more enterprising but the fact remains that after the introduction of road licensing they showed more initiative, both as regards fares and facilities, than at any time since the war. This was especially true of their medium- and long-distance services which were the ones most susceptible to road competition.[41]

The Road Traffic Act of 1930 was not a model piece of legislation by any means but then very few legislative Acts are. But some form of control over the road transport industry was necessary by the 1930s to protect the public interest. Many of the criticisms expressed about the operation of the licensing system have not been based on very firm evidence and, as we have shown, they cannot readily be substantiated. A careful reading of the Commissioners' reports, for instance, shows that the needs of the public were given much greater priority than the critics have been willing to concede. It is the belief that the licensing system as implemented by the Traffic Commissioners did more good than harm so that on balance the public gained from control. Indeed, it might be argued that after the chaotic conditions of the 1920s any form of control would have been an improvement.

NOTES

1   Later reduced to 10 for England and Wales

2   Ministry of Transport and Civil Aviation, *Report of the Committee on the Licensing of Road Passenger Services* (HMSO, 1953)

3   D.N. Chester, *Public Control of Road Passenger Transport* (1936); J. Hibbs, *Transport for Passengers* (1971)

4   Hibbs, op cit, 49

5   Ibid, 51

6   *Report of the Traffic Commissioners: Southern Traffic Area*
     (1932-3), 82

7   Ibid, *Yorkshire Traffic Area* (1931-2), 20

8   Ibid, *Western Traffic Area* (1931-2), 62

9   Ibid, *Northern Scotland Traffic Area* (1931-2), 95-6

10   Ibid, *West Midland Traffic Area* (1931-2), 34-5

11   Ibid, *Western Traffic Area* (1931-2), 62

12   Ibid, *East Midland Traffic Area* (1931-2), 43

13   Ibid, *Metropolitan Traffic Area* (1932-3), 90

14   For examples see *East Midland Traffic Area* (1932-3), 59;
     Yorkshire Traffic Area (1934-5), 25-7

15   *Transport in Lancashire.* Papers and Proceedings at a Conference
     held 5 July 1938 in Manchester (1938), 24; G.M. Higgins and
     W.J. MacKenzie, 'The Coordination of Public Passenger Transport
     in South-East Lancashire', *The Manchester School* (1954)

16   J. Sleeman, 'The Rise and Decline of Municipal Transport',
     Scottish Journal of Political Economy, 9 (1962), 52-3

17   The sharp rise in traffic during and shortly after the war was a
     purely temporary phenomenon occasioned by the severe restric-
     tions on private motoring

18   *Metropolitan Traffic Area* (1932-3), 90

19   *Eastern Traffic Area* (1935-6), 56

20   *Northern Traffic Area* (1934-5), 17

21   *North Western Traffic Area* (1932-3), 41

22   *Yorkshire Traffic Area* (1931-2), 21, and (1932-3), 34

23   For example, the West Midland Commissioners reduced the
      Midland Red Company's 6 services on the London-Birmingham
      route to 3, but passengers still had a choice of some 20 other road
      services to and from London by day in winter, and m re in
      summer, plus 4 services in the small hours of the morn. ng. In
      addition, of course, there were 12 trains a day in each direction.
      West Midland Traffic Area (1931-2), 40

24   *South Eastern Traffic Area* (1936-7), 74

25   The service, along with others, had been acquired from a small
      operator in 1935

26   *South Eastern Traffic Area* (1936-7), 74

27   *Northern Traffic Area* (1934-5), 16

28   *Metropolitan Traffic Area* (1932-3), 90

29   *Southern Traffic Area* (1931-2), 71

30   *South Wales Traffic Area* (1934-5), 61

31   *Yorkshire Traffic Area* (1931-2), 25

32   *Southern Scotland Traffic Area* (1935-6), 96

33   *Northern Traffic Area* (1936-7), 14

34   *North Western Traffic Area* (1936-7), 26-7

35   *West Midland Traffic Area* (1933-4), 41

36   *East Midland Traffic Area* (1937-8), 49; *South Wales Traffic
      Area* (1936-7), 59

37   *South Wales Traffic Area* (1937-8), 64

38   *West Midland Traffic Area* (1934-5), 42-3

39   *Southern Scotland Traffic Area* (1934-5), 93

40 See *North Western Traffic Area* (1932-3), 42-3; *West Midland Traffic Area* (1932-3), 51

41 A point discussed more fully in D.H. Aldcroft, *British Railways in Transition* (1968), 80-1

9   Britain's Internal Airways: The Pioneer Stage of the 1930s

First published in Business History, *6 (1964)*

During the 1920s Britain's external air services developed rapidly particularly from 1924 onwards when Imperial Airways, the Government's 'chosen instrument', was given a monopoly of subsidised operations. In contrast air services within Great Britain failed to 'get off the ground' and for most of the period regular internal air services were virtually non-existent. In the following decade, however, this section of the industry was favoured with greater success. A number of new independent companies appeared on the scene and by the outbreak of the Second World War they had managed to establish a network of commercial air services within the country. Unfortunately the efforts of these pioneers were unaccompanied by financial reward, for none of the companies made any profits. When writing this paper the chief aim in mind has been to throw some light upon the difficulties which the operators faced in their pioneering days. Although the content of the essay is largely historical it is hoped that, in view of the problems regarding the present optimum structure of the industry, its implications will have more than a historical significance.

I

There are several obvious reasons why internal civil aviation proved to be a non-starter in the 1920s. In the first place, ground organisation and navigational aids were far from adequate for the performance of such services. Aerodromes were conspicuous by their absence and until 1922 Croydon was the only aerodrome from which regular passenger services

operated.[1] A large number of strategically sited landing
places is essential of course before proper internal air services
can be established and this point requires no further elabor-
ation. In addition, the shortage of experienced pilots, the
adverse climatic conditions in Britain and the rather uninter-
ested attitude of the British public towards flying all helped
to retard development. These factors apart, however, it is
unlikely that the poor performance and high costs of operation of the early commercial aircraft would have provided
a strong enough inducement to establish air services in a
country in which distances were short and where competition
of a highly developed surface transport system had to be
faced. In the case of Britain the features of internal air transport are somewhat different from those of external operations.
As early as 1929 Fenelon observed[2] that air transport shows
to the greatest advantage when (a) long distances are involved
(b) ground transport is hindered by geographical factors (c)
speed is essential and (d) sea crossings are involved. Most of
these factors operated on international routes but in Britain
only the last was really important and it is significant that
many of the internal airline operators of the 1930s, in fact
the majority of them at one stage, were flying partly over
water. In other words, internal flying only really became
attractive when it could offer appreciable savings in time over
surface transport. In practice, as was discovered later, this
was only possible on relatively long journeys with high-speed
aircraft, and on the more difficult routes. Thus until the
technical performance of British aircraft was improved internal
aviation could not hope to exploit fully its greatest asset.

In the later 1920s and early 1930s conditions became
sufficiently favourable to permit the establishment of regular
internal air services. With the development of international
aviation many of the initial difficulties were being solved and
flying was becoming more popular as the public's distrust of
the new form of transport diminished. Another favourable
factor was the rapid increase in the number of aerodromes
particularly after 1928 when the municipal authorities began

their building programmes. Between 1929 and 1935 the number of aerodromes doubled and of the total of 95 in the latter year almost one-third belonged to local authorities. In addition, the rapid progress in aircraft technology made possible the construction of faster, safer and much more economical machines which were more suitable for internal services.[3] Thus whereas for most of the 1920s the average cruising speed was 100mph or below, by the beginning of 1934 airliners attaining cruising speeds varying from 140 to 200mph were available.[4] At the same time navigational aids under the direction of the Air Ministry improved albeit somewhat slowly. In 1933, for example, the only wireless stations available, other than those serving continental routes, were those of Manchester and Renfrew, of which the former alone communicated with aircraft. Early in 1934 the Air Ministry launched a plan for the provision of a network of radio stations to serve internal traffic and by the end of 1936 the number of wireless stations in the UK providing communication with aircraft was 21. Finally in 1934 the Post Office declared its willingness to utilise internal air services for the carriage of mail.

It is not surprising therefore, that from 1931 onwards several new companies were formed to establish internal air services. One of the first was that of Hillman Airways which began a summer service between Romford and Clacton in 1932 and in the following year extended its operations to Paris. Other companies soon followed and among the most important creations were Blackpool and West Coast Services, Eastern Air Services, Jersey Airways, Spartan Airlines (London to Cowes), Northern and Scottish Airways and Highland Airways. The last of these undertakings secured the first internal mail contract from the Post Office (May 1934) for its service between Inverness and the Orkney Islands. No additional charge was made for the service and the Post Office announced that in future it would be willing to use for the carriage of first class mail, without extra surcharge to the public, any regular internal service which was capable of

giving an acceleration in delivery. New companies continued
to be formed in 1934 and 1935 but the most important event
was the penetration of the railways into air transport. The
railways had acquired powers in 1929 to operate aircraft but
did not attempt to enter the field until air transport looked
like threatening their own interests. In the spring of 1933 the
first experimental railway air service between Cardiff and
Plymouth was inaugurated by Imperial Airways on behalf of
the Great Western Railway. In March of the following year
Railway Air Services was formed with a capital of £50,000
for the purpose of providing such internal air services as the
four British railway companies might require. The new company quickly established services on five important routes
which at first were operated on their behalf by Imperial
Airways.[5]

Thus by the middle of the 1930s a network of internal
air services had been established in Great Britain. In 1935
there were nearly a score of companies operating some 76
services in all. All the major town centres in Great Britain
were provided with air services and many of the islands around
the coast had been linked to the mainland by air. Miles flown
and passengers carried increased from 28,396 and 3,260
respectively in 1932 to 3,463,000 and 158,000 in 1936 and
in the latter year freight and mail shipments amounted to
nearly 1,200 tons. The scope for the further extension of
services was already becoming limited, however. In fact,
between 1935 and 1936, route mileage operated actually fell,
and though it rose again in subsequent years it never recovered
to its former level. After 1936 total miles flown and passengers
carried levelled off and remained more or less stationary
(see Table 1, page 212).

II

Despite the fairly rapid increase in traffic, internal aviation
was far from being a profitable venture; indeed internal air
services were almost certainly less profitable than external
ones though of course the former were not subsidised. The

TABLE 1
Air Services in Great Britain 1932-8

Year	Route Mileage	Miles Flown	Passengers Carried	Tons of Freight & Mail Carried	Number of Companies	Services Operated
1932	na	28,396	3,260	—	5	na
1933	1,220	442,100	22,017	13.7	13	18
1934	3,265	1,559,000	72,441	402	15	34
1935	5,810	3,037,000	121,559	885	19	76
1936	5,000	3,463,000	158,000	1,200	16	54
1937	4,500	3,300,000	161,500	1,300	14	na
1938	5,300	3,267,000	147,500	1,200	16	na

Source: *Report on Civil Aviation*, Cd 5351 (1937), and *Reports on the Progress of Civil Aviation* (HMSO annually)

Maybury Committee stated that most companies were making losses which, in the case of one company in 1934, amounted to £44,000.[6] In fact, no single airline operating within Great Britain ever made a profit during the period in question, and if the results of Railways Air Services are anything to go by the deficits incurred tended to increase rather than diminish. The total losses of the company increased from £14,541 in 1934 to £43,196 in 1935 and to £51,468 in 1937, and in most years the company was losing around 80 per cent of its subscribed capital. It has been estimated that the private companies (other than Imperial Airways) which operated between 1924 and 1939 earned a revenue of £1,721,700 and incurred an expenditure of £3,231,000 leaving a net deficit of £1,509,300.[7]

The financial insolvency of the internal airline operators should occasion no great surprise in view of the experience of the pioneer companies a decade before in the international field.[8] What is surprising is the fact that the companies kept going at all in the face of such adverse financial results. Although conditions were improving in the 1930s it is quite evident that they never became sufficiently favourable to allow profitable operation. A discussion of some of the major difficulties which internal operators encountered will enable the reader to appreciate their problems more easily.

Contrary to original expectations the companies derived the bulk of their revenue from carrying passengers. In a way this was unfortunate, since this type of traffic fluctuated sharply and tended to be concentrated in the summer months and in the day-time, though this was largely because the airlines were often unable to provide a transport service acceptable to the public during the winter months or at night. On the other hand, operators found difficulty in maintaining continuous services because of the adverse climatic conditions, the inadequacy of many aerodromes and the lack of navigational facilities. Most of the aerodromes, particularly the municipal ones, had defects of some sort; they were either too small, had poor surfaces or lacked proper equipment to facilitate flying at night or in bad conditions. By the end of 1938 only 3 of the 100 or more civil aerodromes possessed equipment for assisting landings in bad visibility (a not infrequent occurrence in this country), only one of which, Liverpool, was available solely for the benefit of internal traffic. Moreover, in view of the fact that very few aerodromes were fully equipped for night flying it is not surprising to find that the first night air service in Britain did not begin until October 1938. As one observer remarked: 'Nobody will fly at night because there are no facilities and nobody will put up any facilities because there is no flying at night'. It could of course be argued that the companies should have provided their own facilities and in so far as they failed to do so they had only themselves to blame. Nevertheless the fact remains that given such conditions it was practically impossible to maintain punctual, all-weather day and night services. In 1935 for example less than one-ninth of the services were operated without any break at all. Regularity tended to decrease further north, especially in winter when only about 60 per cent of the scheduled flights were carried out. It follows therefore that the fixed equipment of the airline companies was very much under-utilised. Most operators found it difficult to employ their aircraft for more than about 600 hours per annum despite the fact that to ensure profitable operations it was necessary to use them for at least double that length of time. In 1935 it was estimated that aircraft on internal routes were grounded for about 90 per cent of the time and that a 14-seater aircraft standing idle cost its operator roughly 10s per hour.[10] Moreover, the load factors of most internal airlines were very low indeed even in the peak period. The optimum or break-even load factor was probably in the region of 100 per cent but few companies managed to exceed even 50 per cent. One company recorded a load factor of 30 per cent in 1935 and in July of that year 5 companies recorded load factors as low as 20 per cent. The overall average load factor of the private operating companies (including British Airways) between 1924 and 1939 was only 35 per cent compared with 68 per cent for Imperial Airways, and even this did not enable the latter to break even.[11] Thus the amount of traffic, when averaged throughout the year, was spread very thinly and the revenue derived from it had to meet not only current operating costs but also bear the burden of heavy fixed charges[12] on equipment which for much of the time remained idle. The resulting high fares charged naturally tended to discourage traffic which in turn made it difficult to maintain load factors. Passenger fares ranged from 3d to 10d per mile compared with just over 1d by rail and slightly less by road transport. Nor were the airlines able to offer any appreciable percentage reductions on return fares since 'the high operating cost of aircraft would seem to militate against any attempt to establish single and return fares upon a basis comparable to the older forms of transport, at least on internal services'.[13]

Price was not the only factor which deterred people from going by air. Air travel was often inferior in speed, comfort and frequency of service compared to that of rail. It is true that a marked saving of time was shown on stages serving outlying parts of Britain and on those crossing water though it is doubtful whether the time saved was always worth the additional expense involved. On the other hand, air services which competed with efficient railway services were slower than the train on stages of a little over 100 miles and saved about one and a half hours on stages of nearly 200 miles. In practice most of the stages were much shorter than this — averaging around 60 to 80 miles — and on many of them the speed and frequency of train services was better. Even on routes which did not cross water and where the average speed of trains was less than 30mph air stages of under 50 miles were slower than the fastest train whilst air stages of about 100 miles showed a saving of approximately one hour.[14] However, the frequency of train services was six times higher than that of air services. The Maybury Committee found that the saving in time by air on the London-Liverpool run (180 miles) was a mere 45 minutes and even on the London-Glasgow journey (417 miles) the saving only amounted to just over two hours. In contrast it was 17 minutes faster by rail on the London-Birmingham route (101 miles). In other words there was a limit to the extent to which air transport could be substituted for rail.[15] On the longest and most difficult routes (particularly those involving a water crossing) the possibilities of substitution were greatest but the potential traffic thinnest; traffic was heaviest on intermediate stages between large town areas but here surface transport was very efficient and air transport least competitive. The position was summed up neatly by the Maybury Committee:[16]

> Out of the total traffic offering between two points, only a small proportion will demand the higher speed which air travel can offer or be able to bear its cost. That proportion is likely to be highest between those centres where population is greatest, but it is precisely between those centres that facilities offered by surface transport are already highly developed.
> Over short distances where surface communications are fast and frequent, an airline can offer little saving in time. On cross-country journeys where the airline could offer greater advantages in time, no strong demand for fast travel seems to

exist, if we may judge from the frequency and speed of
surface facilities and perhaps the paucity of traffic is inherent
in the present conditions.

The airline companies would probably have fared better
had they been able to carry more freight and mail since this
type of traffic is less subject to fluctuations. Unfortunately
their ability to do so was limited. The aircraft used were not
designed to carry large freight loads and, in any case, surface
transport was even more competitive in this field than on the
passenger side. Passenger traffic continued therefore to bulk
large and only urgent freight of high value went by air. As
regards the carriage of mail the airlines were again restricted
in their scope by the mere fact that the bulk of the inland
mail was collected by day and required night conveyance, a
service which they were least capable of performing. Thus in
view of the difficulties involved in this respect and the
excellence of rail facilities the Post Office was reluctant to
entrust the airlines with more than a limited amount of mail
to carry.

III

The situation was made much worse than it might have
been by the atomistic structure of the industry. There were
far too many companies chasing too little traffic. In 1933, 13
companies operated a route mileage of 1,220 and carried a
total of 22,017 passengers. Some improvement in the position
took place in the following years but even by 1935 there
were 19 companies covering a route mileage of under 6,000
and carrying an average of less than 6,400 passengers apiece
per annum. During that time there occurred a substantial
increase in route mileage flown in competition, from 5.2 per
cent in 1933 to 31.1 per cent in 1936. Nor did the policy of
the Post Office with regard to mail contracts do anything to
lessen the force of competition. The practice was to accept
the lowest tender for short-term contracts which usually
meant that the companies could only carry them out at a

loss. This was certainly not a policy conducive to the long-term stability and progress of internal civil aviation.

By the middle of the 1930s it was becoming quite evident that if internal aviation was ever to approach anywhere near solvency the existing structure of the industry would have to be altered radically. Most of the firms were very small and unstable and lacked adequate resources to carry out efficient and profitable operations even under the most favourable conditions. The life of some of the companies was extremely short and many of them 'flitted like brief shadows across the scene'.[17] By 1937, 12 of the 31 companies which had begun scheduled services had already disappeared. The Maybury Committee in their report felt that the conditions under which internal services had hitherto been carried on offered no reliable guide as to whether profitable operations could be obtained in the future. Accordingly they recommended the elimination of cut-throat competition on the grounds that 'so long as wasteful competition continues and services are unduly limited in their frequency, regularity and convenience, it seems unlikely that air transport will pay its way'.[18] The obvious solution to the problem appeared to be a consolidation and rationalisation of the interests concerned.

In point of fact this is just what was happening. As early as October 1935 a merger was announced between Hillman Airways, United Airways, Spartan Airlines and British and Continental Airways with the intention of promoting a well-financed and compact organisation called British Airways. The chief aims of the company were claimed to be the reduction of competition and operating costs and the co-ordination of services as far as possible. It was intended that the new concern should operate the main unsubsidised services in Great Britain, but in actual fact British Airways became the Government's second 'chosen instrument' for the development of continental air routes. Consequently the company soon devoted its energies to this task and, in July 1936, all its internal services were taken over by Northern and Scottish Airways and Highland Airways.[19] From then on it was the railways, fearing the threat of air transport, which took the major initiative in the process of rationalisation. Eventually they acquired a dominating interest in a large proportion of the airline undertakings and by the end of 1938 only five important companies, the services of which for the most part offered little potential threat to the railways, remained outside their direct control. Altogether 24 out of the 40-odd companies created between 1933 and 1939 had either failed or been absorbed. But the number of companies still remained high partly because in 1938, as a result of agreements between the railways and certain financial groups, several new companies were formed to take the place of the older competing concerns.

It seems unlikely that the process of rationalisation brought much improvement to the situation. Though it certainly reduced the amount of competition by eliminating some duplicate services, internal aviation still remained unprofitable. If the financial results of Railway Air Services are anything to go by the industry was doing just as badly as before. The fact was that there were still far too many companies in a field where one or two would have been enough. As the largest single interest group the railways were in an ideal position to bring the process of consolidation to its logical conclusion. Yet no attempt was made to combine their interests into one large undertaking. The railways were content to remain influential shareholders in a large number of undertakings each of which retained its separate identity much as before. It might be argued that up to 1939 the railways had little time to reorganise their new interests efficiently. It would perhaps be far nearer the truth to suggest that they had little intention of doing so. The railways were far more interested in acquiring a controlling interest in the airline companies to restrict competition than they were in promoting an orderly expansion of the industry. This negative attitude is reflected clearly in the action they took in 1933 to restrict the growth of new airlines. The railways refused to recognise travel agencies which dealt in airline tickets other than those

of Imperial Airways and foreign airlines.[20] The 'booking ban'
as it was called continued until 1938 when the Government
intimated that it would take action to curtail it if not removed.
Moreover, if the railways had really been interested in con-
solidating air services under one large efficient undertaking
it seems highly unlikely that they would have fostered the
creation of new companies as they did in 1938. On the other
hand these criticisms may perhaps be a little unjust. Railway
participation does seem to have brought about some improvement in air services particularly as regards the coordination of
travel facilities.[21] In fact the Cadman Committee felt that
the railway companies, though no doubt influenced by a consideration of their own interests, were making a useful
contribution to civil air development and had 'provided capital
and experience in a proper and constructive manner'.[22]

IV

As we have seen the Maybury Committee were strongly
favour of some measure of restriction to avoid the 'indiscriminate multiplication of services'. This could be achieved, they
hoped, by licensing aircraft operators and by establishing
their Junction Aerodrome Scheme whereby selected routes
would be regulated with a view to ensuring that suitable
conditions might be secured for the operation of air services.
The scheme was to be applied experimentally over a restricted
number of routes where everything would be done to make
air transport as safe, regular and efficient as possible. Instead
of indiscriminate services between various points in the United
Kingdom there were to be intermediate services to and from
the base point or junction aerodrome situated either in
Manchester or Liverpool.[23] In effect this would cut down the
route mileage between main towns from 2,900 to 900 miles.
Although it would undoubtedly have involved slightly longer
flights and a certain amount of double hauling it was reckoned
that the scheme would help to raise the average load factors
of the operating companies concerned.[24]

The Government accepted the plan in principle but it was

never put into effect since the airlines themselves were opposed
to it. Eventually in 1938 the Government gave belated ack-
nowledgement to the difficulties of the industry. In that year
a licensing system was introduced and internal aviation
received a subsidy for the first time. From 1 November air
operators had to obtain a licence from the newly created Air
Transport Licensing Authority for all services in the United
Kingdom on which passengers and goods were carried for
payment. At the same time the Air Navigation (Financial
Provisions) Act provided a sum not exceeding £100,000 per
annum 'to help those companies which are suffering losses to
establish themselves on a sound commercial footing'.[25] The
subsidy was only to be paid to these companies on the clear
understanding they would attempt to become paying propositions within a five-year period. Only companies operating
regular services licensed by the ATLA could receive financial
assistance and initially 11 companies were eligible for it.[26]
The subsidy payments were made on the basis of capacity-
ton-mileage[27] flown on approved routes so as to encourage
operators towards larger aircraft and higher frequencies.

Unfortunately the outbreak of the war cut short the
implementation of the new scheme so it is impossible to tell
what effect it might have had. However it appears very
unlikely that either the subsidy or the licensing arrangements
would have enabled the airlines to pay their way. Internal
aviation was even less capable of flying by itself than international aviation where one company, Imperial Airways,
held a monopoly of subsidised operations for much of the
time. In view of this it seems extraordinary that the Government should have attempted to keep around a dozen companies afloat in the internal field. In the case of many of the
companies the subsidy payments alone would only have
covered a portion of their deficits. The total payment to any
one company was limited to a maximum of £15,000 per
annum and on the basis of 1937 this would have covered less
than one-third of the total deficit incurred by the railway air
transport undertaking.

The Licensing Authority did little — and indeed could do little — to improve the situation. Altogether it issued 47 licences to no less than 14 companies. To some extent its hands were tied by the fact the Government had granted subsidies to 11 companies, which of course had to be licensed. But in any case its powers were severely limited. It possessed no powers of initiative as regards the planning of air routes or as regards reforming the structure of the industry. The order which brought it into being assumed that there would be sufficient applications by various operators to provide what services were necessary and confined itself to laying down the methods and principles by which the Authority should act. In other words the Authority could only consider applications for licences and either grant or refuse them, or consider, if they were granted, the conditions to be attached to them.[28] In reviewing applications the Authority had to take into account certain considerations such as the coordination and development of air services with the object of ensuring the most efficient services to the public without unnecessary over-lapping; the degree of efficiency and regularity of air services already provided and the extent to which it was probable that the applicant would be able to provide a satisfactory service in respect of continuity, regularity of operation, frequency, punctuality and reasonableness of charges. In so far as these principles were applied it could be claimed that some ration-alisation of air services was achieved. It is quite clear, however, from the details of the inquiries which were released that the Authority had difficulty in interpreting and applying these principles particularly when opposing interests required reconciliation. When Scottish Airways and Allied Airways applied for licences to run services in the North of Scotland the Authority decided, against all evidence to the contrary, that competition was necessary for the best results and split the services between them. On the other hand, when a new company, Night Air Transport, sought permission to inaugurate a night service for mail and goods between Grangemouth and London a licence was refused because

Railway Air Services and North Eastern Airways contended that they should be given the first opportunity to introduce such a service. It need hardly be added that they had little intention of doing so. Thus in view of its restricted scope and powers, together with its inexperience, it is not surprising that the Authority was content to give a *carte-blanche* to established operators and that little attempt was made to reorganise the structure of the industry in the light of previous experience or on the basis of the principles laid down by order.

In view of the difficult conditions which obtained during the 1930s it is perhaps hardly surprising that internal air operators failed to break even. Conditions today are, of course, vastly different but the historical experience is too good to be ignored. In many respects the recently established Air Transport Licensing Board is faced with a similar situation to that which prevailed in the 1930s. To date it has licensed no less than 24 independent companies over half of which are making losses. Before the Board's generosity goes too far it is to be hoped that it will pause for a moment to consider the valuable lessons of history.

NOTES

1   L.H. Savile, 'Aerodromes for Civil Aviation', *Journal of the Institute of Transport* (February 1935), 146

2   K.G. Fenelon, *Transport Co-ordination* (1929), 44

3   Brooks has estimated that for each decade of the period 1919-59 the following improvements in aircraft performance took place: specific operating costs were reduced on average by about one-third; vehicle size and carrying capacity doubled; speed rose by about two-thirds and there was a rapid improvement in safety, reliability and standards of passenger accommodation. P. Brooks, *The Modern Airliner* (1961), 30. See also C. and W. Isard, 'Economic Implications of Aircraft', *Quarterly Journal of Economics* (February 1945), 150-1

4   A. Plummer, *New British Industries in the Twentieth Century* (1937), 164

5   A. Plummer, op cit, 163

6   *Report of the Committee to Consider the Development of Civil Aviation in the United Kingdom*, Cd 5351 (1937), 12

7   This calculation includes British Airways which was concerned mainly with continental operations after 1936. P.G. Masefield, 'Some Economic Factors in Air Transport Operation', *Journal of the Institute of Transport* (March 1951), 88

8   It may be recalled that by early 1921 the four pioneer companies had suspended all overseas operations and it was only a Government subsidy which saved the situation

9   *Hansard* (21 March 1935), 299, col 1468

10 F.C. Shelmerdine, 'Air Transport in Great Britain — Some Problems and Needs', *Journal of the Institute of Transport* (December 1935), 103

11 P.G. Masefield, op cit, 87

12 Fixed costs formed around 50 per cent of total costs. Depreciation charges were high since aircraft soon became obsolete. Twenty per cent per annum was not unusual. On a machine costing anything up to £80,000 this was a heavy charge on revenue

13 J.F. Parke, 'Co-ordination of Air and Surface Transport', *Journal of the Institute of Transport* (May-June 1945), 109

14 One has to bear in mind that the journey between town and aerodrome, which could take up to half an hour each way, greatly reduced the saving in time by air particularly on short and medium distances

15 The distances given are for the air routes and are measured between town centres and not between aerodromes. The distances by rail are 201, 402 and 113 miles respectively

16   Cd 5351, 26

17   P.G. Masefield, op cit, 83

18   Cd 5351, 35

19   Just over a year later these two companies amalgamated to form Scottish Airways based on Renfrew with railway interests participating alongside Whitehall Securities

20   Imperial Airways secured this favoured treatment partly because their services were non-competitive with the railways and partly on account of the fact that the Company had an interest in Railway Air Services

21   *Flight* (20 January 1938), 64

22   *Report of the Committee of Inquiry into Civil Aviation*, Cd 5685 (1938), 21

23   The main centres included in the scheme were Belfast, Glasgow, Edinburgh, Newcastle, London, Southampton, Portsmouth and Bristol

24   The Committee also recommended that the Government should provide and maintain a standard organisation throughout the country, of radio facilities, weather information and air traffic control for all forms of civil aviation. This responsibility was accepted by the Government and put into effect almost immediately

25   *Hansard* (18 May 1938), 336, col 427

26   Details of the scheme and the companies involved can be found in *Civil Air Transport Services: Internal Air Lines*, Cd 5894 (1938), and *The Aeroplane* (4 May 1938), 546 and (21 December 1938), 823

27   Being the pay-load capacity in tons of the aircraft used multiplied by the number of miles flown

28   Such conditions included the places between which passengers and goods might be carried; the places at which intermediate

landings could be made; the observance of time-tables; the
suitability and capacity of aircraft to be used and the maximum
fares to be charged to passengers

10 The Railways and Air Transport, 1933-9

First published in the Scottish Journal of
Political Economy, *12 (1965)*

In view of the wealth of material available it is surprising
what little work has been done on the early history of air
transport in Great Britain. Apart from Higham's book on
Imperial Air Routes[1] and Birkhead's excellent articles on the
early pioneer companies in the international field[2] there is
very little scholarly work worth speaking of. Internal aviation
has suffered even greater neglect and it still remains a virgin
field for the student of aeronautics.

For a variety of reasons Britain's internal air services were
slow to materialise after the First World War. A few attempts
were made in the 1920s to establish regular services but all of
them ended in failure. In the following decade conditions
were more favourable for the introduction of such services.
As a result a large number of companies were established and
by the outbreak of the Second World War Britain possessed a
fairly elaborate network of air services. A particular feature
of this development was the part played by the railways.
Their participation in air transport has been criticised from
various quarters on the grounds that the railway companies
were merely furthering or protecting their own interests. The
purpose of this article therefore is to examine in some detail
the development of the railways' air services and to try to
determine exactly what contribution they made to this new
form of transport.

There can be no doubt that the entry of the railways into
air transport was determined by outside developments in the
field. They had obtained air transport powers in 1929 but
made no attempt to use them until the establishment of

internal air services by private operators in the early 1930s appeared to threaten their own interests. Early in 1934 Sir Josiah Stamp, chairman of the LMS railway company, made it clear that the railways were not going to sit back and let the airlines rob them of their traffic. 'The matter', he said, 'has assumed some urgency with us, owing to the more recent activities of certain established airway companies and their preparations for the inauguration of regular commercial services between important centres in competition with our rail services. It is desirable for the four main line companies to act in co-operation.'[3] The railways were obviously determined not to make the same mistake they had made with road transport in the 1920s when they had allowed the new competitor to establish a strong foothold before participating themselves. Indeed the railways themselves admitted that the main reason for the promotion of the Railway (Air Transport) Bills in 1928-9 was so that they might be at 'liberty to take a share in the inevitable development of air transport and avoid a repetition of their experience in regard to road transport'.[4] As the organ of the air world, *Flight*, remarked somewhat later, 'the railway companies, still sore from their battle with road transport, are prepared to fight any rivalry from the air'.[5]

The first experimental railway air service was made by the Great Western Company in April 1933 when it began a daily service between Cardiff, Torquay and Plymouth (later extended to Birmingham), a notoriously difficult route by rail.[6] The service was actually operated by Imperial Airways on behalf of the company, the latter taking care of the booking and advertising arrangements.[7] On 15 May the Post Office granted the company permission to carry the mails by air. The venture could hardly be called a success, however, and in September of the same year it was discontinued. Despite the appreciable saving in time by air only 714 passengers were carried together with a small amount of cargo and the Great Western lost £6,526 on the operation.[8]

Meanwhile the other railway companies had been trying

to secure the co-operation of the private air lines with the idea
of establishing joint services. Negotiations proved unsuccessful
however and the railways decided to strike out alone. In
March 1934 a company known as Railway Air Services was
established with a capital of £50,000 for the purpose of
providing such air services as the railway companies might
require. The four railway companies and Imperial Airways
each held one-fifth of the shares and the latter company
undertook to operate the services until such time as the new
company obtained its own aircraft.[9] At the same time it was
agreed that Railway Air Services would confine its activities
to Great Britain and in return Imperial Airways promised not
to invade the internal field. Thus the new company not only
secured the assistance and co-operation of an already
experienced air operator but they also acquired the services
of the assistant general manager of Imperial Airways,
Lieutenant-Colonel H. Burchall, who was seconded to the
board of Railway Air Services.[10]

One of the first actions of the new company was to resume
the service between Birmingham, Cardiff, Torquay and
Plymouth (with an additional extension to Liverpool) which
had been operated by the Great Western in the previous year.
A link was provided between Cardiff and Bristol by arrangement with Norman Edgar (Western Airways), a private
company which operated a service between Bristol and
Bournemouth.[11] In the following May, Railway Air Services
arranged with Spartan Air Lines a joint service between
London, Ryde and Cowes, a route which the latter airline
had operated independently in the summer of 1933. The
delivery of a fleet of four-engined planes two months later
enabled the new company to make a considerable expansion
in its services. A twice-daily service was started between
Birmingham, Bristol, Southampton and Cowes[12] and was
soon followed by the 'main line' service between London-
Belfast-Glasgow *via* Birmingham and Manchester which was
to form the backbone of the company's routes. The introduction of this flight was no doubt occasioned by the fact

that a private company, Midland & Scottish Air Ferries Ltd, had opened a service on this route in April 1934 and the railways feared that this might lead to a fall off in their cross-channel traffic between Liverpool and Belfast.[13] There was every justification for this assumption for although air transport was much dearer an appreciable saving in time could be made on flights involving a water crossing. The journey between London and Belfast took about five hours by air compared with a surface time of 12 hours or more.[14]

On all these routes Railway Air Services obtained mail contracts from the Post Office. At the time the only other airline company permitted to carry mail in Great Britain was Highland Airways[15] and it appeared to many private operators as if the railways were being accorded favoured treatment. The Post Office's explanation did little to allay the dissatisfaction of the private companies on this matter. It was argued that the railway companies had been given the contracts because they had a great deal of experience in carrying mail bags in trains and an intimate knowledge of the ground organisation of the Post Office.[16] However, in the following year the Post Office adopted the policy of tendering for mail contracts which were awarded to the lowest bidder offering a reliable service. This was an unsatisfactory policy since it meant many of the tenders accepted could only be carried out at a loss, and though Hillman Airways managed to secure the contract for the London-Belfast route in 1935 the combined resources of the railways were able to undercut the private operators in subsequent years.[17]

The services established in the summer of 1934 formed the framework of the railways' air routes. In the following winter (1934-5) when traffic fell off all of them were suspended except for the London-Belfast-Glasgow flight and as from the November Birmingham and Manchester were dropped as internal stops in favour of Liverpool. It is true that the London-Isle of Wight service was continued but it was operated independently by Spartan Air Lines in the winter months. In the summer of 1935 the suspended services were revived

and further additions were made to the network. Nottingham
and Birmingham were connected by air services and Manchester and Liverpool were linked with Blackpool from which a
service to the Isle of Man operated.[18] Numerous extensions
were made in 1936. The Company established direct connections between the Isle of Man and Carlisle, Glasgow,
Belfast, Liverpool and Manchester, and Leeds and Bradford
were brought into the network. In the West Country and the
South a number of new services were introduced linking
Bristol and Cardiff with Weston-super-Mare, Bristol with
Brighton and Brighton with Southampton and the Isle of
Wight.[19] By this time Railway Air Services had a fleet of 14
aircraft and were operating about 62 different services on
seven main routes.[20] Most of the services except the London-
Belfast-Glasgow and those to the Isle of Man operated in the
summer months only. Few significant changes were made in
1937.

Thus by 1937 the route mileage of Railway Air Services
was largely completed. For the most part air services were
confined to the territory covered by the LMS and Great
Western railway companies. The venture could hardly be
called a financial success. Deficits were incurred in every year
and showed little signs of decreasing. Altogether the company
lost £192,545 on its air services between 1934 and 1938
(see Table 1 opposite). This is not really surprising for although
traffic increased load factors remained at a very low level
throughout this period *(see Table 2 opposite).* The average
load factor of the company was little more than 35 per cent
which was probably less than half the break-even figure. The
reasons for the failure of internal air operators in general to
secure break-even load factors in the 1930s have been
examined elsewhere and need not detain us here.[21] What
should be noted, however, is the fact that the traffic figures
of Railway Air Services fell off appreciably after 1937. This
is largely due to the fact that certain services were hived off
into separate undertakings, the most notable of which was
Great Western & Southern Airlines established in 1938, and

TABLE I
FINANCIAL RESULTS OF RAILWAY AIR SERVICES,
1933-8

Year	Gross receipts £	Expenditure £	Net receipts £
1933	1,665	8,191	6,526 Dr [a]
1934	13,319	27,860	14,541 Dr [b]
1935	16,005	59,203	43,198 Dr
1936	24,665	65,607	40,942 Dr
1937	32,500	83,968	51,468 Dr
1938	21,684	64,080	42,396 Dr

Notes: [a] Great Western Railway only
[b] Includes LMS limestone quarry

Source: Ministry of Transport, *Railway Returns, 1933-1938* (HMSO)

TABLE 2
RAILWAY AIR SERVICES
Traffic Statistics, 1934-9

	Passengers	Mail lb	Cargo lb[b]	Miles flown	Load factor
1934[a]	2,237	5,625	6,000	210,857	12.6%
1935	13,293	21,631	167,498	655,972	35.5%
1936	22,076	385,027	39,862	905,297	42 %
1937	25,523	454,926	117,934	1,004,196	39.1%
1938	7,082	490,917	48,459	570,160	43.5%
1939	5,313	309,406	50,049	397,875	39 %

[a] From 7 May [b] Includes excess baggage

Source: J. Stroud, *Annals of British and Commonwealth Air Transport*
(1962), 631, quoted by permission of the publishers, Putnam
& Co Ltd

to the fact that the railways had by this time secured considerable interests in private airway concerns.

The air activities of the railways were by no means confined
to the services carried on by the company which had been
formed in 1934. Almost from the very beginning the railways
sought to acquire an interest in the numerous private companies
which were formed in the 1930s to operate internal air
services. By 1935 there were nearly a score of companies
operating within the United Kingdom and some of these
competed both with railways' ground transport system and
with Railway Air Services. On the London-Liverpool route,
for example, RAS faced direct competition from United
Airways and Hillman Airways and similar conditions prevailed
on the Liverpool-Belfast-Glasgow route. It was in the railways'
own interest therefore to try and weaken this competition by
acquiring an interest in the undertakings concerned.

The financial structure of the internal air transport industry
became extremely complicated in the later 1930s and only
the more important changes affecting the railways can be
noted here. The first move was made early in 1935 when a
company called Channel Island Airways was formed to take
over the services previously operated by Jersey Airways. This
new company, two-thirds of whose capital was held by the
railway companies and the financial trust Whitehall Securities,
later acquired control of Guernsey Airways.[22] Meanwhile
Whitehall Securities had secretly been buying shares in a
number of airline companies and by the autumn of 1935 they
had secured a substantial interest in Spartan Air Lines, United
Airways, Hillman Airways, Highland Airways, Northern &
Scottish Airways and of course Channel Island Airways. In
October of that year the first three companies were amalgamated to form British Airways, and when in the following year
the Government designated this company as its second
'chosen instrument' for the development of international
routes, the company's internal services were handed over to
Northern & Scottish Airways and Highland Airways both
of which were affiliated to Whitehall Securities. Thus the

trust became the most important rival of the railways who were anxious lest it should cut the ground from under their own feet. The problem was solved however in 1937 when Clive Pearson, the chairman of Whitehall Securities, became a director of Southern Railways. Henceforth competition between the two groups diminished. Almost immediately Highland Airways and Northern & Scottish Airways were merged into a single company, Scottish Airways, which was jointly owned by the railway companies and Whitehall Securities. In September of that year competition was reduced on the west coast by the formation of Isle of Man Air Services Ltd with a capital of £75,000 which was held equally by the LMS railway company, the Isle of Man Steam Packet Company and Olley Air Services Ltd.[23] The railways completed their financial deals in 1938 when they secured a substantial interest in Olley Air Services Ltd which was a holding company comprising Air Commerce, Channel Air Ferries and West Coast Air Services (formerly Blackpool & West Coast Air Services). Thus by the end of 1938 the railways had secured a financial interest, though not necessarily a controlling interest, in all but 5 of the 16 companies operating air services within the United Kingdom.[24] Whitehall Securities remained the other large holding organisation.

The railways obviously played a dominating role in the development of Britain's air services but their participation was not always welcomed. In fact contemporaries were often very critical about the air activities of the railways. It was alleged that they neglected certain routes, that they did little to rationalise or coordinate their services and that the railways were mainly interested in stifling the competition of independent operators. *Flight* for example complained that their air services showed little evidence of rationalisation[25] and the paper's leader writer, A. *Viator*, was convinced that 'the railway monopoly of airlines will be bad, for railways are their major concern, and air lines, properly run by people in competition, will eventually show up the railways in quite a number of ways. Naturally, this will never be done by the railways themselves, *who are looking for a commercial machine to fly slower than their star expresses'*[26] (author's italics). One MP, W.R.D. Perkins, accused the railways of adopting a policy towards aviation similar to that which they had practised with the canals in the nineteenth century. 'Our quarrel with the railway companies is not that they are not trying to run aviation but that they are not trying to run it wholeheartedly. They are stepping in to get control and are slowly strangling it, just as they did with the canals.'[27] On the other hand, the Maybury Committee on internal aviation found no reason to indict Railway Air Services[28] and the Cadman Committee of 1938 felt that the railways were making a useful contribution to internal air transport and that they had 'provided capital and experience in a proper and constructive manner'.[29] As we shall see in due course both these views require some modification since neither of them can be substantiated fully in the light of the evidence available.

Little criticism can be made about the actual services operated by the railways. In terms of speed, frequency and regularity of service and prices charged the facilities offered by Railway Air Services were as good if not better than those provided by private operators.[30] According to the chairman of the LMS the aim was to provide 'nothing less than the best available in air transport',[31] and even *Flight* had to admit that 'they (RAS) offer a frequency of service on most of the routes which will add greatly to the attractions of air transport'.[32] The company used the most up-to-date aircraft and they were often in the forefront with technical improvements. On some routes speeds of 160-170 mph were being attained as early as 1935 and the railways were the first to use wireless equipment in their aircraft for ground communication.[33] Moreover, there is no evidence to suggest that services deteriorated as the railways emerged as the dominant group in air transport; if anything they improved. The railways also made considerable effort to co-ordinate rail and air services particularly in the later 1930s.

Late in 1937 they held a conference with five of their main associated companies to arrange *inter alia* through-booking facilities over much of the UK, the coordination of ticket facilities, the issue of comprehensive time-tables covering the whole network and the planning of circular tours by different means of transport.[34] Even before this, however, serious attempts had been made to coordinate ground and air transport facilities and in some cases Railway Air Services had actively cooperated with the independent airlines. The company ran joint services with a number of private airlines and in 1935 agreements as to time-table coordination were made with Norman Edgar (Western Airways).[35]

As regards the routes served by Railway Air Services there is cause for more concern. It is noticeable that the bulk of the company's services were concentrated in the western half of Great Britain in a line running from London to Glasgow, that is largely in the territory covered by the LMS and Great Western railway companies. In contrast, the eastern side of the country was almost completely neglected by the railways. The explanation seems clear enough. In the west and north-west the railways faced much more competition from private air operators than in the east. The London-Liverpool-Isle of Man-Belfast route was particularly vulnerable as the railways still monopolised the long-distance surface transport on this route. But on the east coast route to the north there were few private air services operating except North Eastern Airways and Aberdeen Airways (later Allied Airways), both of which confined their activities mainly to Scotland and for the most part did not offer a serious threat to the railways. In consequence the LNER had little cause to retaliate since its traffic was scarcely affected by competition from the air. Moreover, it should be remembered that the LNER was not involved in water services off the north-east coast as the LMS was in the west and that the Scottish main line services were particularly efficient especially after 1935 when new streamlined services were introduced.[36]

It can be argued therefore that the railways concentrated

their air services on those routes most subject to air competition and at the same time avoided wherever possible establishing air services on main line railway routes. This did not
happen in every case of course but it was particularly true of
the London-Belfast-Glasgow service. Here the railways
encountered serious competition and consequently they
devoted most attention to this route. What is significant is
that they avoided introducing a direct air link between
London and Glasgow *via* Manchester until 1938. It was
contended that there was no good prospect of direct traffic
between London and Glasgow or Manchester and Glasgow,
a conclusion that ran counter to the opinion of the Maybury
Committee. It is true, of course, that flights involving water
crossings were likely to attract the heaviest traffic simply
because the travelling time saved was quite substantial. But
this argument is irrelevant here for it is inconceivable that it
was quicker or convenient to fly to Glasgow *via* Belfast rather
than direct. The only conclusion we can draw from this is
that the railways delayed introducing a direct service until
private operators entered the field. Had they done so alone
it would merely have creamed traffic from their own ground
facilities.[37]

Apart from one or two cases, notably Midland & Scottish
Air Ferries and possibly North Eastern Airways,[38] there
appears to be little evidence to confirm the belief that
the railways deliberately tried to strangle private operators.
On the other hand they did endeavour to gain control by
acquiring a financial interest in private air companies and
eventually only a few remained outside the railway grouping.
It is significant, moreover, that none of the five companies
which remained independent seriously interfered with railway
interests. Nevertheless railway control was not necessarily
detrimental to internal aviation as a whole. There is no doubt
that railway participation brought about a reduction of competition through a rationalisation of services. By allocating
routes to various companies a certain amount of duplication
was avoided. But this was by no means a bad thing. Few

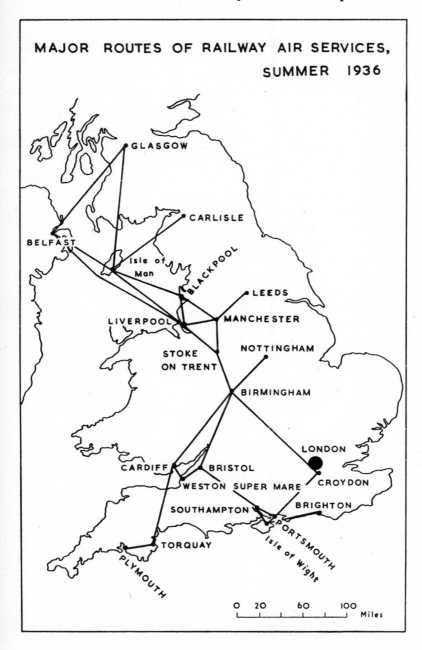

MAJOR ROUTES OF RAILWAY AIR SERVICES,
SUMMER 1936

routes could support even one airline company properly and anything which would raise load factors was to be welcomed. The only pity is that the railways did not carry the policy further and adopt the Maybury Committee's Central Airport Plan.[39] Nor is there any evidence to suggest that this policy led to a deterioration in services. On the contrary, facilities appear to have improved in the later 1930s partly as a result of the railways' influence. The grouping of the Isle of Man services, for example, provided improved schedules in 1938 whilst the link with Scottish Airways led to improved through services to the north of Scotland. Coordination of travel facilities especially between air and rail was made easier and was actively encouraged by the railway companies. More could no doubt have been done in this respect but one should not forget the fact that the railways rarely held more than a third of the capital of the companies in which they had a financial interest so that there was a limit to what they could do. Moreover, the fact that the railways held less than a controlling interest meant they were never in a position to impose an unduly restrictive policy on the companies concerned particularly as Whitehall Securities was often an influential shareholder in many of them.

On the other hand, there are grounds for believing that the policy of the railways was not always constructive either. There were far too many separate companies operating in the internal field and one would have thought it would have been in the railways' own interest to try and create one large undertaking for the whole country. This would have allowed a much more intensive use of the costly capital equipment and at the same time produced considerable administrative economies. Yet they did little to bring this about; indeed by 1937-8 they were promoting new companies such as Great Western & Southern Airlines and Western Isles Airways Ltd, thus negating the beneficial effects of earlier mergers. Of course it can be argued that they were limited by the fact that they owned few of the companies outright but there would surely have been little difficulty in acquiring complete control had the railways been determined to do so. In view of the fact that Whitehall Securities was an influential shareholder in some of the companies it seems surprising that no attempt was made to secure their cooperation in this matter which would have been in the financial interests of both parties.

On balance it may be concluded that the railways made a significant contribution to the development of air transport. Though they had secured a semi-monopoly of air transport services within Great Britain by the late 1930s it would be wrong to suggest that they openly abused their favourable position. Nevertheless the attitude of the railways was far from impartial and, as we have seen, policy was often determined by a consideration of their own interests. Perhaps the most serious objection which might be made was that the railways did little to reorganise or rationalise the structure of the industry. Possibly this would have been done in time yet the very fact that the railways were engaged in promoting new companies in 1937-8 suggests that they had little intention of grouping the various undertakings into one large company.

NOTES

1   R. Higham, *Britain's Imperial Air Routes, 1918-1939* (1960)

2   E. Birkhead, 'The Daimler Airway', *Journal of Transport History* (November 1958) and 'The Financial Failure of British Air Transport Companies, 1919-24', ibid (May 1960)

3   *Report of the Proceedings at the 11th Ordinary General Meeting of the Proprietors of the LMS Railway Company* (23 February 1934), 14. A copy of this report can be found in the Historical Records Department of the British Railways Board

4   *Statement on Behalf of the Promoters in support of a Second Reading of the Air Transport Bills, 1928-29* and *Memorandum submitted to the Minister of Transport* (20 November 1928),

Archives of British Railways Board. See also *Railway Gazette* (8 November 1935), 765

5   *Flight* (1 March 1934), 192

6   For details of the service see *Great Western Railway Magazine* (May 1933), 197-202, and (June 1934), 265

7   *Railway Gazette* (7 April 1933), 493, and (19 May 1933), 684. This was the beginning of a fruitful partnership between the railways and Imperial Airways. It had been foreshadowed as early as April 1931 when the four main-line companies had reached an agreement with IA for combined air-rail freight services

8   *Railway Returns* (HMSO, 1933)

9   After the company had acquired its own aircraft Imperial Airways continued to supply the pilots and maintain the machines. R. Finch, *The World's Airways* (1938), 112

10   *The Times* (29 March 1934). The other members of the board were S.B. Collett (GWR), squadron-leader of the City of London Squadron of the Auxiliary Air Force, Sir Harold Hartley (LMS), chairman, O.H. Corble (LNER) and G.S. Szlumper (SR)

11   *The Times* (24 March 1934)

12   *Railway Magazine* (December 1934), 439-40

13   *Flight* (5 April 1934), 318

14   Ibid (13 September 1934), 959

15   Apart from Western Airways which because of its close association with Railway Air Services received a sub-contract to carry mail between Cardiff and Bristol

16   *Flight* (11 October 1934), 1066

17   *Railway Gazette* (24 December 1937), 1223

18   *Railway Magazine* (December 1935), 395-6

19   See *Report on the Progress of Civil Aviation 1936* (HMSO, 1937), 12

20   *The Air Annual of the British Empire* (1938), 606, and *Flight* (23 April 1936), 465

21   Derek H. Aldcroft, 'Britain's Internal Airways: The Pioneer Stage of the 1930s', *Business History* (June 1964) (see pp 208-25 above)

22   *Railway Gazette* (February 1935), 183 and 217

23   *Motor Transport Year Book and Directory, 1938-9,* Vol 23

24   For details see *Civil Air Transport Services: Internal Air Lines*, Cd 5894 (1938) and *The Aeroplane* (21 December 1938), 823 and (4 May 1938), 546

25   *Flight* (23 April 1936), 451

26   Ibid (20 January 1938), 64

27   *Hansard* (22 July 1939), Vol 350, col 1314. Cf P.G. Masefield, 'Some Economic Factors in Air Transport Operation', *Journal of the Institute of Transport* (March 1951), 84

28   *Report of the Committee to Consider the Development of Civil Aviation in the United Kingdom*, Cd 5351 (1937)

29   *Report of the Committee of Inquiry into Civil Aviation*, Cd 5685 (1938), 21

30   *Flight* (12 May 1938), 477, and *Report on the Progress of Civil Aviation, 1934* (HMSO, 1935), 15-16

31   *Report of the Proceedings at the 12th Ordinary General Meeting of the LMS Railway Company* (1 March 1935), 28, Archives of the British Railways Board

32   *Flight* (23 April 1936), 451

33   *Railway Magazine* (August 1935), 125-6

34   *The Aeroplane* (19 January 1938), 81, and *Flight* (20 January

1938), 64

35   *Railway Magazine* (August 1935), 139-40

36   *Railway Gazette* (20 September 1935), 451

37   When introduced in 1938 the direct link between London and Glasgow provided a service between three and four hours which was less than half the time taken by surface transport. *Flight* (17 February 1938), 162 and (12 May 1938), 477

38   For North Eastern Airways I merely quote the opinion of Masefield. I am inclined to believe that he is not altogether correct on this point for I have found no concrete evidence to support his remark

39   For a discussion of this scheme see Aldcroft, loc cit

11 Innovation on the Railways: The Lag in Diesel and Electric Traction

First published in the Journal of Transport Economics and Policy, *3 (1969)*

Although two new forms of traction power were available to the railways by the early twentieth century, little attempt was made in Britain to abandon the steam locomotive until well after the Second World War. Before 1939 only the Southern Railway Company invested in electrification on any consider-able scale, and diesel power was hardly used at all by any of the four main-line companies. Even as late as 1955, when the British Transport Commission launched its famous Modern-isation Plan for the railways, steam power still reigned supreme: steam accounted for 87 per cent of the total traction miles run, compared with 10 per cent for electric and 3 per cent for diesel traction. The majority of the diesel and electric services consisted of multiple units operating over short distances. Most main-line services were still performed by the steam locomotive. Altogether British Railways possessed only just over 500 diesel and electric locomotives, as against nearly 18,000 steam ones.[1] Only in the last decade or so have the railways really made the switch from steam to diesel and electric traction.[2]

This provides an interesting case study of delayed response in the application of new techniques. Nearly half a century elapsed after the new technology was shown to be technically feasible before it was applied extensively to Britain's railways. In few other countries was progress so slow. Many continental countries made much greater headway with electrification both before and after 1939; in America diesel traction gained ground rapidly from the middle of the 1930s. By 1946 diesel power was responsible for one-eighth of the ton mileage, one-quarter of the passenger car mileage and one-third of the shunting and marshalling mileage on American railroads, and the American companies had practically abandoned the construction of new steam locomotives.[3]

Given the advantages of diesel and electric traction it is difficult, at least from the standpoint of the 1960s, to see why they were neglected so long. Over the last few years British Railways have reaped their main economies from the replacement of steam by new forms of power, and most people would agree that services have improved considerably as a result. Could not the substitution have been made earlier? Most of the technical problems had been solved by the 1930s, and many of the benefits, especially of electrification, were apparent well before 1939. There is no need to list these benefits in great detail.[4] The most obvious were cleaner, faster and more frequent services at lower cost. In particular, multiple units were very suitable for short-distance commuter services because of their flexibility. Moreover, there was every prospect that improved services would bring an increase in traffic, an important consideration at a time when road competition was becoming severe. The experience of the Southern Railway left little doubt about the advantages. The chairman of the company, Sir Herbert Walker, was extolling the virtues of electrification as early as the 1920s, and it was largely because of his enterprise that the Southern Railway made such rapid progress with the new form of traction in the 1930s. By 1939 just over 30 per cent of the company's route mileage had been converted, involving a capital outlay of £20.5 million, and electric services accounted for no less than 60 per cent of the total mileage run. The Southern electric trains became noted for their reliability, frequency, punctuality and comfort, and in every case traffic increased. Over the period 1930-9 passenger journeys on electrified lines rose by 12½ million, compared with a drop of one million on the remaining steam services. Operating costs were one-third to one-half less than those of steam, the main savings being made on labour and maintenance costs. On the basis of data for

1936 the difference in haulage costs per train mile between steam and electric was nearly 11 pence, giving an overall saving of nearly £1.4 million on the total train mileage operated. An allowance has been made for interest charges in this estimate; the return on capital expended to 1936 (£16 million) works out at roughly 8.8 per cent.[5]

Although these figures are only approximate, there seems little doubt about the economic benefits of electrification. The company was well satisfied with the results, and claimed that modernisation schemes were started only after careful investigation had ascertained that they would yield a reasonable return.[6] Yet outside the Southern region and the London Passenger Transport Board there was virtually no electrification at all. The other three companies possessed a mere 190 miles of electrified route by 1939, and most of this consisted of local suburban lines such as those around Tyneside, Merseyside and Manchester. Altogether only about 5 per cent of the total route mileage had been electrified, including little which could be classed as main-line.[7]

By 1955 there had been little further extension of the electrified system. Nor had much progress been made with diesel traction. The latter possessed many of the advantages of electrification; the main differences were that the capital costs were lower and diesel units could be introduced progressively on existing track, whereas electrification required extensive reconstruction of the track and structures.[8] The diesel locomotive was developed somewhat later than the electric, but the main problems were overcome by the later 1930s.

Why, then, did British railways take so long to make the break with steam? Can the delay be explained purely in economic terms, or were there other reasons?

Constraints on Technological Progress
In theory a decision to invest in new technology will be taken only if it promises a clear economic gain. In general this will require average operating costs to be below those of the old

technology,[9] whilst the net return must be sufficiently large
to meet any interest charges on the new investment. Even if
these conditions are met there is no guarantee that the investment will be made, since investors will generally expect a
rate of return more than marginally above that which could
be secured from continuing the old techniques. And, even if
the new technology is economically attractive, there are a
number of factors which may prevent or delay its adoption.
Some of these possibilities are as follows:

(i)   The structure of the industry and the nature of its
output may be such as to retard the adoption of new processes.
To take a specific example: the limited use made of the ring
spindle and automatic loom in the cotton industry before
1939 was due to the fact that these machines were not particularly suited to producing the kind of products Lancashire
specialised in. This type of situation may, however, result in
partial adoption.

(ii)   If the capital components of the industry are highly
interrelated it may be difficult to introduce new techniques
in a piecemeal fashion because of the need to alter other
assets or installations at the same time. The more closely
related the capital assets are, the greater will be the cost of
introducing innovations. If the assets are related to those of
other industries there is the problem of sharing joint costs
and profits.

(iii)   The application of new techniques may depend upon
the state of the market and the availability of finance. If
economic conditions are depressed innovations will tend to
be received unfavourably, even though they might produce
significant economic gains: entrepreneurs may be reluctant
to innovate, either because cash reserves are low or because
they consider long-term prospects to be unfavourable.[10]
Alternatively, the financial requirements might be so great
that it would be impossible to clear the demand without
extensive borrowing. Successful borrowing will depend on (a)
the availability of finance and the strength of competing
claims for it, and (b) the soundness of the borrower in the

long term.

(iv) Relative factor prices may be such as to discourage the adoption of capital-intensive techniques.

(v) The industry may be faced with external competition. The railways, for example, have faced serious competition from the growth of motor transport since the First World War. It is difficult to say precisely what effect this will have. The threatened industry may have recourse to innovation and improvement in an effort to combat competition. On the other hand, if the industry shifts into the competing field innovation in its own sector may be delayed.

(vi) There is the possibility that the leaders of the industry will maintain a continued faith in old techniques and distrust the new, with which they are not familiar. This is particularly so where much capital has been sunk in equipment which may still be in good condition. Such conditions may produce a defensive reaction which could lead to attempts to revamp or improve old techniques.

This is an imposing, though by no means exhaustive, list of factors which might impede the introduction of new techniques even if they are economically attractive. We shall now proceed to examine the economics of the new forms of railway traction and the other constraints upon their introduction.

Electric Traction
The most convenient starting point is the middle of the inter-war period. Before that time electric and diesel traction were still mainly in the experimental phase. We shall start with electrification, since it tended to be technically more advanced than diesel power.

There is little evidence that much detailed investigation was made into the costs of electrification before 1931. In that year the Weir Committee produced its report on mainline electrification.[11] Having satisfied itself that the average traffic density on the railways was above the critical minimum necessary for electrification, the committee produced a fairly detailed study of the costs of the operation. It estimated that conversion of the whole main-line system would cost £261 million. Operating savings were expected to be about £17.6 million a year, giving a return of 6.7 per cent on the capital invested. This may have been an underestimate, however, since no proper allowance was made for the likely increase in traffic. Given the high capital costs of conversion, the railways could not be expected to carry out the programme without borrowing. On the assumption that the investment would be spread over 20 years, the expected rate of return after payment of interest was around 2 per cent. 'Such a return taken by itself would not appear from a business point of view to warrant the adoption of a scheme of such exceptional magnitude. The margin would, in our view, be too narrow for the risks and contingencies involved.'[12]

The Weir Committee's verdict was hardly likely to encourage the railways to press forward with electrification. The rate of return was too low to justify full-scale conversion, which the committee favoured in spite of its conclusion.[13] Electrification of some of the dense traffic routes would no doubt have paid, but there were other routes where the rate of return would have been well below the average. To take an extreme case: in 1938 the Great Western Railway costed its Taunton-Penzance route and found that the return from electrification would be a mere 0.75 per cent.[14] The main drawback to the Weir report was that it lumped the whole system together and envisaged the conversion of many uneconomic lines. In economic terms only part of the system was suitable for electrification. This was borne out by a later study published in 1951. Although conditions had changed somewhat by then, it was found that on the basis of 1948 traffic densities only between 4,000 and 5,000 route miles were suitable for conversion.[15] Even then it was by no means certain that the rate of return would be reasonable or high enough to justify any scheme of electrification.[16] Economically there would seem to have been little justification for investing heavily in electrification either before or after the war.

But cost was not the only deterrent. Electrification presented problems of an institutional nature. It would have involved extensive scrapping of rolling stock and structures. Moreover, before the war, it would have required cooperation between the four railway companies and the electricity-generating authorities in order to achieve uniformity. In short, the interrelated nature of the capital assets presented a barrier to rapid innovation. Furthermore, the Weir report came at the worst possible time from the trading point of view — in the middle of the depression, when railway receipts were falling rapidly. With falling receipts, depressed trade and growing competition from road transport, the railways were not encouraged to embark on large-scale capital projects.

There was also the question of finance. It is true that the companies' reserves were quite high after the Great War, and net receipts were by no means negligible in the 1920s. But most of these resources were used either for overtaking arrears of maintenance accumulated during the war or for paying dividends.[17] Possibly dividends could have been slashed and the money used for investment, but in view of the Weir report the railways were probably reluctant to sacrifice their shareholders' immediate interests to a risky investment programme. The uncertain financial prospects of the railways would have made it difficult to raise sufficient cash in the market.[18] After the Second World War the problem of finance became more acute because of the official restrictions on capital investment.

A less important point, though still an unfavourable one, was the trend in factor prices. Coal and labour, the two most important operating costs, remained relatively cheap throughout the period. In fact labour and fuel costs fell relative to the cost of capital.[19] Hence there was no strong incentive to invest in capital-intensive techniques which would produce savings in labour and fuel. With the shortage of labour and fuel during and after the Second World War the position altered somewhat; but by then other factors came into play, notably Government restrictions on investment, which prevented the railways from exploiting new techniques. This point will be considered later.

If the dice were loaded so heavily against electrification, why was the Southern Railway Company so attracted by it? The main answer is that its traffic was generally more suited to electric traction than that of the other companies. About 78 per cent of the Southern's total revenue came from passenger traffic, compared with a national average of 46 per cent.[20] Much of it consisted of dense flows over relatively short distances at peak hours of the day. This type of traffic required rapid transit to avoid congestion, and here the multiple electric unit, with its speed, acceleration and flexibility, scored heavily over the cumbersome steam train. The nature of the traffic also made it very susceptible to competition from motor transport. Even before 1914 road competition was affecting receipts, and its rapid growth after the war was an important influence in the company's decision to electrify.[21] 'It was only electrification and the reduced operating costs which allowed better services at cheaper fares. By those means rail transport was once more in a competitive position and new traffic was created.'[22] In addition, the Southern Railway was financially better off in this period than the other three companies[23] and could more easily afford to be progressive. It was fortunate too in having a very able chairman.

Though the reasons given for the lag in electrification outside the south are convincing, they are not necessarily the only ones. It is quite possible that the lag would have occurred even if the unfavourable factors had not existed. This point may be clarified by examining the case for diesel traction.

Diesel Traction
The most potent arguments against electrification were the high cost (and low return) coupled with the highly complex nature of the new technology, which required extensive adaptation of the railway structure. Diesel traction possessed many of the advantages of electrification without its chief drawbacks. A fairly elaborate study of the comparative costs

of steam, electric and diesel traction was published in *Modern Transport* soon after the Weir report.[24] The net cost of applying diesel traction over the same network was estimated at about £154 million, considerably lower than for electrification. The annual saving in operating costs compared with steam would have been around £22.8 million (assuming the price of oil to be £3 per ton), producing a return of nearly 15 per cent on the capital invested. If the investment had been phased over a lengthy period the rate of return, after allowing for interest charges, would still have been in the region of 10 per cent. Moreover, the great advantage of diesel traction was that it could replace steam rolling stock when it became obsolete. It was also economically superior to electric traction at lower traffic densities.

Technically the switch to diesel traction was known to be feasible at this time, since successful experiments had already been made. By the early 1930s about 250 diesel locomotives were in use on British railways,[25] whilst American railroads made considerable headway with the diesel traction in the later 1930s and early 1940s. Why then the delay in Britain?

The cost, in terms of either the rate of return or the supply of finance, could hardly have been a deterrent, since each unit could be installed separately with little additional outlay on interrelated assets such as track and signalling. This was equally true both before and after the Second World War. It could be argued that during the war the railways were in no position to exploit new techniques and that for many years after 1945 they were occupied with the backlog of maintenance and renewal, whilst the Government accorded the railways a low priority in investment allocations. Well into the 1950s the British Transport Commission claimed that the backlog of maintenance, coupled with shortages of materials and labour and restrictions on investment, prevented the application of new techniques. In its report for 1953 the Commission lamented that 'even the arrears of maintenance due to the extensive use made of the railways during the war have hardly yet been made good. Not only has the trend of

rising costs outstripped the financial provision made during
the period of Government control to meet these special
arrears of maintenance, but physical limitations upon
re-equipment have intervened . . . It has in fact been possible
to do little more than continue certain major works started
before the war, such as the Manchester-Sheffield-Wath
electrification; to deal with cases of war damage and extreme
dilapidation; and to make a limited number of improvements
on, essentially, a "make-do-and-mend" basis, rather than as
stages of a master development plan'.[26]

Given the severe economic conditions prevailing at the
time, the Commission's argument sounded convincing. And
in terms of electrification it certainly was. But it does not
readily explain the neglect of diesel power. Despite the
economic austerity, diesel traction could easily have been
introduced as part of normal replacement policy. The railways did not cease to build new locomotives altogether after
the war, but their replacement policy was based solely on
steam. For many years after 1945 the mass production of
steam locomotives was continued, and virtually no attempt
was made to explore the possibilities of diesel traction until
well into the following decade. In part this was a reflection
of the general approach to the railways. Despite the antiquated
nature of the railway system after the war, the Commission
made little attempt to draw up long-term plans for modernising it until well into the 1950s. No doubt economic
circumstances would inevitably have involved curtailment or
modification of any plans submitted by the Commission, but
such a delay in presenting plans in the first place was 'quite
inexcusable . . . on the part of a body supposed to be devoting
its whole energy to matters of major policy'.[27]

Effect of Competition
There is clearly no good economic reason to explain the delay
in developing diesel traction. It cannot be explained on
grounds of cost, or on account of items (i), (ii) and (iii) in our
list of factors, because these items had little bearing on diesel

traction. Changes in relative factor prices were of only
marginal importance, and then mainly before 1939. By a
process of elimination we are left with items (v) and (vi).

The first of these relates to external competition and can
be dealt with quite easily. By the 1930s the railways were
faced with two new competitors, road and air transport.
Road transport was by far the more important; it affected
mainly passenger and merchandise traffic over short and
medium distances, though by the later 1930s competition was
being pushed further afield as a result of improvements in
the performance of the motor vehicle. Competition prevailed
both in service and in price. Motor transport generally provided a more flexible and convenient type of service, especially
on difficult cross-country routes; in many cases the prices
charged were lower than those of the railways, partly because
they were based on the costs of operation, whereas the railways adhered to a pricing policy which inadequately reflected
costs.[28] Thus road operators tended to concentrate their
activities on the dense and profitable traffic routes on which
they could undercut their competitors. As a result they
creamed off the best traffic and left the railways with the
bad or high-cost traffic on the thinly populated routes.[29]

If anything the development of road transport presented a
distraction rather than a competitive spur to the railways.
Only the Southern Railway attempted to meet the competition by a shift along the technological front. The other three
railway companies adopted two policies, neither of which was
entirely satisfactory. To combat road competition they
reduced charges sharply in the later 1920s and 1930s, largely
by extending the number of exceptional rates and sub-standard
fares. But these reductions tended to be across-the-board cuts,
with little regard to variations in the degree of competition or
to the costs of operation of different services.[30] Thus overall
net revenue tended to decline, since charges were reduced
alike on the profitable and on the unprofitable, on both competitive and non-competitive traffic.[31] The correct solution
was not an overall non-discriminatory lowering of charges,[32]

but selected changes which took account of differences in profitability and competition. A few of the possibilities were as follows. On the profitable long-distance trunk routes charges could have been maintained or even raised without loss of revenue, since they were only marginally affected by road competition. On the high-cost marginal traffic routes charges should have been raised, either to cover costs or to drive traffic away so that the routes could have been closed. But on some of the short- and medium-distance routes, where traffic was dense and competition severe, charges could have been reduced to prevent losses of traffic to the road.

The second line of attack was for the railways to make a direct move into the road transport business. It was not until after 1928, however, that they made any serious attempt to do so. Initially they concentrated on the passenger side and their chief method of entry was to buy up, or acquire financial interests in, established bus companies. They soon secured substantial interests in many of the larger companies, and by the end of 1931 they were associated in one way or another with 19,500 buses out of a total of 41,500 on British roads — that is, about 47 per cent. The atomistic structure of the road haulage industry made it difficult for the railways to adopt the same approach there. Hence, apart from the purchase of one or two old-established companies such as Pickfords and Carter Paterson, the railways confined their road haulage activities to buying and operating their own vehicles. By 1938 they owned about 10,000 goods vehicles out of a total of nearly half a million.

It is doubtful if the railways gained much from this venture. In fact they probably wasted a great deal of energy and capital which could have been expended more profitably in improving rail services.[33] Their interests in road transport were insufficient, especially on the haulage side, to give them power to curb the degree of competition to any significant extent,[34] and they could not repeat the episode of the canals. But the amount spent on road transport was quite substantial and the return small. Altogether they spent nearly £15 million

— £4.6 million on their own vehicles and about £10 million
on investment in bus companies — money which could
have been spent more profitably. For in 1938 net receipts
from the railways' road transport activities amounted to just
over £130,000, equivalent to a return of less than 3 per cent
on the capital invested.[35]

A similar thing happened in air transport, though to a much
smaller degree. Internal air services were practically non-existent
in the 1920s; and even in the following decade, when a network of trunk services was established, competition with
surface transport was confined to long-distance routes. On
these routes the railways did make an attempt to improve
their services, though this largely took the form of speeding
up their steam passenger trains. But the railways were worried
by the potential threat of air competition and were determined
not to make the same mistake they had made with road transport in the 1920s, when they allowed the new competitor to
establish a strong foothold before participating themselves.
Thus they very soon entered the air transport business, and
by the end of the 1930s had secured a controlling interest in
most of the long-distance air services operating within Great.
Britain. Although the actual capital invested was quite small,
there were persistent losses; in 1937 the loss amounted to
over £51,000.[36]

In sum, therefore, road and air competition probably
tended to divert the attention of the railway companies from
technological improvements. After 1939 this explanation
ceases to apply, since war conditions necessitated Government
control of transport and restricted the scope for investment.
The same partly holds true for the post-war period, since
nationalisation brought together competing forms of transport.

Faith in Steam
This brings us to the final point, item (vi), namely, continued
faith in the old technology by the leaders of the industry.
There seem to be good grounds for arguing that this was an
important factor in delaying the adoption of new forms of

traction both before and after 1939. Before the war railway
opinion was fairly sceptical about the merits of electric and
diesel traction, particularly diesel.[37] Only the Southern
Railway gave electrification a favourable reception; the
reasons for this were discussed earlier. The other companies,
though not completely hostile, certainly did not welcome it.
The climate of opinion was summed up by the Weir Committee as follows: 'We have been unable to find any strong spirit
of conviction in railway circles to warrant a belief that any
schemes, comprehensive or sectional, dealing with main lines
are likely to be adopted.'[38]

In part this reaction could be explained by the fact that in
the 1930s there was still too little known about the comparative costs and advantages of steam, diesel and electric traction.
A number of estimates had been made (notably those of the
Weir Committee and *Modern Transport*), but these dealt
with the railway system as a whole rather than with individual
routes. Of course it could be argued that it was up to the
railways to make a more detailed breakdown in costs in order
to determine the routes on which the new technology could
be introduced economically. Yet, apart from one or two
individual case studies, neither the private companies before
1939 nor the British Transport Commission after the war
made thorough investigations into the comparative costs of
the three forms of traction for individual routes.[39]

But perhaps a more important reason was that the railways
continued to maintain their faith in steam. Generations of
railwaymen — directors, engineers, traffic managers and
workmen alike — had been reared in the era of steam traction,
and they were reluctant to depart from established practice.
This feeling was no doubt reinforced by the fact that considerable capital was locked up in steam traction, which had not
yet been proved obsolete. Reaction to the new techniques
tended, therefore, to be defensive in the sense that serious
attempts were made, especially in the 1930s, to improve the
performance of the locomotive and speed up existing steam
services. Improvements were concentrated primarily on the

main trunk routes with the introduction of the famous stream-
liner trains such as the *Cheltenham Flyer*, the *Silver Jubilee*
and the *Coronation Scot*. The introduction of these crack
expresses brought substantial reductions in journey times on
some of the main-line services; two hours and fifteen minutes
was knocked off the London-Edinburgh run and 95 minutes
off the London-Glasgow service. The London Midland &
Scottish Railway Company set the pace in this respect. By
1938 it had 63 passenger services covering 6,317 miles
scheduled at an average start-to-stop speed of 60 miles per
hour, as against only three such services covering 418 miles in
1932.[40] As a result of these improvements the railways firmly
believed that the steam locomotive still had a future and that
it could be made competitive with the new forms of traction.
They therefore saw little need to explore new possibilities.[41]

This faith in steam traction continued to prevail after the
war, no doubt largely because the Railway Executive of the
British Transport Commission was staffed mainly with railwaymen of the steam era. This appears to be the only really
convincing explanation of the Commission's policy of placing
orders for nothing but steam locomotives for nearly a decade
after the war.[42] As one prominent writer on railway history
has recently pointed out: 'The insistence of the Railway
Executive's engineers that really worthwhile economies could
be achieved by one more reappraisal of steam locomotive
design was symptomatic of the inward-looking traditionalism
of the railway industry.'[43]

Conclusion
It is debatable whether economic factors alone caused the
long delay in the application of electric and diesel traction to
Britain's railways. Certainly in the case of electrification the
economic prospects were doubtful, especially after the rather
unfavourable pronouncements of the Weir Committee. But
the economic case for diesel traction was much stronger, and
this suggests that other constraints were operative. The dis-
tracting effect of competing forms of transport was not

unimportant before 1939, but lost much of its force after the war. The availability of finance presented a problem after 1945, but this does not adequately explain the neglect of diesel traction. The only permanent element, operative both before and after the war, seems to have been the railway leaders' attachment to, or faith in, steam traction. This situation probably resulted from the fact that railway management was largely inbred. Both before and after nationalisation the higher echelons of management were drawn mainly from men who had been in the railway business since boyhood. The failure to recruit managerial staff from outside the profession, at least until recently, meant that the prospects for questioning traditional railway practice were limited. If the railways are to safeguard against similar problems of technological stagnation in the future they will need to draw much more widely than hitherto on outside talent and advice.[44]

NOTES

1   See the *Annual Reports and Accounts* of the British Transport Commission and D.L. Munby, 'The Future of British Railways', *London and Cambridge Economic Bulletin*, 49 (1964), xv

2   For the railway background in general see D.H. Aldcroft, *British Railways in Transition: The Economic Problems of Britain's Railways since 1914* (1968)

3   C.J. Allen, *Locomotive Practice and Performance in the Twentieth Century* (1949), 233

4   A fairly full summary of the benefits can be found in E.C. Cox, 'The Progress of the Southern Railway Electrification', *Journal of the Institute of Transport* (January 1937)

5   For full details see G.T. Moody, *Southern Electric* (1960), and H.P. White, *A Regional History of the Railways of Great Britain: Vol 2: Southern England* (1961)

6   *Railway Gazette* (1 April 1938), 685

7   Ibid (28 April 1939), 39 (Electric Traction Supplement) and
    K.H. Johnston, *British Railways and Economic Recovery* (1949),
    328

8   On the other hand, operating costs of electric traction are lower
    than those of diesel traction

9   Even if average operating costs are the same in both cases the new
    technology may be introduced if it produces economies external
    to the actual production process. For example, a new machine
    may be capable of producing the same number of units of a
    particular product at exactly the same cost as the one replaced,
    but, because it produces them in a more convenient size and
    shape, handling and distribution costs are lowered. These economies
    may not accrue directly to the firm producing the product, but
    indirectly it may stand to benefit from an increase in demand
    resulting from lower distribution costs and a more attractive
    format

10 This may not always be the case, however. Lower capital costs in
    the downswing of the cycle may encourage innovation

11 Ministry of Transport, *Report of the Committee on Main-Line
    Electrification* (1931)

12 Ibid, 21

13 Ibid, 16

14 *Railway Gazette* (19 May 1939), 808 (Supplement), and (26 May
    1939), 54 (Supplement)

15 British Transport Commission, *Electrification of Railways*
    (1951), 8, 14-15

16 See the discussion in the *Report of the Select Committee on
    Nationalised Industries: British Railways*, H of C 254 (1960), l-liii

17 T. Watson Collin, 'Railway Finance in the Light of the Railways
    Act, 1921', *The Accountant*, 86 (1932), 41

18   Outside borrowing would have been necessary for a large-scale
      programme of electrification

19   Between 1924 and 1938 railway wage rates fell by 1 per cent
      and coal prices by 13.3 per cent, whereas the price index of
      capital goods remained stable and steel prices rose by 9.8 per
      cent. London and Cambridge Economic Service, *Key Statistics*
      (1900-1966), and B.R. Mitchell, *Abstract of British Historical
      Statistics* (1962), 351, 477

20   W. Smith, *An Economic Geography of Great Britain* (1953),
      593

21   Moody, op cit, 5

22   White, op cit, 187

23   As a result of its location in the more prosperous south and the
      nature of its traffic. Only a small proportion of the company's
      receipts was derived from those types of traffic (heavy freight)
      which were declining

24   *Modern Transport* (4 and 11 July 1931). See also A. Brown,
      The Railway Problem (1932)

25   Mostly for shunting purposes

26   British Transport Commission, *Annual Report for 1953*, 23

27   W.A. Robson, *Nationalized Industry and Public Ownership*
      (1960), 96

28   Railway freight pricing policy was based on a value system of
      classification, which charged a high rate for valuable goods and
      a low one for cheap commodities. Passengers were charged a
      standard rate per mile. Thus there was no close correspondence
      between charges and costs, and the system as a whole involved
      a considerable amount of cross-subsidisation. In practice this
      meant that charges were higher than they should have been on
      the dense and profitable traffic routes where road competition
      was often severe, and too low on the high-cost routes where road
      transport was less competitive. For a more detailed treatment of
      the basis of railway pricing policy see G. Walker, *Road and Rail*

(1947 ed), and Aldcroft, op cit, 59-68

29   C.I. Savage, *An Economic History of Transport* (1959), 140-2

30   Walker, op cit, 130-1, and B. Williams, 'Transport Act 1947:
      Some Benefits and Dangers', *Journal of the Institute of Transport*
      (May 1951), 154

31   The railways were imbued with the idea of attracting or maintain-
      ing as much traffic as possible, irrespective of the costs of carrying
      it. Any addition to the volume of traffic would raise gross revenue,
      but the railways often overlooked the fact that it might at the
      same time reduce the net return if the costs of carrying the
      additional traffic were greater than the revenue derived from it.
      For a fuller exposition of this point see D.H. Aldcroft, 'The
      Efficiency and Enterprise of British Railways, 1870-1914',
      Explorations in Entrepreneurial History, 5 (1968)

32   A course of action which inevitably led to a failure to achieve
      optimum fare levels. For example, by the middle of the 1930s
      the average fare per passenger mile had been reduced to 0.64
      pence, whereas it has been estimated that an average fare of
      0.904 pence was required to maximise revenue. See E.J. Broster,
      'Railway Passenger Receipts and Fares Policy', *Economic Journal*,
      47 (1937), and 'Variability of Railway Operating Costs', ibid,
      48 (1938)

33   *Final Report of the Royal Commission on Transport*, Cd 3751
      (1931), 41

34   See D.N. Chester, *Public Control of Road Passenger Transport*
      (1936), 209-10

35   That is, on the investment of £4.6 million in their own road
      vehicles. The railway accounts do not specify what was earned
      on investments in road passenger transport concerns. Most of
      the above data have been compiled from the Ministry of Transport
      Railway Returns (1933-8)

36   See D.H. Aldcroft, 'The Railways and Air Transport in Great
      Britain, 1933-1939', *Scottish Journal of Political Economy*,
      12 (1965) (see pp 226-42 above)

37   See *The Economist* (18 April 1936), 120

38   Ministry of Transport, *Report of the Committee on Main-Line Electrification* (1931), 5

39   In the 1950s, for instance, the London Midland electrification scheme was allowed to go forward without any proper examination of the alternative cost of applying diesel traction. See *Select Committee Report* (1960), para 222

40   S.H. Fisher, 'Acceleration of Railway Services', *Journal of the Institute of Transport* (February 1939), 144-5, 152

41   A view no doubt reinforced by the incredible performance of the steam locomotive *Mallard*, which attained a top speed of 125mph on test runs in 1938. This was both a British and a world record for steam

42   It is interesting to point out here that, though just before nationalisation the Southern Railway Company issued a plan (November 1946) to convert all lines east of Portsmouth to electric and diesel traction, it was not until 1959 that the scheme was put in hand.

43   G.F. Allen, *British Rail After Beeching* (1966), 6

44   An important consideration in view of recent technical developments. It now seems likely that the Railways Board and the Government are prepared to finance further research on high-speed trains

_12_ The Changing Pattern of Demand for Passenger Transport in Post-war Britain*

D.H. Aldcroft and P.J. Bemand

In the post-war period there have been many studies of local and regional passenger transport movements which have focussed attention in particular on the decline in public transport and the concomitant problems of urban traffic congestion as a result of the widespread use of the private car. Such studies have been concerned with the factors determining traffic generation and attraction and modal split and have made extensive use of gravity type models.[1] These studies have been primarily directed towards the problems of urban and regional transport planning and there have been few attempts to examine trends in passenger transport movement at the macro level.

This neglect is partly explained by the absence of sufficiently detailed long-run time series data in a form suitable for such an analysis. However, the improvement in the official statistics since the early 1950s makes it possible to carry out a study at the aggregate level for the period up to 1969. The first part of this paper discusses the post-war trends in consumers' expenditure on transport and the allocation of that expenditure between different modes. In the second part an attempt is made to explain these trends and modal split using multiple regression analysis on the data for the period 1956-69.

assistance with the preliminary calculations. The research was greatly assisted by a generous grant from the Houblon-Norman Fund.

Since the war passenger transport has grown rapidly both in absolute and relative terms. Between 1952 and 1969 the total number of passenger miles travelled in Great Britain by the chief modes of transport (air, rail, bus, and private car) has increased from 112.2 thousand million to 242.5 thousand million, an increase of 116.1 per cent.[2] In the same period consumers' expenditure on transport has increased rapidly and its share of total consumers' expenditure has risen from 6.45 per cent to 11.27 per cent.[3]

The trends in consumers' expenditure on transport since the war are given in full in Table 1 *(opposite)* and in Appendix 2 *(see page 300).* The share of expenditure on transport in total consumers' expenditure (at current prices) has risen from 5.95 per cent in 1946 to 11.27 per cent in 1969, an average rate of increase of 2.7 per cent per annum. This is a larger and more sustained increase than for any other major sector of consumers' expenditure.[4] A breakdown between modes of transport shows clearly that this substantial increase has been accounted for entirely by the growth of private transport. In fact the share of public transport in consumers' expenditure on transport has fallen substantially from 46.15 to 18.70 per cent between 1953 and 1969, while that of motoring[5] has increased from 46.77 to 71.34 per cent over the same period. Within the public sector the shares of rail and road have changed very little, their respective proportions being approximately 30 and 70 per cent respectively.

These changes are reflected as might be expected in the shares of different modes in total passenger miles. A glance at Table 2 *(see page 266)* shows that the share of public transport in total passenger mileage has fallen even more sharply than in the case of consumers' expenditure; in 1969 it accounted for only 23.63 per cent as against 63.88 per cent, while that of private motoring has risen from 35.95 to 75.88 per cent between 1953 and 1969. The shares of rail and road within the public sector have again remained relatively constant over the period, with rail accounting for a slightly larger share than in the case of consumers' expenditure.

TABLE 1: *Changes in Consumers' Expenditure on Transport in UK 1946-69*

	Consumers' expenditure on transport as % of total consumers' expenditure	Expenditure on public transport as % of total consumers' expenditure on transport	Expenditure on motoring as % of total consumers' expenditure on transport	Expenditure on rail as % of consumers' expenditure on public transport	Expenditure on Bus and Coach travel as % of consumers' expenditure on public transport
1946	5.95	NA	28.77	NA	NA
1947	5.95	NA	31.58	NA	NA
1948	5.39	NA	22.56	NA	NA
1949	5.67	NA	27.92	NA	NA
1950	5.69	NA	32.34	NA	NA
1951	5.83	NA	34.46	NA	NA
1952	6.45	NA	38.55	NA	NA
1953	6.95	46.15	46.77	29.51	70.49
1954	7.20	42.53	48.85	30.00	70.00
1955	7.81	38.02	54.42	29.20	70.80
1956	7.56	39.27	52.07	29.90	70.10
1957	7.86	37.60	53.37	30.77	69.23
1958	8.57	32.57	59.65	31.15	68.85
1959	9.03	29.95	62.57	30.73	69.27
1960	9.41	28.67	64.12	31.73	68.27
1961	9.14	29.33	62.94	31.80	68.20
1962	9.44	27.62	64.54	31.64	68.36
1963	9.85	25.53	66.48	31.49	68.51
1964	10.28	23.84	68.04	31.37	68.63
1965	10.28	22.96	68.50	31.48	68.52
1966	10.44	22.37	68.70	31.63	68.37
1967	10.97	20.42	70.55	31.87	68.13
1968	11.42	18.64	72.19	31.72	68.28
1969	11.27	18.70	71.34	34.00	66.00

Source: *National Income and Expenditure*

TABLE 2

The Shares of Different Modes in Total Passenger Mileage in GB, 1952-69

	Air	Rail	Road (public service vehicles)	Public Sector (rail & road)	Road (private transport)
	%	%	%	%	%
1952	0.09	21.48	44.65	66.13	33.78
1953	0.17	20.58	43.30	63.88	35.95
1954	0.16	19.90	41.12	61.02	38.82
1955	0.15	18.58	38.88	57.46	42.39
1956	0.21	18.43	36.57	55.02	44.77
1957	0.23	19.62	34.77	54.39	45.38
1958	0.21	17.95	30.54	48.49	51.30
1959	0.26	16.77	28.99	45.76	53.98
1960	0.31	15.64	27.68	43.32	56.37
1961	0.35	14.38	25.72	41.01	59.55
1962	0.40	13.18	24.51	37.69	61.91
1963	0.47	12.43	23.03	35.46	64.07
1964	0.46	11.72	20.53	32.25	67.29
1965	0.60	10.54	18.96	29.40	70.00
1966	0.61	9.95	17.36	27.31	72.18
1967	0.52	9.33	16.28	25.61	73.87
1968	0.51	8.81	15.38	24.19	75.30
1969	0.49	8.91	14.72	23.63	75.88

Source: *Passenger Transport in Great Britain*

The results of the analysis of both consumers' expenditure on transport and passenger mileage data illustrate clearly the sharp decline of the public sector and the corresponding rise of the share of private transport, with rail being affected slightly less adversely within the public sector.

The following analysis seeks to establish the major variables which have influenced (1) the share of total consumers' expenditure devoted to transport, and (2) the allocation of this expenditure between alternative modes.

The chief variables which need to be considered in determining the level of total transport expenditure are disposable income and income distribution, the price of transport relative to the price of other commodities, the size of population, density and spatial distribution of population, the age and sex distribution of population, family size and level of car ownership. All of these factors have usually been included in urban and regional models of traffic flows,[6] but in a macro approach using time series data some of these variables are inappropriate for one reason or another. This is because for one thing the concepts concerned cannot be meaningfully considered in a national context. And secondly, data limitations preclude their use. Thus for instance, income distribution and the spatial and age distributions of the population cannot conveniently be represented by values at the aggregate level for each year without introducing undue complexity in the equations. On the other hand, while population density could obviously be represented by a single figure it is equally obvious that its introduction, in addition to population size, would be meaningless for the simple reason that an increase in population inevitably produces a rise in density on a national basis and would thereby give rise to multicollinearity. Similarly, though data for average family size and the level of car ownership could be introduced without great difficulty it is probable that their influence is more relevant to local and regional traffic studies than in a national context. Effectively, therefore, this leaves us with three primary variables, income, relative prices and population size, with family size and car ownership as possible additional variables.

The exact form of the variables used and the statistical sources are as follows. As the income variable we have used total consumers' expenditure (C) as representing disposable personal income (less savings); this also met our requirements for explaining the share of total transport (C_t) in consumers' expenditure.[7] For population we have used 'De facto or home population mid year estimates' (N).[8] The price relatives posed a more difficult problem. In order to enable a comparison to be made between the price of transport and the price of all commodities it was necessary to use the price variable in an index form. The index of retail prices for 'all items' (P) and for 'transport and vehicles' (P_t) have been used;[9] the latter includes the expenditure on public transport and the running costs and purchase of private motor vehicles; it therefore meets our requirements as determined by the items included in consumers' expenditure on transport. Unfortunately, however, prior to 1956 the interim index of retail prices did not include 'transport and vehicles' as a distinct item but incorporated it under the heading 'Services'. This restricts the span of the time series analysis to the years 1956-69. It might be borne in mind, however, that to push the analysis back further in time would run up against the problem of the abnormal conditions of the early post-war period for which the available statistics are none too reliable. The relative price variable $\frac{P_t}{P}$ was then constructed from these two components.

The general form of the first function could then be written as:
$C_t = f (C, \frac{P_t}{P}, N)$. The linear form of this function was derived as follows:

$$C_t = a + b\,C + b_2\,\frac{P_t}{P} + b_3\,N \quad \dots \dots \dots \dots 1$$

Explanations of the allocation of expenditure between modes was more difficult due to the shortcomings of the available data. First, it was necessary to restrict the analysis to three surface modes, rail, bus and private car, since these are dealt with separately in the consumers' expenditure data whereas expenditure on air travel, taxis and hire cars are included in 'Other Travel'.[10] Secondly it is impossible to separate expenditure on urban and long-distance travel in the case of buses and cars and the equivalent separation of passenger mileage is also difficult, if not impossible, due to the classification of the official statistics.[11] These data problems have prevented an analysis being made of the alternative modes for similar types of journey, eg between rail and car and express coach for long-distance travel, or between car and bus in cities.

The appropriate variables to be considered in explaining modal choice at the aggregate level should not differ markedly from those discussed above in the case of total transport expenditure. The arguments used for the exclusion from consideration of certain variables apply equally here. Important additional variables which might be examined are relative travel times and the quality of service (passenger comfort, frequency of service, inter-service connections etc). It is impossible however to devise meaningful values for relative travel times or to quantify quality of service at the aggregate level.[12]

As the dependent variable for analysis in modal choice the number of passenger miles travelled per year on each mode was considered to be most suitable, on the grounds that passenger miles provides a measure of output in physical terms which enables more precise comparisons to be made between the different modes than would be possible if consumers' expenditure were used.

Four functions were constructed, one for total passenger mileage and one for each of the three modes being considered. The general form of the functions is as follows:[13]

$$PM_t = f(C_t, \frac{P_t}{P}, N) \quad \ldots \ldots \ldots \ldots \ldots 2$$

and

$$PM_i = f(C_t, \frac{P_i}{P}, N) \text{ for mode } i \quad \ldots \ldots \ldots \ldots 3, 4, 5$$

The results of the regression analysis for the five equations given above were as follows:

1   Consumers' Expenditure on transport (C_t)

$$C_t = 2330.84 + 0.175C + 815.855 \frac{P_t}{P} - 0.0882N$$

$R^2 = 0.9958$

2   Total Passenger Miles (PM_t)

$$PM_t = -409.735 + 0.00472C - 37.085\frac{P_t}{P} + 0.0100N$$

$R^2 = 0.9935$

3　Passenger Miles : Rail (PM_r)
$$PM_r = 50.589 + 0.0000503C_t - 15.057\frac{P_r}{P} - 0.0002175N$$
$$R^2 = 0.946$$

4　Passenger Miles : Bus (PM_b)
$$PM_b = 81.452 - 0.00284C_t - 10.790\frac{P_b}{P} - 0.000{\text{·}}19N$$
$$R^2 = 0.942$$

5　Passenger Miles : Car (PM_c)
$$PM_c = 601.794 \div 0.0332C_t - 16.392\frac{P_c}{P} + 0.0125N$$
$$R^2 = 0.9946$$

Tests of 'goodness of fit' of these regression lines showed the calculated F ratios for all five to be substantially greater than the critical value for 3 and 10 degrees of freedom at the 1% level. Calculated values:

Equation 1:　111.96
　　　　　2:　720.29
　　　　　3:　　83.30
　　　　　4:　　77.00
　　　　　5:　856.85
　F (3, 10), 1% level:　6.55

It will be noted that the corrected values for R^2 are also high for all five regression lines. The results of the tests of significance for the individual co-efficients are rather less promising. The calculated 't' values for the five equations are summarised in the table below:

Variable	1	2	3	4	5
(Constant)	0.907	-2.39	1.799	1.73	-3.44
C	9.15	3.69			
C_t			- 0.052	- 1.44	5.022
P_t/P	1.197	- 0.814			
P_r/P_t			-3.59		
P_b/P_t				-1.18	
P_c/P_t					- 0.75
N	-1.47	2.499	- 0.35	- 0.416	3.74

[Critical value for 't' with 10 degrees of freedom at the 5% level is 2.23. Underlined values are significant]

The table shows that of the fifteen explanatory co-efficients, only six are significant. Of the latter, the most powerful variable is consumer expenditure; thus total consumer expenditure is a major factor in the determination of both the level of consumer expenditure on transport (1), and total passenger-miles travelled (2), whilst consumer expenditure on transport is a significant explanatory force in the case of car travel (5). Population growth is significant in the determination of two dependent variables, namely total passenger-mileage (2), and car travel (5). Finally, the price variable is significant in only one case, and somewhat surprisingly, this is travel by rail.

That these results are less negative than may appear at first glance can best be shown by considering each of the equations in turn in the light of the discussion in the first part of the paper. The results for equation (1) show total consumer expenditure as the major force in determining the level of consumer expenditure on transport; neither the price of transport relative to all commodities nor the growth of population are significant. When it is recalled that expenditure on transport has increased at a faster rate than any other major category of consumer expenditure, primarily because of the growth of private transport, these results should occasion no surprise. The rapid rise in the cost of motoring has not checked the spread of car ownership nor the increase in travel by car. It would appear that the insignificance of the price variable in the case of total transport expenditure reflects largely the price inelasticity of travel by car. So far as the population variable is concerned, it may be surmised that the increase in expenditure on transport due to population growth is swamped by the increase in per capita expenditure on transport.

The second equation, for total passenger mileage, illustrates the same situation from a slightly different viewpoint. Again the level of total consumer expenditure is the major significant variable, and the relative price of transport is not significant. Population growth, however, is a significant variable in this equation; the effects of population growth seem to be more directly observable in the case of total passenger miles travelled. This is almost certainly accounted for by the dominant share of the private car in total passenger mileage, and in this case we are not dealing with fare-paying passengers.

Equation (3), relating to passenger-miles travelled by rail, is notable in that it is the only case in which the price variable is significant; furthermore, price is the only significant variable in this equation. The result indicates that price elasticity is the major cause of the declining share of rail travel in total passenger-mileage.[14]

The fourth equation, for passenger-miles travelled by bus, is by far the least satisfactory; the failure to obtain useful results here may be attributed to the impossibility of treating urban and long-distance travel separately as was noted earlier.[15] Indeed, the result for rail travel must also be regarded with caution in view of the comparable difficulty of treating suburban and inter-city travel separately.

The results shown in the last equation, explaining passenger miles travelled by car, have been anticipated in the discussions of the first two equations above; consumer expenditure on transport and population growth are both significant variables, price is not significant.

Taken as a whole, the results of the regression analysis provide confirmation of the trends pointed out in the earlier part of the paper. Two major points have been established here: first, the rapid and continuing growth of expenditure on transport as a share of total consumer expenditure is largely independent of the price of transport relative to the general price level; secondly, this trend in total transport expenditure is explained largely by the dominance established by the private car in passenger travel. Neither of these conclusions can offer much comfort to those concerned with the future development of passenger transport in Britain.

NOTES

1   The literature is extensive and only a selection can be mentioned.
    See for instance W.Y. Oi and P.W. Shuldiner, *An Analysis of*
    Urban Travel Demands (1962), J.F. Kain, 'A Contribution to the
    Urban Transportation Debate: An Econometric Model of Urban
    Residential and Travel Behaviour', *The Review of Economics and*
    Statistics, 46 (1964), F.R. Wilson, *Journey to Work — Modal Split*
    (1967), and M.E. Beesley and J.F. Kain, 'Forecasting Car Owner-
    ship and Use', *Urban Studies*, 2 (November 1965)

2   *Passenger Transport in Great Britain* (HMSO)

3   In current prices. *National Income and Expenditure Blue Books*
    (HMSO)

4   The percentage shares of consumers' expenditure for major
    sectors in 1946 and 1969 is shown below:

		1946	1969
1	Transport and travel	5.95	11.27
2	Food	24.32	20.88
3	Housing	9.06	12.54
4	Fuel and light	3.87	4.97
5	Durable goods (excl vehicle purchases)	2.72	4.11
6	Durable goods (incl vehicle purchases)	3.22	6.84

5   Expenditure on motoring as used here includes purchases of
    motor-cars and motor-cycles and running costs of motor vehicles.
    See *National Accounts Statistics: Sources & Methods* (1968),
    for further details

6   See note 1

7   *National Income and Expenditure Blue Books*

8   *Annual Abstract of Statistics* (1970), 7, Table 6

9   Ibid

10   In any case these modes account for an insignificant part of
     total passenger transport

11 For example, it is not until the early 1960s, when the first
    Motoring Survey was taken, that it becomes possible to make
    such a breakdown for private transport. See 'Motor Car Owner-
    ship and Use', *Economic Trends*, 116 (June 1963), and G.F.
    Ray and C.T. Saunders, 'Problems and Policies for Inland
    Transport', Ch XI, in W. Beckerman *et al, The British
    Economy in 1975* (1965), 341-5

12 Certain aspects of quality of service, eg comfort, would be
    difficult to quantify in any circumstances, even at the local level

13 The notations and sources used for the analysis are as follows:
    C -   Total consumers' expenditure
    C_t -   Consumers' expenditure on transport
    N -   Population
    PM_t -   Total passenger miles travelled
    PM_r -   Passenger miles by rail
    PM_b -   Passenger miles by bus
    PM_c -   Passenger miles by private car
    P -   Price of 'all items'
    P_t -   Price of all transport
    P_r -   Price of rail transport
    P_b -   Price of bus transport
    P_c -   Price of car transport
        The sources for the variables not already covered in equation
    (1) are as follows: the passenger miles data are drawn from
    Passenger Transport in Great Britain, 1963-69. For the price
    indices for rail and bus the average passenger receipts per
    passenger mile figures were calculated from the passenger
    mileage and average passenger receipts data in the *Annual
    Abstract of Statistics* and *Passenger Transport in Great Britain*.
    Similarly for cars, an index of average expenditure per passenger
    mile was derived from total consumers' expenditure on motoring
    and passenger mileage data as given above

14 Cf R. Pryke, *Public Enterprise in Practice* (1971), 230-1

15 Local studies suggest that urban bus traffic is elastic with respect
    to fare increases and a rise in the car stock. See J. S. Wabe and
    O.B. Coles, 'The Economics of Bus Operations in Coventry',
    Warwick Economic Research Papers, 29 (October 1972)

13 Reflections on the Rochdale Inquiry into Shipping

First published in Maritime History, *1 (1971)*

Britain's maritime industries have been well served by govern-
mental committees in recent years. In 1962 the Rochdale
Committee reported on the docks;[1] four years later the
Geddes inquiry surveyed the shipbuilding industry;[2] finally
the turn of shipping came in 1967 when the President of the
Board of Trade appointed a small committee, again under the
chairmanship of Viscount Rochdale, to undertake a wide-
ranging survey of the industry. After considerable delay the
committee duly presented a voluminous report in May 1970.[3]
This was to be, as the President of the Board of Trade noted
on the appearance of the report, the first full-scale investigation of the British shipping industry ever to be undertaken.
Not since the beginning of the twentieth century had shipping
activity been subject to such close scrutiny and even then the
earlier inquiries had been only partial in scope.[4]

Before looking in detail at some of the committee's labours
it might be useful to offer a few general reflections and comments on the report. Despite its length — nearly 500 pages in
all — it would be misleading to describe the document as comprehensive in all respects. It is true that on some topics it is
extraordinarily long: for example, nearly 100 pages,
approaching one-quarter of the effective text, are devoted to
manpower and related problems. This is surely somewhat
disproportionate relative to the importance of the subject
vis à vis others. It would appear that a great deal of the detail
on the training of seamen etc could have been left out without
great loss. On the other hand, some subjects are given short
shrift: conferences are discussed in only twenty pages, the

use of new investment-appraisal techniques are scarcely
mentioned, while international comparisons on many aspects
are excused on the grounds of data limitations.

The report is unlikely to prove a policy-inspiring document.
This is largely because its conclusions are neither controversial nor presented very forcibly. There are almost no startling
revelations and in consequence the report provides rather
unexciting reading. An almost complete absence of 'headline
material' was the way *Fairplay* summed it up.[5] It contrasts
sharply with the ferocious attack which Sturmey launched on
the shipping industry in 1962.[6] The difference in tone is
partly to be explained by the fact that in the years since
Sturmey's analysis the industry has been repairing some of
the mistakes made since the war. But it should also be recognised that the inquiry was carried out by a committee
untrammelled by vested interest and as such it is objective,
fair and free from bias.[7] Perhaps it might be suggested that
the committee, cognisant of the vitriolic attacks made on the
industry in the past, have leaned too far in the other direction
and have taken an unjustifiably complacent view of the
industry's efforts to revitalise itself. As *The Times* leader
rather unkindly remarked, 'the Report might almost have
been written by the industry itself.[8]

Indeed few industries subject to official inquiry can have
emerged so unscathed as the shipping industry does from the
investigations of Lord Rochdale and his team. The committee
make many recommendations but few, if any, are of the kind
which require major changes in the structure of the industry
or in government policy towards it. The absence of drastic
policy changes is reflected in the relatively mild interest it
has aroused in shipping circles, a sharp contrast to the furore
which Sturmey's book caused in the early 1960s. The report
was generally warmly welcomed by shipowners as a vindi-
cation of their latest efforts,[9] while the shipping journals
devoted a remarkably small amount of space to it. On the
basis of inspired leaks, *Shipping World and Shipbuilder*
summarily dismissed the report three months before it

appeared as being not worthwhile, and later argued, in a mere half column, that the speed of the industry's adaptation to change had overtaken the inquiry.[10] Only *The Economist* appears to have given it reasonable coverage.[11]

To appreciate the significance of the Rochdale Report the shipping industry's problems need to be placed in historical perspective. In the latter half of the nineteenth century British shipping expanded rapidly on the basis of new techniques, notably steam, iron and later steel. Britain became by far the largest maritime power and she had few serious rivals. In the two or three decades before 1914 Britain owned some 40-50 per cent of the world's steam tonnage, that is four times as much as the nearest competitor, Germany. In addition, about half of the world's seaborne trade and two-thirds of British trade was carried in British vessels, while up to two-thirds of the new ships launched were built in this country.[12]

Yet there were signs, even at this early date, that British supremacy in this field was beginning to crumble. During the 1890s the growth of the British fleet began to slacken off and contemporaries noted with mild alarm that certain foreign fleets, especially those of Germany and later Japan, were advancing more rapidly and beginning to encroach on British sea routes. The subsequent intervention of war had a serious effect on British shipping; a large amount of tonnage was lost, and though handsome profits were made these were dissipated frivolously in the immediate post-war boom. By 1920 the British fleet had barely regained the pre-war level whereas there had been a substantial expansion in world shipping generally. During the inter-war period British shipping marked time. The slower growth in trade compared with before 1914, low profits, excess capacity and severe foreign competition as a result of nationalistic maritime policies on the part of foreign governments, reduced the incentive to invest and expand the fleet. As a result the volume of shipping owned by the UK remained almost static and by 1939 Britain's share of the total had fallen to 28 per cent or less, compared with 44 per cent in 1914.

Despite the external constraints on expansion, however, it is also clear that the difficulties of British shipowners were partly self-inflicted. They were certainly less enterprising than their foreign counterparts, both subsidised and non-subsidised, as regards exploiting new trades and new techniques. Openings in non-British and non-liner trades were available had the trouble been taken to exploit them, while the adoption of new technology, in the form of oil-driven ships, would have reduced costs and made British shipowners more competitive. But for the most part such opportunities were missed. British shipowners invested in traditional techniques rather than in new ones. Thus, for instance, while Scandinavian owners were building diesel-engined tankers, fruit-carriers and cargo ships suitable for charter to liner companies, UK tramp owners continued to favour the traditional 9-10 knot dry-cargo steamships. It is significant that non-subsidised Scandinavian tonnage more than doubled between 1919 and 1939 (from 3.6 to 7.6 million gross tons) and Norway in particular managed to capture a substantial proportion of trade once carried by British vessels.[13]

The relative decline of the British fleet has continued almost unchecked post-1945. Though there has been a small absolute rise in the tonnage owned since the late 1930s and compared with the early post-war low, by the end of the 1960s the UK tonnage was no greater than it had been in 1930. This compares very unfavourably when set against the rapid growth in the world fleet, from 60.1 million gross tons in September 1939 to 179.5 million at the end of December 1968. In consequence Britain's share of world tonnage has slumped from 28 to 11.5 per cent over the same period, though by the latter date Britain was still, by a narrow margin, the largest shipowner outside the 'flags of convenience' countries.[14]

It was perhaps only to be expected that Britain would suffer some loss of importance after the war with the rapid development of new shipping powers, some of which were backed strongly by government assistance, and with the emergence of flags of convenience, protective policies and the slower growth in British trade compared with that of the world as a whole. But it is difficult to conceive that these factors fully explain the sharp decline, or the fact that British tonnage has stagnated since 1930 given the rapid rise in sea-borne trade since the war and the openings for shipping created by new trades and new technology. Professor Sturmey's argument was that the decline was largely self-generated through the unenterprising internal structure of the shipping companies. Unfortunately the Rochdale Committee do not address themselves to this issue directly but focus their main attention on the poor profitability record of British shipping. Indirectly they attempt to answer the question though it is necessary to consult many chapters of the report to obtain a coherent review. In many respects their findings do not differ markedly from those of Sturmey, but they are expressed in more moderate language, they are dispersed over several chapters, and, what is more important, they detect signs of revival since the commencement of their inquiry. This latter finding together with the absence of strong recommendations probably account for the welcome accorded to the report by shipowners.

As regards external constraints on British shipping the committee deal with this subject fairly succinctly in Chapter 4 on 'Foreign Competition'. Shipowners have long argued that external factors such as subsidisation of fleets, flag discrimination, the growth of flags of convenience and the creation of new national fleets have been largely responsible for their difficulties. There is some truth in this assertion but it cannot explain the very poor record at a time of rapidly expanding world trade and opportunities for the employment of shipping. For one thing those countries practising some of the more blatant forms of protection, such as flag discrimination and subsidies, have not done very well either. The fleets of France, Italy and the United States increased only by between 27 and 32 per cent over the period 1958-68 as against an increase of 79 per cent in world tonnage. Similarly, the main flag discriminators, the Latin American countries, have also had a poor record.

On the other hand, many west European and Scandinavian countries have managed to expand their fleets considerably without the aid of protection to any significant degree. Thus over the same period the Norwegian fleet doubled, that of Greece quadrupled, while those of Sweden, Denmark, Finland, West Germany and Portugal have all done very much better than the British. The Japanese fleet, though assisted by liberal credit facilities, has expanded by no less than 245 per cent during the same time. The fleets flying flags of convenience — operating from tax havens — Liberia and Lebanon in particular, have done very much better than the average, but these fleets do not compete with liner services and their existence has not prevented a significant expansion of the tanker and tramp fleets of those countries which do not grant any protection at all. Yet despite capital subsidies, which curiously enough the committee do not recognise as such, Britain has had virtually the worst record of any country, and had it not been for the increased operations of overseas-owned and merchant companies the fleet would have declined absolutely.

It would be erroneous, therefore, to attribute the stagnation in shipping simply to unfavourable external influences. But it is not until very much later — in fact nearly some 300 pages on — that the committee get to the crux of the matter, namely profitability. The return on capital employed in shipping has been extremely low; an independent study carried out for the committee showed that it averaged roughly 3.6 per cent (before tax) over the period 1958-69, that is well less than a third of the average return for all companies.[15] Such low returns can hardly have provided owners with much incentive to invest. 'In view of their experience, it is not surprising that they did not extend their fleets more in the period under review; rather it may be considered surprising that they continued to invest in new vessels as much as they did.'[16] The committee went on to express the view that if much higher returns could not be earned in the future shipowners would be acting in the best interests of the shareholders if they decided to run down their investments in shipping activities.[17] The committee, however, did not feel disposed to make any specific recommendation along these lines.

Unfortunately the committee's analysis at this point leaves much to be desired and it is necessary to draw on information presented earlier to get a proper overview of the problem. There are many questions that require answering before argument along these lines can be sustained. First, how do recent returns compare with those of the past and with those of foreign fleets? It is generally assumed that shipowners have been prepared to operate at lower returns than those for industry as a whole though there is little historical information to substantiate this point. As regards international comparisons the committee were unable to collect sufficient informatio to provide a reliable yardstick. Thus we are left very much in the dark on this point, which is a pity since if returns abroad were equally low then we should need some alternative explanation as to why British tonnage stagnated. Second, why were profits so low? Was it due to a general over-investment in tonnage, poor utilisation of ships through defective management, bad investment decisions, inappropriate pricing policies or to unavoidable fluctuations? Here the committee are very diffuse in their analysis and on some points they have little to offer in the way of concrete information. Finally, if investment in shipping is allowed to be run down as the committee seem to feel is desirable, how far must this be carried before returns are raised to a reasonable level? And what is to be regarded as reasonable in this context? If, on the assumption that excess capacity is not the problem, the fleet has to be pruned severely in order to raise returns, then this may increase external costs considerably. Presumably shippers would suffer delays in exporting and importing goods (unless foreign fleets were pure substitutes) and the cost of employing foreign shipping services would be borne by the balance of payments, a matter to which the committee devote considerable attention later on in the report. Incidentally, the question about excess capacity and how much (cf the railways), and there must surely be some, was never explicitly considered.

Since there are so many unknowns it is difficult to determine exactly what blame to lay on shipowners for their poor performance. If returns are generally low (both at home and abroad) because of excess tonnage, then it could be argued that British shipowners were doing the right thing in not investing excessively. Conversely, if British returns are low compared with those on foreign fleets, and there is indirect evidence to suggest that this was the case, then it suggests that some of the blame can be attributed to internal management of British companies. There are several possible routes by which defective management might lead to low returns. Investment may be made in the wrong technology, operating costs may be higher than they should be because of poor capacity utilisation and low levels of productivity generally, or charges may be insufficient to cover full costs and yield normal profits. It should be instructive to examine these points in the light of the available evidence.

As regards technology it is clear that in the last decade or more shipping has experienced changes which 'are probably no less significant than the replacement in the nineteenth century of the wooden ship with that of iron, and of sail by steam'.[18] The days of the general purpose tramp are numbered, the majestic passenger liners of the nineteenth century are giving way rapidly to civil aviation, while the traditional cargo liner is steadily becoming outdated. The ships of the present and future comprise tankers, many of which are owned by oil companies, specialised ore and other bulk carriers and container vessels. The size of vessels has increased enormously in the last few years with significant savings in operating costs. For example, the savings in cost per ton-mile from using very large bulk carriers, as compared with the average-sized general purpose tramp, may be as high as 75 per cent.[19] It is in this field that the highest returns have been made in recent years, more especially ore carriers which netted a return on capital of 12-18 per cent during 1966-9.

Yet British shipowners have been very slow to move into this area of operation. In 1968 over three-quarters of the sea-borne trade of five major bulk commodities (iron ore, grain, coal, bauxite and alumina, and phosphate rock) was carried in bulk carriers of over 18,000 dead-weight tons, whereas only 14 per cent of the UK fleet consisted of such ships.[20] Until recently a large part of the investment in shipping went into the traditional type of ship; between 1958 and 1967 over 40 per cent of total investment was absorbed by the relatively small traditional cargo vessel and over 22 per cent went into general purpose tramps, areas where the returns have been lowest.[21] In those branches of activity where returns have been relatively high, that is bulk carriers of one kind or another, the proportion of investment has been very low indeed, under 10 per cent of the total. Tankers, which now account for around one-half of the world's shipping tonnage, have been relatively neglected by shipping companies in the past with the result that some of the largest British ship-owners are now oil companies. Returns on tankers have not been good by any means but they have been slightly better than those on cargo liners and general purpose tramps.

It appears then that British owners have neglected the faster growing and more profitable sectors of the trade. This neglect can scarcely be attributed to a shortage of finance despite low returns. Much of the past investment has been internally financed and shipowners both at home and abroad had access to readily available supplies of cheap credit. There have been considerable changes in the terms on which credit facilities and capital allowances have been made but, generally speaking, shipping has been favoured compared with other industries, and the facilities available have been on a par with, if not better than, those obtained by most of our competitors. Indeed the system in operation from 1965 to 1966 is generous to a degree. The investment allowance was abolished in favour of an investment grant which consisted of a cash payment of 20 per cent (temporarily raised to 25 per cent in 1967 and 1968) of the cost of a new ship; the remaining 80 per cent was financed by cheap credit made available from the banks. In addition, from April 1965 free depreciation of ships (deferment of tax liability) in any year was allowed without limit. In effect, under the present system shipowners need do no more than break even and initially all they need to find is the 20 per cent cash deposit until the Government makes payment.

The combined effect of these terms tends to encourage a diversion of resources to shipping investment — probably to an uneconomic degree as it allows the industry to operate on lower margins than other commercial activities which are less favoured. Moreover, grants and cheap credit facilities have, in the past at least, been granted rather indiscriminately to efficient and inefficient firms alike and regardless of the desirability of distinguishing between sound and unsound investments. Cheap credit the world over has probably had a detrimental effect in that it has led to excessive investment in shipping in boom periods. The committee recognised the adverse effects that the present system has on efficiency and the allocation of investment resources between shipping and other industries and therefore suggested a return to the investment allowance system in operation before 1966, under which the owner received a subsidy as a deduction from tax but only providing the company was making profits. They were not, however, prepared to contemplate any significant reduction in the financial facilities available to shipping, which is somewhat surprising in view of the fact that shipping has been treated rather generously over the last decade or so.

Finance cannot be regarded as the main stumbling block to innovation. More likely the neglect of new fields can be attributed to the failure of management to recognise the importance of the new opportunities offered. In this respect as in others (eg research and development in which the past record has been poor) management has not been in a position, partly because of a lack of qualified personnel both on the technical and economic side, to appreciate the importance of new changes and the alternative investment choices thereby presented. Many companies, for example, have failed to follow through the full financial implications of their invest-ment proposals, and there has been a marked reluctance to employ modern investment-appraisal techniques using discounted cash-flow analysis.[22] Rather surprisingly the com-mittee have not attempted to appraise the wisdom of more recent investment decisions by the industry.

Even this does not settle the matter completely. Had the bulk of past investment been switched from traditional fields to bulk carriers and tankers no doubt the rate of return on capital would have improved, but it would still probably have been low compared with that of industry as a whole. However, the crucial question is perhaps how rates of return on shipping would have compared with those earned by foreign shipping companies. Other factors could intervene to reduce the profitability of home enterprise. The management of shipping operations may be inefficient, leading to higher operating costs *vis à vis* those abroad. On this matter the Rochdale Committee has little to contribute. There are scattered refer-ences to crew costs, productivity and value added in shipping but there is little concrete information which would allow us to say whether shipping operations on the basis of the chosen technology have been grossly mismanaged.

By all accounts productivity has been rising quite rapidly in recent years, a judgement no doubt based on the sharp reduc-tion in manpower which has taken place over the last decade, but the committee confess that for lack of adequate data they were unable to prove it.[23] Admittedly the concept of producti-vity measurement is difficult in shipping and the data far from satisfactory. But this seems to be a surprising admission of failure to construct a productivity series. And it is all the more surprising given the recent attempts to construct productivity measurements for eighteenth- and nineteenth-century shipping[24] and the work on transport productivity,

including sea transport, for the period 1952-65 carried out by
Deakin and Seward. The latter show that total factor productivity rose only slowly up to 1958 but then accelerated
appreciably through to 1965.[25] Later estimates are not
available but in all probability it is still rising rapidly.

The third source of shipowners' difficulties may lie in
pricing policy. Even if investment decisions were correct and
shipping operations were managed efficiently, low returns
might still result if charges for services were fixed at such a
level that would prevent normal profits being made. Of course,
the assumption that an optimal pricing policy can be pursued
depends very much on the extent of cross-subsidisation and
.on the market in relation to capacity. We know very little
about the extent of the former but it is hard to conceive that
it did not exist. We do know a little more about price structures. Presumably for passenger liners and general purpose
tramps the market relationships were such that charges were
determined by external forces and shipowners had little
leeway in which to manoeuvre. Again in the case of bulk
carriers and tankers (excluding oil company tankers) contract
rates were fixed for lengthy periods, and, in any case, since
average returns on capital were reasonable for this group we
need not probe deeply into the freight structure. But a third
or more of the UK fleet in 1968 still consisted of multi-deck
dry-cargo vessels of the traditional type, the freight rates for
which were fixed in conference.

On the relationship between freights and costs in conference the committee have little to offer on the grounds that
the data are inadequate and the differences in conference
procedure. But one feels again that they should have
pursued their studies further. It is possible, as McLachlan has
shown,[26] to construct an index of British liner freights, and,
in any case, the currently published German index provides a
reasonable approximation. From the information available it
is possible to state that between 1948 and 1961 liner rates
moved closely with shipping costs and this helped to stabilise
the level of profits of liner companies compared with those

of tramps. But since the conferences did not generally use their power to obtain abnormal profits in boom periods the rewards of restraint have been limited. The annual average gross profits per ton of a sample of liner companies were little better than the corresponding figures for a sample of tramp companies.[27] It seems, therefore, that cargo liner companies paid a high price for relative stability in freights and that these on average have been fixed at too low a level.

Other than this we can say very little about the pricing policy of shipping lines. Do they base freights on average or marginal costs and what degree of cross-subsidisation is involved? As for the activities of conferences we are told no more than we already know. The old hoary arguments for and against conferences, familiar to those who have studied the report and evidence of the Royal Commission on Shipping Rings of 1909, are trotted out, after which the committee conclude, on the basis of somewhat slender evidence, that no other system would provide the same regularity and continuity of service to shippers.[28] Perhaps in their wisdom the committee secretly feel that with the decline of the traditional cargo liner services and the growth of bulk carriers and tankers on contract rates, the conference system is steadily becoming something of an anachronism, though if this were the case it is surprising that they bothered to recommend the framing of a published code of conference practice.[29]

We can now summarise the argument so far for the poor performance of British shipping. External constraints, such as protection abroad, may be considered partly responsible though it might be more realistic to argue that there need have been no lagging and certainly no stagnation given the fact that unassisted fleets managed to grow more rapidly and increase their proportionate share of the world fleet in some cases. Low profits no doubt reduced the incentive to invest but since these in turn stemmed partly from a misallocation of investment resources, that is a strong predilection, at least well into the 1960s, to invest in traditional techniques, low profits can be regarded as both cause and effect. Profits were also depressed by relatively high operating costs, which were partly the result of higher crew costs compared with abroad, but were probably more due to the failure to improve significantly the efficiency of shipping operations, at least in the 1950s when productivity growth was slow. The small productivity gains were a product of the slowness with which a shift was made to new techniques, for example better and bigger ships such as bulk carriers, and a failure to utilise existing capacity to the fullest extent. To some extent defective pricing policy may also have contributed to lowering returns, especially in the case of cargo liners, though given severe foreign competition from more efficient operators there was probably a limit to which rising costs could be matched by adjustments in freights. In sum therefore, the management of shipping has left much to be desired. There have been too many small and disintegrated units of management of a type unsuited to grasping new opportunities and, as the committee point out, 'higher financial returns have been achieved by those companies with good management as reflected by an ability to take prompt advantage of opportunities which have presented themselves'.[30]

The conclusions do not depart radically from those presented by Sturmey in 1962. But the committee do not emphasise them unduly since they are obviously more impressed with the 'new spirit of enterprise evident in the management of many shipping companies, which is leading to greater efficiency in operation and a greater awareness of, and willingness to exploit, the opportunities offered by recent technological developments'.[31] The beginning of this improvement can probably be dated somewhere in the early 1960s, when productivity performance began to improve appreciably,[32] rather than since the committee began its deliberations as *The Economist* suggested.[33] But the full force of it certainly came in the big spending spree of the late 1960s. By September 1969 British owners had nearly eight million gross tons of shipping on order, the most significant feature of which was that nearly all of it comprised orders for either bulk carriers, tankers or cellular container ships.[34]

It is doubtful if this sharp response was solely the fruit of mounting criticism in the past, though this must surely have played some part. However, there were other influences which spurred shipowners to invest heavily, notably a rising trend in profits, the general shipping and shipbuilding boom abroad in the later 1960s, and, above all, a new and more generous system of subsidies or investment grants introduced in January 1966. Altogether, up to 30 September 1969 the total investment grants paid or due to be paid for ships already on order amounted to the colossal sum of £285 million. As the committee remarked, 'We cannot but recognise that the introduction of investment grants has played a major part in the decisions of UK shipping companies to order very substantial tonnages of new vessels over the last three years, although other major influences have also been at work.'[35] Whether the industry has been prudent to embark on such a large spending spree in such a short space of time remains to be seen, but at least this time it has ordered the right sort of ships.

The remaining sections of the report may be dealt with quite briefly. As we have already noted, there is a lengthy discourse on manpower and related problems, which goes into great detail about the training and recruitment of seamen and shore staff, but which also seems to be largely unrelated to the main theme of the report and might well have con- stituted the subject of a separate inquiry. The chapters on the role of government policy provide a useful summary of the current position but they add very little to what is already known. Of the remaining sections those on the balance of payments and shipping statistics are the most interesting and merit some attention.

Historically the shipping industry has been a substantial earner of foreign exchange and, to a lesser extent, it still is today. The Chamber of Shipping has argued for some time that the official presentation of the shipping account in the

balance of payments severely understates the contribution of
the industry in this direction since it debits payments made
by UK residents to foreign shipowners and fails to recognise
that the industry is also an import saver as well as an export
earner. Secondly, the Chamber maintains that the industry
converts domestic resources into foreign exchange more
effectively than most other industries and therefore earns
substantial foreign exchange at relatively low cost.

The committee examined both these propositions in some
detail. In collaboration with the Chamber of Shipping and
the Central Statistical Office, the balance of payments
shipping account was reworked to allow for the above items.
The results of this analysis produced a figure of £333 million
for the industry's direct contribution to the balance of payments for 1966 compared with only £2 million as recorded
in the official accounts. The revised estimate for 1968 was
even higher — £500 million.[36] However, these calculations
are somewhat meaningless in themselves and a similar method
of calculating the import savings and export earnings needs
to be applied to other industries for purposes of comparison.
Discounting freight on UK imports paid to overseas owners
is equivalent to foreign exchange paid for imports of products into Britain and which can be produced at home, while
the definition of import-saving as the freight paid by UK
residents for the services of British shipping is similar to the
import-saving derived by industries producing for the home
market. Moreover, no estimate is made of indirect transactions,
including ship sales and purchases, and interest and profits
transferred by a UK company to its foreign owners, the net
effect of which would be to reduce the total exchange
earnings.

As regards the second question, the committee found,
after making a number of not altogether convincing calculations on the basis of 1963 data, that compared with other
industries the cost of converting resources into foreign exchange
was relatively high for shipping. One suspects, however, that
the committee were in some doubt about the validity of their

results since they expressed uncertainty as to the benefits to be derived from switching resources from shipping into other uses.[37] Furthermore, they declined to recommend any reduction in the special assistance accorded to the industry.

The committee perform a useful task in highlighting the deficiencies in shipping statistics. Many of the statistics published are defective in some respects while information on a number of important matters is conspicuous by its absence. For instance, the Board of Trade, the Chamber of Shipping and Lloyd's Register all publish data on shipping tonnage but the coverage of the figures is different in all three cases. Moreover, most tonnage figures provide a very inadequate measure of shipping capacity. There are no published world figures for trade carried by ships of different flags, either in total or on particular routes, while the total carryings of the home fleet are not known. Similarly, there is no currently published index of British liner freights and reliable figures for employment in the industry are difficult to obtain. Data on output, productivity and profits are also very fragmentary. Yet, while the committee note these omissions with some regret, it should be emphasised that they rather underestimate the uses to which the available information can be put, and they have not made a great deal of effort to repair the deficiencies. In particular, it has been shown recently that it is possible to construct productivity estimates for sea transport, while the preparation of a liner freight index is a feasible proposition. One must surely ask why the committee did not undertake the task of providing some of the more valuable statistical series in order to provide empirical foundation for their intuitive guesses.

In all over ninety recommendations are made, but many of these are of only minor importance and one-third or more relate to manpower. Even the main ones are not such as to occasion any surprise and they can be summarised briefly. The committee stress at several points the need for a greater consolidation of interests among shipowning companies so as to produce larger groups adapted to exploiting new opportunities fully. They also urge the development of effective corporate machinery for analysing economic trends and other influences which affect the industry. An overall recruitment policy is advocated and stress is placed on the desirability of appointing more graduates for management. The importance of research into technical matters, on which the industry in the past has had a poor record, is given due emphasis, and to this end they recommend the establishment of a 'Ship Research and Development Institute'. Finally, as regards government policy towards the industry three recommendations deserve mention. Largely on balance of payments grounds, and surprising perhaps in view of their rather equivocal analysis on this subject, they recommend that special assistance to the industry should remain broadly unchanged, though with a shift to investment allowances as soon as practicable. The Government should encourage the rapid adoption of a code of conduct by conferences the details of which should be made public. And thirdly, they urge the Government in conjunction with the industry to explore the possibilities of improving the quality and quantity of shipping statistics.

Given its past record the shipping industry has obviously been let down very lightly. Buried in the report are flashes of criticism but the committee are clearly more taken with the recent display of enterprise, and judging from their recommendations they are prepared to let bygones be bygones. With the prospect of increasingly competitive conditions in the future and challenging new opportunites, it is to be hoped that this newly found spirit of enterprise does not evaporate in the light of the committee's benevolence. Despite the length of the report the committee leave many areas untrodden or inadequately explored and many questions unanswered. There is still room for further research into the economics of shipping.

NOTES

1   *Report of the Committee of Inquiry into the Major Ports of Great Britain*, Cd 1824 (1962)

2   *Report of the Shipbuilding Inquiry Committee, 1965-6*, Cd 2937 (1966)

3   *Report of the Committee of Inquiry into Shipping*, Cd 4337 (1970)

4   See, for example, the *Report of the Select Committee on Steamship Subsidies*, H of C 385 (1902), and the *Report of the Royal Commission on Shipping Rings*, Cd 4668 (1909)

5   *Fairplay* (14 May 1970), 9

6   S.G. Sturmey, *British Shipping and World Competition* (1962). The reviewer in *The Guardian* (25 October 1962) described it as a 'ferocious book'

7   None of the six signatories had any direct connection with shipping

8   *The Times* (7 May 1970)

9   *The Financial Times* (7 May 1970)

10   *Shipping World and Shipbuilder* (February 1970), 266, and (June 1970), 759. 'So, for the expenditure of £111,000 of public money, Mr Wilson has the empty satisfaction of a report telling him, more or less exactly, what the industry tried to tell him three years ago.'

11   *The Economist* (9 May 1970), 64-5

12   H.J. Dyos and D.H. Aldcroft, *British Transport: An Economic Survey from the Seventeenth Century to the Twentieth* (1969), 232

13   Ibid, 326

14   *Report*, 18, Table 2.3

15   Ibid, 334

16   Ibid, para 1277

17   Ibid, para 1278

18   Ibid, para 1580

19   Ibid, para 491

20   Ibid, para 103, Table 3.2, and para 489

21   Ibid, para 1261 and p 476, Table 9

22   Ibid, paras 1280-2

23   Ibid, para 13

24   D.C. North, 'Sources of Productivity Change in Ocean Shipping,
      1660-1850', *Journal of Political Economy*, 76 (1968); G.M.
      Walton, 'Sources of Productivity Change in American Colonial
      Shipping, 1675-1775', *Economic History Review*, 20 (1967);
      R. Knauerhase, 'The Compound Steam Engine and Productivity
      Changes in the German Merchant Marine Fleet, 1871-1887',
      Journal of Economic History, 28 (1968); and the critical comment
      by G.M. Walton, 'Productivity Change in Ocean Shipping after
      1870: A Comment', ibid, 30 (1970)

25   B.M. Deakin and T. Seward, *Productivity in Transport: A Study
      of Employment, Capital, Output, Productivity and Technical
      Change* (1969), 128, Table 4.7

26   D.L.M. McLachlan, 'Index Numbers of Liner Freight Rates in
      the United Kingdom, 1946-57', *Yorkshire Bulletin of Economic
      and Social Research*, 10 (1958)

27   D.L.M. McLachlan, 'The Price Policy of Liner Conferences',
      Scottish Journal of Political Economy, 10 (1963), 329, 333, 335.
      See also D. Maxwell, 'Shipping Conferences — A New Look
      Needed', *The Statist* (15 May 1964), 494

28   *Report*, para 476

29   Ibid, para 485

30   Ibid, para 1172

31   Ibid, para 219

32   Deakin and Seward, op cit, 128

33   *The Economist* (9 May 1970), 65

34   *Report*, para 105, Table 3.3

35   Ibid, para 1378

36   Ibid, paras 1293-4

37   Ibid, paras 1345 and 1353

Appendices

Appendix 1 (Chap 3)

British and National Share of Entrances and Countries (with cargoes)

		1850			1860			1870			1880		
		Nat.	Br.	Other	Nat.	Br.	Other	Nat.	Br.	Other	Nat.	Br.	Other
UK	(all)		65·1			56·4			68·8			70·4	29·6
	(steam)		81·6			84·3			88·5			83·2	16·8
Norway	(all)				74·5	2·0	23·5	70·0	11·6	18·4	68·2	11·8	20·0
	(steam)							25·2	53·0	21·8	40·8	26·6	32·6
Sweden	(all)				40·3			31·8			37·2	13·5	49·3
	(steam)										39·8	23·3	36·9
Germany	(all)							35·9			39·1	38·1	22·8
	(steam)							15·0			34·4	49·2	16·4
Holland	(all)				39·5	37·2	23·3	28·4	53·8	17·8	30·9	49·8	19·3
	(steam)				31·2	68·1	0·7	19·1	77·9	3·0	29·0	61·6	9·4
Belgium	(all)				11·4	34·3	54·3	6·4	56·8	36·8	11·6	59·4	29·0
	(steam)				18·4	68·6	13·0	9·3	78·9	11·8	14·3	65·8	19·9
France	(all)				41·4	29·8	28·8	31·5	39·8	28·7	30·0	40·6	29·4
	(steam)				40·0			32·1			35·6		
Italy	(all)							36·5	25·8	37·7	34·8	34·4	30·9
	(steam)							19·7	36·0	44·3	23·3	43·3	33·4
US	(all)				70·8	23·9	5·3	38·1	50·5	11·4	20·4	51·7	27·9
	(steam)							33·1	46·1	20·8	15·5	67·7	16·8
Chile	(all)										0·7	79·9	19·4
	(steam)										1·0	89·7	9·3
Argentina	(all)										11·1	37·8	51·1
	(steam)										12·6	44·2	43·2
Japan	(all)										21·7		
	(steam)										27·9		
Canada	(all)											65·4	34·6
	(steam)											61·3	38·7
New Zealand	(all)					71·7	28·3		92·6	7·4		88·0	12·0
	(steam)												
Denmark	(all)										52·1	11·4	36·5
	(steam)										61·0	16·3	22·7
Portugal	(all)							11·8	66·7	21·5	6·5	63·0	30·5
	(steam)							5·2	86·9	7·9	3·1	72·5	24·4
Spain	(all)										26·6		
	(steam)												
South Africa	(all)											85·6	14·4
	(steam)												
India	(all)										9·1	79·1	11·8
	(steam)										0·6	92·6	6·8
British possessions	(all)					84·8	15·2		88·5	11·5		87·1	12·9

Source: Board of Trade, *Progress of Merchant Shipping Returns*

...arances in Foreign Trade at Ports in Certain
  in ballast)

Nat.	1890 Br.	Other	Nat.	1900 Br.	Other	Nat.	1905 Br.	Other	Nat.	1911 Br.	Other		
	72·7	27·3		63·7	36·3		63·3	36·7		58·9	41·1	UK	(all)
	79·5	20·5		66·8	33·2		65·5	34·5		60·0	40·0		(steam)
·8	14·6	20·6	67·8	10·9	21·3	56·7	12·6	30·7	52·7	9·8	37·5	Norway	(all)
·3	21·4	27·3	60·0	15·2	24·8	52·0	14·9	33·1	50·7	10·7	38·6		(steam)
·7	20·5	45·8	41·6	9·9	48·5	48·5	6·7	48·8	49·8	5·4	44·8	Sweden	(all)
·3	27·8	41·9	39·0	11·1	49·9	47·5	7·7	44·8	49·4	5·9	44·7		(steam)
·9	35·4	20·7	49·0	26·9	24·1	48·7	27·1	24·2	50·3	23·0	26·7	Germany	(all)
·2	38·3	17·5	50·2	28·6	21·2	48·9	28·7	22·4	50·4	24·0	25·6		(steam)
·8	52·3	18·9	25·3	41·7	33·0	27·9	34·7	37·4	26·6	30·5	42·9	Holland	(all)
·5	55·0	16·5	25·2	42·3	32·5	28·0	35·2	36·8	26·5	31·1	42·4		(steam)
·0	53·2	27·8	16·3	44·6	39·1	11·5	47·2	41·3	13·0	44·1	42·9	Belgium	(all)
·0	53·4	26·6	16·9	44·3	38·8	11·8	47·1	41·1	13·2	44·4	42·4		(steam)
·9	44·0	24·1	26·1	40·6	33·3	27·3	35·2	37·5	24·0	36·1	39·9	France	(all)
·0			25·6	42·1	32·3	26·7	36·1	37·2	23·6	36·6	39·8		(steam)
·4	49·4	26·2	49·8	19·7	30·5	26·0	29·7	44·3	27·0	28·7	44·3	Italy	(all)
·2	55·9	25·9	48·6	20·3	31·1	23·5	30·9	45·6	25·4	29·4	45·2		(steam)
·1	52·8	25·1	16·9	52·8	30·3	15·8	50·5	33·7	13·5	50·1	36·4	US	(all)
·5	59·0	22·5	15·0	55·6	29·4	15·7	51·7	32·6	12·7	50·7	36·6		(steam)
·8	47·1	38·1	8·6	50·1	41·3	6·5	48·6	44·9	6·1	50·7	43·2	Chile	(all)
·9	41·3	39·8	11·1	50·9	38·0	7·4	49·4	43·2	6·4	53·4	40·2		(steam)
1	42·2	30·7	33·4	29·3	37·3	35·5	32·4	32·1	43·4	33·5	23·1	Argentina	(all)
·1	45·6	25·3	31·9	31·2	36·9	34·3	33·9	31·8	40·1	36·4	23·5		(steam)
·2			34·9	38·9	26·2	12·9	47·0	40·1	47·2	30·5	22·3	Japan	(all)
·7			35·0	38·9	26·1	12·5	47·3	40·2	47·0	30·6	22·4		(steam)
	51·6	48·4		61·0	39·0		66·1	33·9		69·9	30·1	Canada	(all)
	53·1	46·9		64·8	35·2		68·4	31·6		73·6	26·4		(steam)
	87·4	12·6		91·8	8·2		84·6	15·4		96·8	3·2	New Zealand	(all)
	88·0	12·0		94·7	5·3		85·9	14·1		98·8	1·2		(steam)
·2	11·5	30·3	56·1	7·8	36·1	54·9	6·7	38·4	54·2	5·1	40·7	Denmark	(all)
·5	13·7	24·8	60·1	9·0	30·9	58·1	7·4	34·5	56·4	5·5	38·1		(steam)
·0	53·5	39·5	5·4	56·8	37·8	2·8	51·3	45·4	2·0	47·6	50·4	Portugal	(all)
·3	56·7	37·0	4·7	58·1	37·2	2·5	52·3	45·2	1·8	47·8	50·4		(steam)
·8			47·4	27·6	25·0	43·1	26·8	30·1	37·7	26·2	36·1	Spain	(all)
5			47·8	28·0	24·2	43·3	27·1	29·6	37·8	26·4	35·8		(steam)
	87·9	12·1		89·8	10·2		85·7	14·3		80·0	20·0	South Africa	(all)
	96·4	3·6		94·3	5·7		88·5	11·5		81·3	18·7		(steam)
·6	82·4	12·0	3·3	79·0	17·7	1·4	80·6	18·0	3·0	76·6	20·4	India	(all)
·0	89·9	10·1	0·8	81·9	17·3	0·0	82·3	17·7	2·1	77·5	20·4		(steam)
	88·6	11·4		90·5	9·5		91·9	8·1				British possessions	(all)

Appendix 2 (Chap 12)

CONSUMER EXPENDITURE ON TRANSPORT and TRAVEL IN UK, 1946-69 (£mm)

| | GDP at Market Prices | Total consumer expenditure (Current Prices) | Expenditure on motor cars & motor cycles new & secondhand | Running costs of motor vehicles | Expenditure on Travel | | | | Total expenditure on motor vehicles (3 + 4) | Total consumer expenditure on transport (8 + 9) | Total expenditure on rail, bus, coach & tram (5 + 6) | Expenditure on running costs as % of motoring expenditure |
					Rail	Bus, coach & tram	Other	Total				
1946	10,302	7,239	36	88	108		199	307	124	431		70.97
1947	11,177	7,988	49	101	90		227	325	150	475		67.33
1948	11,962	8,552	48	56	106		251	357	104	461		53.85
1949	12,586	8,907	61	80	103		262	364	141	505		56.74
1950	13,013	9,400	64	109	98		264	362	173	535		63.06
1951	15,102	10,150	74	130	99		289	388	204	592		63.73
1952	15,805	10,691	117	149	107		317	424	266	690		56.02
1953	16,987	11,402	186	169	108	258	72	438	355	793	366	47.61
1954	17,884	12,091	234	191	111	259	75	445	425	870	370	44.94
1955	19,418	13,038	310	244	113	274	77	464	554	1018	387	44.04
1956	20,621	13,744	268	273	122	286	90	498	541	1039	408	50.46
1957	21,796	14,509	320	289	132	297	103	532	609	1141	429	47.45

Appendix 2 continued

Year	GDP at Market Prices	Total consumer expenditure (Current Prices)	Expenditure on motor cars & motor cycles new & secondhand	Running costs of motor vehicles	Expenditure on Travel				Total expenditure on motor vehicles (2 + 3)	Total consumer expenditure on transport (7 + 8)	Total expenditure on rail, bus, coach & tram (4 + 5)	Expenditure on running costs as % of motoring expenditure
					Rail	Bus, coach & tram	Other	Total				
1958	22,649	15,296	425	357	133	294	102	529	782	1311	427	45.65
1959	24,028	16,117	506	405	134	302	109	545	911	1456	436	44.46
1960	25,895	16,933	568	454	145	312	115	572	1022	1594	457	44.42
1961	27,361	17,830	500	526	152	326	126	604	1026	1630	478	51.27
1962	28,619	18,910	538	614	156	337	140	633	1152	1785	493	53.30
1963	30,376	20,087	633	682	159	346	158	663	1315	1978	505	51.86
1964	33,477	21,459	723	778	165	361	179	705	1501	2206	526	51.83
1965	35,633	22,885	697	914	170	370	201	741	1611	2352	540	56.73
1966	37,775	24,232	693	1045	179	387	226	792	1738	2530	566	60.13
1967	40,092	25,362	784	1178	181	387	251	819	1962	2781	568	60.02
1968	42,917	27,113	867	1368	183	394	284	861	2235	3096	577	61.21
1969	44,957	28,618	782	1518	205	398	321	924	2300	3224	603	66.00

Source: National Income and Expenditure

Appendix 3 (Chap 12)

Total Passenger Mileage in Great Britain, 1952-69 (000 million miles)
(estimated passenger mileage)

	Air inc NI & CI	Rail	Public Service Vehicles[1]	Private Transport[2]	TOTAL
1952	0.1	24.1	50.1	37.9	112.2
1953	0.2	24.1	50.7	42.1	117.1
1954	0.2	24.2	50.0	47.2	121.6
1955	0.2	23.8	49.8	54.3	128.1
1956	0.3	24.5	48.6	59.5	132.9
1957	0.3	25.9	45.9	59.9	132.0
1958	0.3	25.5	43.4	72.9	142.1
1959	0.4	25.5	44.1	82.1	152.1
1960	0.5	24.8	43.9	89.4	158.6
1961	0.6	24.1	43.1	99.8	167.6
1962	0.7	22.8	42.4	107.1	173.0
1963	0.8	22.4	41.5	115.5	180.2
1964	0.9	23.0	40.3	132.1	196.3
1965	1.0	21.8	39.2	144.7	206.7
1966	1.1	21.5	37.5	155.9	216.0
1967	1.2	21.2	37.0	167.9	227.3
1968	1.2	20.8	36.3	177.7	236.0
1969	1.2	21.6	35.7	185.0	242.5

1   Estimated from operator's returns including data on number of passengers carried, passenger receipts and vehicle mileage

2   Based on statistics of vehicle mileages derived from traffic and estimates of average number of persons per vehicle derived from the Motoring and National Travel Surveys

Index 309